Mexico
a travel survival kit

Mexico — a travel survival kit

Published by
Lonely Planet Publications
PO Box 88, South Yarra
Victoria 3141, Australia

Printed by
Colorcraft, Hong Kong

Photographs by
Doug Richmond

This edition
October 1982

National Library of Australia
Cataloguing in Publication Data

Richmond, Doug.
    Mexico, a travel survival kit.

    Includes index.
    ISBN 0 908086 36 9.

    1. Mexico — Description and travel — 1951- —
Guide-books. I. Title.

917.2'04833

Doug Richmond is an inveterate traveller who has lived and worked in Mexico intermittently since the mid 1940s. Having never had much money he has always travelled on the cheap. This experience and a lifelong interest in Mexican history led him to write this guidebook. His other writing has included travel guides to Central America and Baja California. When not travelling, Doug Richmond keeps an address in Oakland, California.

Contents

Introduction

I've long thought that the official motto of the United Mexican States should be *'No hay regulas fijas'* (there are no fixed rules). And this saying prevails throughout the fabric of Mexican life, from the Customs Guard at the border to the menu at a favourite restaurant. More than any single factor this is enough to make Mexico more unlike the rest of North America — and Europe, as well — than Costa Rica, Spain or Chile.

The majority of the people are Spanish-speaking Mestizos, a mixture of indigenous tribes and European, with a generous leavening of all the other races and nationalities under the sun. But there are still more native-language speakers in Mexico today than there are inhabitants in Guatemala, people living entirely outside the money economy.

Mexico has about 70 million people, half of whom are 15 years of age or younger. The 1981 World Almanac lists the unemployment and under-employment rate as approximately 50%. The disparity in wealth between the very rich and the very poor is extreme, and the gap appears to be widening. But there is probably no group of people on earth that treats the stranger in its midst as warmly as do Mexicans, and everywhere the person who makes mistakes — inevitable! — in his attempts at speaking Mexican Spanish will be gently corrected, not ridiculed as is the individual who essays his poor French in Paris.

Mexico is an industralized country in which mechanized devices, from faucets to locomotives, seem to take a malicious delight in breaking down at the most inopportune times, a situation that bothers no one unduly. When something becomes *discompuesto* it is regarded by the locals as a petty annoyance not worth becoming upset over. This remark applies whether we are talking about a two-room hotel in a little no-plaza village out in the wilderness or a posh establishment on the Reforma in Mexico City.

And there is no country on earth that can offer so much for so little money to the foreigner traveller as Mexico.

Facts about the Country

HISTORY

It is difficult to pinpoint exactly the date that can be truly said to be the beginning of modern Mexico, but I would place it as Good Friday 1519, the day on which Hernan Cortés arrived on the foreshore of what became Villa Rica de Vera Cruz, and a more sanguine and hard-bitten little group of freebooters has probably never existed in a particular place before or since!

There were something like 500 men and 16 horses that had arrived from Cuba in several ships, which Cortés promptly burned to discourage dissention, back-sliding and desertion among the other ranks. In effect, this single act insured the success of the undertaking as it forced the Spaniards to conquer or die, and conquer they did. Most of them, especially the officers, were scions of impoverished lesser nobility, and they tended to hail from Extramadura and, to a somewhat lesser degree, from Andalucia. Both regions were noted more for their lack of opportunity and general poverty than anything else. This pattern of emigration from Spain to Mexico persisted for centuries and is largely responsible for the fact that Mexican Spanish differs sharply from the Castilian which is the language of the so-called 'better classes'.

At the time he made his propitious landing Cortés had no idea of the immense number of Indians he was facing, but in point of fact he and his men were pitted against hundreds of thousands of Aztecs alone, plus uncounted hordes of other tribes. The Aztecs were the dominant nation, but their rule was maintained through constant warfare with their neighbours, a situation on which Cortés and his men capitalized neatly, fostering alliances as they went, often after pitched battles.

Cortés was greatly aided in his conquest of Mexico — by which we mean the Aztecs — by the fact that the Indians regarded both the Europeans and their horses with superstitious awe which lasted until the Spaniards had a fairly secure toehold on the Aztec capital of Tenochtitlán and had made the Aztec Emperor, Moctezuma, a prisoner. To give some idea of the magnitude of the task let me point out that Tenochtitlán was larger than either the London or Paris of that time, with an estimated 300,000 inhabitants, and the Spanish had fewer than 500 men under arms, including priests, and half that number usually disabled by diarrhea! Which is not to say that the Aztecs simply give up their cause without a struggle. There were skirmishes between the Spaniards and Indians, and also between Cortés' forces and other Spaniards sent out from Cuba to punish him.

On St John's day, 24 June 1520, there occurred a battle between the Europeans and the Aztecs, during the course of which Moctezuma was struck in the head by a flung stone and killed. The direct cause of this fight is forgotten, but there is every reason to suspect that the Aztecs were irritated beyond endurance by the Spaniard's edict prohibiting human sacrifice. By 30 June things were looking very bad for Cortés, so he began a retreat over a causeway to Tacuba with a force consisting of 3-4000 Tlaxcala Indian allies and about 1000 Spaniards — by this time he had received some reinforcements. The retreat was intended to be secret, but a wakeful Indian woman saw their flight and sounded the alarm. Thousands of Indians were killed, along with several hundred Spaniards in the ensuing battle, but the Europeans put up an excellent rear guard action and Cortés wound up with about 400 European survivors, approximately the number with which he had mounted his expedition. The retreat is remembered in Mexican history as the *Noche Triste* (sad night), and the bloody causeway is commemorated on the maps of modern Mexico city as the street 'Punte de Alvarado' (Alvarado's bridge) in honour of Cortés' second-in-command.

A year later, after numerous battles with members of the various Indian tribes, and the addition of around 200 more European reinforcements, Cortés was back at Tenochtitlán. He defeated the Aztecs once and for all and effectively made himself ruler of Mexico. He tore down the temples which the Aztecs had used for making human sacrifices and used the stone to construct churches and homes, the foundations of what is now the world's largest city.

Although the Conquistadores' stated purpose in conquering Mexico was to spread the word of God and convert the Indians, and only incidentally to make money, I suspect that the latter endeavour was probably regarded privately as the most compelling, and those early Spaniards who survived wound up fabulously wealthy men. Many of them returned to their native Extramadura and built immense manor houses, some of which are in daily use in Cáceres and Mérida to this day.

Then followed 300 years of Spanish colonisation and rule in Mexico, years which the energetic Spaniards put to good use. Nearly every city of any consequence in the country was surveyed and planned during the 16th century; cities were built around a central plaza on which were located the church and government offices, with the remaining frontage being taken up by the business establishments of the leading merchants and professional people, a system which is followed to this day. In time, these bare-ground plazas, originally used much of the time for parade grounds, acquired stately trees, ornate fountains and even bandstands. Now they are both the central park and the focal point for social activities and provide much of Mexico's charm. Called the plaza, zócolo, plaza de armas or parque centro it is the single feature that sets a Spanish-designed town apart from its equivalents in the United States and Canada. About the nastiest thing one can call a Mexican town these days is a 'no-plaza village', for without the zócolo a town in Mexico doesn't really amount to much.

It didn't take very long for the population to take on its present ethnic characteristics, for the virile Spaniards soon mixed with the indigenous population and created the Mestizo, today the predominant ethnic group in the country. The degree of intermixture is amazing when you consider that there were never more than 20,000 Spaniards in Mexico at any one time.

Spain was an efficient ruler. It had to be, for it controlled Mexico for some 300 years, but the way it looked on Mexico as a cow to be milked irritated the Mexicans no end. For example, only Peninsulares or Gachupines (the Mexican term for Spaniards born in Spain) could hold high office. All wine had to be shipped in from the mother country, although it was well known that the colony was able to make wines of equal quality. The Spanish rule of thumb was 'What is good for Spain is good for Mexico'.

Eventually these, plus hundreds of other indignities, became too much for the Mexicans to bear, and a parish priest, Miguel Hidalgo y Costilla, raised the cry for Mexican independence, the famous 'Grito' that is repeated each 14 September by the leading political lights of the country, both national and local: 'Long live the Virgin of Guadalupe! Death to the Gachupines!' Unfortunately Father Hidalgo was a much better schemer than he was a soldier, and it didn't take too long for the hated Gachupines to capture and execute him along with three of his cohorts and put their heads up on hooks at the four corners of the Alhóndiga, a large public granary in Guanajuato.

The rebels persevered, and in 1821 Mexico became a free and independent nation and entered into years of political fecklessness, typical of the freed Spanish colonies in North, South and Central America. For example, when Mexico became a free and independent nation it inherited the Spanish holdings and tax collection methods, but by means of diligent mismanagement it was able to dissipate its wealth and default on its foreign obligations within a very few years. In 1836 the fledgling republic lost a great deal of its holdings when Texas revolted. Mexico was unable to overcome the Texans who were outnumbered by the Mexicans by about the same ratio as the Aztecs had outnumbered the Spaniards some three centuries previously.

By 1846 relations between the United States and Mexico had reached an impasse over unpaid debts — a perennial problem besetting countries dealing with Mexico before and since — and over the objections Mexico had to the United States annex-treatment of US citizens in Mexico, and many other differences. Most people today think that the ensuing war was a one-sided mismatch with the odds greatly favouring the United States, but such was by no means the case. In fact, European military experts and politicians were sure that Mexico would win the war hands down and in very short order. Mexico had a modern, supposedly well-trained army, a dashing officer corps, flamboyant uniforms, and a very short supply line, whereas the United States was blessed with none of these supposed advantages.

When the war got under way Santa Ana, the disgraced, one-legged politician-cum-soldier who had been instrumental in losing Texas to the Mexicans, was in disgrace in Cuba. He promptly contacted the US Government and suggested that he be smuggled into Mexico where he was sure he could persuade the Mexicans to call off hostilities on terms favourable to the US. The United States ostensibly fell in with his line of reasoning and returned him to Mexico via Vera Cruz — probably the dirtiest and most subtle trick a country ever played on an enemy. Immediately Santa Ana arrived in Mexico he convinced the government to appoint him commander-in-chief of all Mexican forces, and also to make him president several times. By means of gross ineptitude in the conduct of military operations, the Mexicans managed to lose the crucial battles of Buena Vista, Cerro Gordo and the ultimate struggle for Mexico City itself. This not only cost them the war, but also the parts of their northern territory that became the US states of California, Arizona, Utah and Nevada, plus parts of New Mexico, Colorado and Wyoming.

Incidentally, this war is pretty much neglected in the history lessons in the schools of both the United States and Mexico, although it was far and away the most important struggle ever undertaken by either of the antagonists.

In 1857 a Zapotec Indian from Oaxaca named Benito Juárez, whose statue today graces nearly every plaza in Mexico, took over as presidente and a three-year civil war began. It ended with the Juaristas passing laws disestablishing the Catholic Church as the official religion. Civil registration of marriages, births and deaths become compulsory, and the huge wealth of the Church was expropriated.

Juárez was still running the country when the French, with the assistance of Spain and England, invaded Mexico for the same old reason — non-payment of justly contracted debts. That is, England and Spain were strictly on a bill-collecting mission, but the French were after bigger game — the whole country. To this end they installed as emperor one Maximilian of Austria who should have been suspicious of the whole enterprise when he discovered that he would have to give up his claims to the Austrian crown if he accepted the crown of Mexico.

The upshot was that Mexico got another emperor, its second, and for a while Maximilian ruled Mexico, and fairly ably too. Among the monuments to his brief reign are Mexico City's famous Reforma, the boulevards he conceived and executed as the focal point of the city, patterned after the Champs Elysées in Paris. Another enduring legacy of Emperor Maximilian is the *Code Napoleon*, still the basis of Mexican law. But Maximilian and his scatty wife, Carlotta, had badly misjudged Mexico and the determination of the Mexicans and, worse, he had lodged his trust in a French emperor, Napoleon III, who, when push came to shove, abandoned his protégé to his fate which was to be stood up on a hill between two of his faithful generals and shot. The hill was called 'The Hill of Bells' and is located on the outskirts of Querétero. Today there is a chapel marking the spot, built by the Austrian government. Fittingly enough, the little chapel is called 'The Chapel of Expiation'.

Díaz, who had served as a general under Juárez, followed his leader as president. He, like Juárez, was an Indian, and he ruled Mexico with an iron fist for some 30 years. These were the three decades during which Mexico made the greatest material advances since the days of Spanish rule. Under the aegis of Díaz railroads were built, highways constructed and many of the capital improvements serving Mexico today were created. But the poor people suffered at the expense of the rich, and in 1911 the little brown men put on the armbands and took up their rifles and threw the rascals out.

The revolution had as its avowed aim the alleviation of the miserable conditions of the poor, and especially the rural poor, the redistribution of land, and the destruction of the huge haciendas. The rallying cry of one of its leaders, Zapata, 'Tierra y Libertad', is still a force in the land. The revolution lasted until 1927, with flare-ups until the 1930s, and during that period Mexico essentially lapsed into anarchy. This was the period that many people still think of when you mention Mexico. It was the land of bandidos and crossed bandoliers and big hats and wiry horses. During the final days of the revolution the country was plagued by roving gangs of bandits; the sacking of towns and the robbery and murder of wayfarers was commonplace. And it was during this final period that some of the most bloody fighting occured between the Cristeros and the proponents of secular government.

During the latter 1930s Mexico expropriated the oil industry which was to prove a bonanza forty years later when an immense pool of oil was discovered in the areas around Villahermosa and Coatzalcoalcos. The country now ranks among the leading oil-producing nations, but it has done the average Mexicano very little good. One reason for this is that under Mexican law the oil belongs to the state and not to the owner of the land over the oil. This means that an oil strike is just about the worst thing that can befall a small farmer, and as a direct result of the ongoing oil boom hundreds and hundreds of farmers and ranchers lost their land. The small effect on the general population of all this new money is compounded by the republic's national debt of around US$40 billion, a crushing amount for what is essentially an underdeveloped and overpopulated country. If it weren't for the oil strike the country would have gone bankrupt long ago.

Mexico has a tendency to squander huge amounts of money on projects that are unnecessary, never completed, and poorly conceived. For instance, Mexico is dickering to buy a dozen F-5 war planes from the United States, despite the fact that it has no enemy worth mentioning and only one airport in the country from which these ultra-modern aircraft can operate. Another case is the huge steel mill at Las Truchas, a Pacific coast town that doesn't even appear on most maps. The mill was apparently designed with ouija boards and everything about it was totally wrong, from its location far from existing or potential markets, to the selection of machinery which didn't work well together, or sometimes at all. All in all the Government admits to spending about US$4 billion on this white elephant which is still woefully inefficient and totally incapable of producing steel competitively.

A legacy of the colonial days is buried in the psyche of Mexican politicians to this day, and most politicos look on public office as a license to steal for themselves, their families, and their friends. The tourist will likely first encounter this at the border when the immigration officer casually requests a dollar or two for providing a document that is plainly stamped *gratis*. Done in precisely this way, the payment is called *mordida* which translates as 'little bite', and it's done all over Mexico, at all levels of government. The mordida is often confused with the *propina* by the foreigner, but the two are entirely different. The mordida is really a bribe, but the propina is an out and out gratuity, a tip. Or to put it another way, the traffic cop gets a mordida, a taxi driver or waiter receives a propina. The traffic policeman who is lucky can make maybe 250 pesos a day in mordida, but the brother of a recent president is rumoured by his fellow countrymen to have wound up with millions of US dollars!

Today Mexico has a stable government dominated by a single party, the *Partido Revolucionario Institutional*, commonly abbreviated PRI and pronounced 'Pree'. To give the semblance of multi-party rule, PRI actually supports the other political parties with sub rosa donations, but it is thoroughly understood by all concerned the PRI runs — and milks — Mexico.

The President is elected to a six-year term, and one of the most important planks in the Constitution of 1917 is 'no re-election'. This is so highly regarded in Mexico that it is not uncommon to encounter streets named 'No Re-election'. The President of Mexico has a great deal more power than his counterpart in the United States, which is bad for the country in a way because each President tends to junk the programmes of his predecessors. For instance, during the 1950s the President embarked on a programme of replacing the machinery in the inefficient sugar industry, but before the machinery could be installed his term ended, and the incoming President simply forgot the whole thing. When the expensive machinery arrived from here and there around the world it was not unpacked, or even properly stored. In the early 1970s President Díaz-Ordaz remembered it, but by this time it was nothing but a mass of rusted junk, so of course the whole thing was forgotten. Forgotten, that is, until 1980 when the world price of sugar soared and Mexico was not only unable to take advantage of the higher price but couldn't make enough sugar for its own needs and had to use some more oil money to buy sugar.

There are hundreds of these stories and as you travel in Mexico you will encounter dozens of examples of inefficient planning and execution such as the new, modern cement plant that has never crushed a piece of limestone, or the dozens of idle locomotives cannibalized because nobody could bestir himself to order parts while the government-run railroads are chronically short of motive power.

CLIMATE & GEOGRAPHY

A great deal has been written about the various climates of Mexico, complete with tables giving the average temperatures for each month of the year at various places, but the traveller has to remember only two things: the lower the altitude and/or the closer the ocean the hotter and muggier the climate, and the higher the elevation and/or the greater the distance from the ocean the more salubrious the climate!

The Spaniards were well aware of the effect of altitude on climate, and to this day Mexico has no large city on the coast and the few ports all serve an inland metropolis in the high country behind them. Vera Cruz on the gulf and Acapulco on the Pacific both serve Mexico City. Guaymas serves the State of Sonora, and the factories, mills and smelters of Monterrey and Saltillo now get their ocean freight through Tampico.

Mexico, the fourth-largest country in the Americas, is shaped sort of like a bent cornucopia with a bump near the small end jutting out into the Caribbean. It begins by running south from the US border, then curves more and more towards the east and finally to the north so that, Mérida, Yucatan, is slightly further north than Mexico City and due south of New Orleans. The Sierra Madre Oriental and Sierra Madre Occidental mountain ranges are parallel to the two coasts, with a high mesa containing Mexico's most important cities, and the most interesting places. Below Mexico City the two ranges merge and continue down into Central America as one.

This quirk of geography makes Mexico the ideal place for the traveller. As every experienced wanderer knows, extremes of weather can do more than any single thing to ruin a trip, but in Mexico a change in weather can be had for the trifling price of a short bus ride.

This climatic variability makes it difficult to recommend clothing — it takes radically different outfits for the different altitudes, but the Central California-style clothes I take pretty well cover the whole spectrum.

Fortunately for the *viajero* the strip along the United States frontier is mostly uninteresting, with the possible exception of the area next to the California border. Except for those arriving in Mexico via the Tijuana crossing — far and away Mexico's busiest border port of entry — very few travellers even stay overnight in a Mexican border town.

ROUTES

There are four routes from the US into the interior of Mexico: through Baja from Tijuana and then by ferry or air across the Sea of Cortés; from Tijuana around the northern end of the Sea of Cortés, meeting the route south from Nogales at Santa Ana; south from Juárez down the high-altitude backbone of the country; and south from Nuevo Laredo down through Monterrey and San Luis Potosí. There is really a fifth route, running down the east coast to Poza Rica and then up to Mexico City, but it is hot, sultry and uninteresting in summer, and uninteresting and subject to bone-chilling northers during the winter. It is a route that I would not recommend to my worst enemy and no more mention of it will be made in these pages.

Facts for the Visitor

MONEY

The peso is the Mexican monetary unit. In this book it is also written as M$. In Mexico it is indicated just by $, almost identical to the sign used for the US and other dollars. Under some circumstances this can cause confusion, so occasionally the peso amount is followed by MN, which means *Moneda Nacional* (national money). $1000MN translates as a thousand Mexican pesos — other countries use pesos, too. But US$100 can also be written $100US, or $100dls, or even $100MA, this last meaning *Moneda Americano*.

The peso is divided into 100 centavos, abbreviated ctvos now and then. Because of the debasement of the peso, 20 ctvo coins are the smallest you are likely to encounter. Other coins are the 50 ctvo, occasionally referred to as a *tostón*, and one, five, 10 and 20 peso coins which are rapidly replacing the less durable paper currency of equivalent value.

Currently the peso is around 46 to the US dollar. Approximate rates are:

US$1 = M$46	M$100 = US$2.17
£1 = M$82	M$100 = £1.21

Before the devaluation early in 1982, the rate had been around 25 to the US dollar. As the value of the peso could drop further, it is advisable to change US$ to pesos only as needed.

Because of Mexico's extremely close economic ties with the US, the US$ is well known and readily negotiable almost anywhere in Mexico, but other currencies such as francs or British pounds are unfamiliar to the locals, especially in the smaller, out-of-the-way places, and could very well cause problems come conversion time. It is technically illegal to use foreign currency in Mexico, but you wouldn't know it around the US border where dollars are common as pesos.

Cash is easier to convert than travellers' cheques, but try to avoid offering torn banknotes. Even in the fair-size city of Lagos de Moreno I had several banks refuse to exchange a torn US$100 bill, simply because it was ripped half-way across its face. (In fact a ragged US banknote is worth just exactly the same as one in pristine condition.) I usually carry cash on my travels in US$50 and $100 bills concealed in a leather money belt that looks just like any other belt a man uses to support his pants. (These belts are available in luggage stores, mens' shops, and by mail from L L Bean, among others.) If you get one, be sure that the zipper-closed hidden pocket inside the belt is long enough for its intended purpose.

It is important, except in the expensive tourist-oriented areas, always to have a few small-denomination Mexican bills in hand. The smaller businesses are chronically short of cash for change, and unable to come up with change for bills as large as M$100. Out in the hinterlands it is always wise to have a few M$50 notes in reserve at all times.

Travellers' cheques are not nearly as acceptable and readily negotiable as their vendors would lead you to believe, and the farther one gets from large cities the less acceptable they are. Even in a major city like Guadalajara banks might not want to cash them for non-depositors. They are accepted by the larger tourist-oriented hotels such as the Sheraton, Fenix and Holiday Inn, but these places tend to charge a fee for the service and at some you have to be a guest which can make it an expensive way indeed to get a travellers' cheque cashed.

When a bank condescends to accept travellers' cheques at all it may only do it as a service for depositors. It isn't all that hard to open an account in a Mexican bank, but it will take at least a couple of hours and require the counter-signatures of half the bank's staff, including the managing director. If you are going to spend some time in a given area, it would be worth opening an account for the sake of convenience, if nothing else, but I would make it a practice to keep my peso account low because of the extreme likelihood of devaluation.

Credit cards are not too popular in Mexico, although they are gradually catching on. (Part of the problem is that a local must have an income, generally of at least M$20,000 a month to qualify for a card, putting it well out of reach of the vast majority of the population.) The most popular credit cards are the bank credit cards — Visa and Mastercharge — but their use is pretty well limited to the more expensive establishments. American Express comes in a distant third, followed by Diners Club and Carte Blanche. Credit cards are not generally accepted for bus, ferry and train tickets, but airlines accept them as a matter of course. Many travellers carry American Express so they can receive mail at Amex offices, but in Mexico this is not too important because the country is so huge and there are so few American Express offices. Experienced travellers simply receive their mail at their hotel or via the *Lista de Correos* at the local post office.

In your travels around Mexico you will see sign after sign touting extremely high interest rates paid on deposits in banks and other financial institutiions. At the time of writing almost any bank will pay 27-30% on peso accounts, and around 16% on dollar accounts. Before putting your money into a peso account be aware that in this sort of deposit you will wind up with pesos only, whereas in the lower-paying dollar accounts you are supposed to receive US dollars when the account is closed. Actually the real advantage in doing this sort of investing is that Mexico has tough secrecy laws, which means that they don't make a practice of informing foreign governments — and especially the US government — of financial transactions, so that a non-Mexican citizen is left to decide for himself whether or not he will declare his gains to the tax collector back home. The Mexican government withholds its own tax out of the interest, but this is a mere bagatelle compared to the vicious bite of the English-speaking countries.

Finally, the black market. I haven't forgotten it, but as the peso is freely exchangable with any currency in the world, banks are the place to exchange money.

PRICES

Inflation is rampant in Mexico, and hotel rates change almost monthly. In the following chapters, hotels have been classified into the following categories (1981 rates):

up to M$100 a night	inexpensive
to M$200 a night	moderate
to M$250 a night	expensive
to M$300 a night	very expensive
Above M$300 a night	ridiculously expensive

Restaurants are classified similarly, based on the cost of the comida corrida or an order of the standard *encheladas Suizas* served by about 95% of the restaurants in Mexico: up to M$50, inexpensive; to M$80, moderate; to M$100, expensive;

to M$130, very expensive; and over M$130, ridiculously expensive.

ENTRY FORMALITIES
Because Mexico actively solicits tourist business it is relatively easy to cross the border, especially for citizens of the USA. A 'tourist permit' good for a maximum of 180 days (not 6 months!) may be issued on proof of US citizenship, and the *Migración* people will accept almost anything on paper as documentary proof, even a California driver's license!

Canadians also do not require passports and are admitted for 90 days on proof of citizenship. Nationals of other countries must present a passport and will get a permit for 90 days, or for a shorter period extendable to 90 days.

Tourist permits are also issued by the various non-border tourist offices, but nothing is gained by this, except to waste time. The people who staff the tourist offices are there to do as little as possible to earn their pay, and generally all they know about Mexico is what is on their brochures, if that. For those arriving in Mexico by air the situation is simplified because the airline usually takes care of the paperwork.

Even though US and Canadian citizens do not require a passport in Mexico, I feel that all travellers should carry passports outside their own countries. For one thing, a passport is usually required for financial transactions, such as cashing travellers' cheques, and it is a great help when picking up mail at the post office. For another, people often change their travel plans. If you are in Yucatán you might decide to go through Belize to Guatemala, visit Tikal on the way, and return to the USA via Comitán and San Cristóbal las Casas where the weather is cooler and the scenery more interesting than going back up the east coast of Mexico. Without a passport there is very little chance that you would be admitted to either Belize or Guatemala.

The regulations for US citizens entering Mexico from Belize or Guatemala vary from time to time, and it may be necessary to apply at a Mexican Consulate to obtain a tourist permit. This has happened to me a couple of times, and I have also been issued a 180-day permit at the border at Cuidad Cuauhtémoc as a matter of course. Non-US citizens would be well advised to take no chances and apply at the Mexican consulate first.

Working in Mexico
The 180-day (or less) tourist permit is the most practical of all Mexican travel documents and most Americans residing in Mexico are actually using the temporary tourist permit rather than suffering the additional paperwork necessary to obtain the more complicated *residencia* permit. Similarly, students planning to enter one of Mexico's dozens of schools would, in most cases, be well advised to opt for the easily-obtained tourist permit rather than the student's permit.

Mexico is one of the most xenophobic of nations, and getting a work permit is next door to impossible for foreigners, except for language teachers sponsored by an accredited school of languages, and artists, writers, photographers and the like. Even if you happen to fall into one of the latter categories you will find it is more trouble than it is worth. Also, it is extremely important to realize that an artist working in Mexico under a work permit is usually forbidden to sell his output on the local economy. One of my friends was deported because he made the mistake of photographing and writing — in English! — a brochure for one of the local luxury hotels.

Customs
Mexico is fairly lenient about the amount and type of goods a tourist is allowed to bring in, and as a rule of thumb anything that strikes the customs official as reasonable will be passed without a second glance. But be warned that smuggling into Mexico by Mexican nationals is one of the most severe problems facing the Government and there is a great deal of pressure on the customs people to eliminate the sport. It is forbidden to bring in such commonplace items as toasters, calculators, stereos, portable radios and so on. If you travel with one of those big cassette players-cum-radios the odds are that it will be confiscated on the spot.

When travelling from Tijuana or Mexicali toward Guadalajara there is an inspection station out in the middle of nowhere in the desert east of Sonoita where all vehicles are stopped and the passengers and their belongings are inspected. You must have your tourist permit or other documents, otherwise there is an excellent chance that you will wind up retracing your steps on the next westbound bus. And when you are going through the customs part of this inspection, take a careful look at the rooms full of stereos, adding machines and so on travellers before you have donated to the greater good of the Mexican Government!

HOTELS

In Mexico the minimum wage is around M$150 a day, and an awful lot of workmen don't even make that much! This means that a M$150 hotel room is beyond the wildest dreams of most of the locals. And a travelling mechanic, small-time salesman, truck driver or minor civil servant simply does not rate an expense account that will expand to cover M$350 hotel rooms or M$175 lunches.

Therefore it follows that Mexico must of necessity have a lot of low-price respectable hotels, inexpensive fixed-price lunches and bargain-rate transport. These facilities are intended primarily for the benefit of the local inhabitants, but the foreigner is more than free to take advantage of them. Not only free, but royally welcomed in most cases, and generally a tourist is treated much better in a M$100 (room with bath) hotel than in one of the many M$1000 a night 'international' places that won't even give you a smile or a kind word. It is the smaller hotels intended for locals that will probably assist the motorcyclist to get his steed up over the threshold and into the lobby for the night, or will tell you to catch a bus outside the door for M$2 instead a taxi for 50 times as much.

In Mexico many of the smaller hotels are actually converted mansions left over from Colonial times, with flower-bedecked patios and high, high ceilings. In the range of M$75 and up you can count on an attached bath most of the time, although the water may never get very warm. But the expensive hotels don't necessarily have hot water either, and they seldom spend much design time on ambience. It is extremely rare for a small hotel catering to the local population to have anyone who speaks anything other than Spanish, but this is no great problem. Hotels are anxious to do business, and will understand perfectly when you ask for a room in English, or German, or Japanese. 'If you don't want a room why are you standing there with your bag in front of the désk?' is their line of reasoning.

By and large the smaller the town the less expensive the hotels, and there are instances where it will actually pay to stay at a smaller outlying town rather than a major city. In Mexico I rarely pay more than M$250 a night for a room with attached bath, and most of the time pay around M$150 or less.

In this book I have tried to list hotels in the region of M$150 pesos single, M$200 double, bath attached. Or even less. 'Double', by the way means two people in a double bed, a cama matrimonio. If twin beds are desired it will cost more.

Hotel rates are price-controlled in Mexico, and you will probably see a price list posted in your room, but if you are charged more than the stated price don't jump to the conclusion that you're being ripped off. Because of the ferocious inflation the Government has relaxed or revised its rulings in many cases. If there is not a list in your room you can see a copy in the office, but it is largely a waste of time anyway. It is better to look at the hotel and the room and decide for yourself if it suits your pocketful without recourse to price lists. After about a week in small hotels in Mexico you will be able to tell almost just by walking past what the rates are likely to be.

Even when the rates are posted you can often get a lower price by polite haggling. Or the establishment may have automatically shown you the most expensive room in the house because they assume this is what a rich tourist would want. It is no disgrace to ask for something cheaper — it's a way of life for the locals. So don't hesitate to ask for a cheaper room if you think one is available. Just say, 'Tiene otro cuarto mas barato?'

My favourite type of hotel is a Spanish-built converted mansion, the older the better. These have thick stone walls and are usually built around a shady central courtyard that often boasts flowers and a fountain. These heavy walls have a sort of thermal flywheel effect in that they take all day to heat and in turn give the warmth back during the chill of the night. This is important because fuel is terribly expensive by local standards and most buildings do not have heating facilities. This applies to many expensive hotels, too.

Air-conditioning usually costs extra, sometimes as much as M$100 a night, but many rooms come with a big slow-turning ceiling fan, often provided with a 10-speed control. I prefer the fan hands down because the air-conditioner often makes more noise than cooling, and I have yet to encounter a Humphrey Bogart fan (remember *Casablanca?*) that didn't work. The trick is to turn the fan on when you retire, and crawl under a single sheet. The sheet shields the body from the direct blast of the fan, which otherwise can leave you chilled in some areas and sweating-hot in others.

Electricity is expensive in Mexico, and it's rare, even in fairly expensive hotels, for the room lighting — usually only a 25 watt bulb — to be adequate for reading. The solution is to carry your own 60 or 75 watt bulb. However don't expect to use devices drawing eight or 10 amps or so — the wiring and fuses simply aren't up to it. I've known several travellers who caused fulmination and consternation by attempting to use their hand-held hair dryers in small-town hotels.

Hotels are so inexpensive in Mexico that I am completely at a loss to account for the popularity of motor homes and caravans among the English-speaking North Americans who visit the country. These outfits cost an arm and a leg and are an awful lot of trouble, too, because the campgrounds they require aren't at all common in Mexico. When finally located they are invariably on the outskirts of town where land is cheap, away from the centre of town which is where the action is plus being the most charming part of the area.

ELECTRICITY

Electric service in Mexico is nominally the same as in the US — 117 volts, 60 Hz. Outlets take the common parallel-bladed plug found on US appliance cords, except that a U-ground outlet is extremely rare. Light bulbs are the same US 'regular' with Edison Medium Screw bases. Bayonet-type bases similar to European practice are rarely encountered.

Voltage goes up and down like a yo-yo and can get so low at times that a NiCad battery charger won't work! In fact, constant-voltage transformers are almost standard equipment for owners of television sets to prevent low voltage from shrinking the picture to postage-stamp size, or even eliminating it altogether.

FOOD

Most Mexican breakfasts are the approximate equivalent of the Continental Breakfast favoured by Europeans, and a popular selection is *café con leche* (coffee with milk) with *pan dulce* (small semi-sweet cakes). The latter are generally placed in a wicker basket on the breakfast table, and you pay for what you eat.

Most Mexicans prefer to have their main meal of the day at lunch, usually served during the first half of the afternoon. If dinner is eaten it is the same as lunch — separate menus are almost unheard-of — and it is served until quite late, say 11 pm or so. The eating bargain for lunch, sometimes available at dinnertime as well, is the multi-course *comida corrida* (set meal). Some places list it as *menu turistica*. Usually the comida corrida offers four or five courses, with a limited selection of entrees, and it costs about half as much as the same items when ordered à la carte, or even less.

Maíz (corn or maize) is the basic ingredient of the native diet. Anyone returning to Mexico after an absence of some years will immediately discover that things like tortillas and tamales taste much stronger than before. This is because Mexico has, for economic reasons, ceased importing white corn from the US and switched to the much cheaper yellow corn grown primarily for livestock food. The yellow corn has much more 'corn' flavour than the white. It is sold through the network of Government-operated stores called *Conasupos* which you will see in almost every town of over 1000 population. Originally they were intended as a cut-rate alternative to the price-gouging village stores, and to this day they primarily sell neccesities at subsidized prices.

Most Mexican dishes are not very 'hot' — contrary to the tourists' tales to the contrary. But be very, very cautious in applying the contents of the small bowls of *salsa* (sauce) that grace most tables and restaurants. These can vary in intensity from bland to blistering, with absolutely no difference in appearance. Proceed with extreme caution until the degree of heat is ascertained.

There is no standardization at all in Mexican cooking, and a dish may differ drastically from what has gone before under the same name in another area, or even in another restaurant up the street. Take the well-known tortilla as a prime example. In most of Mexico it is a corn-based unleavened pancake, almost identical to the chapatti of India in size and shape. But in parts of the State of Sonora tortillas are made of wheat flour, about 1-2 mm thick, and as much as 40-50 cm across. Because of their extreme thinness and their large diameters, these tortillas must be hand-made and are gradually losing popularity as a result, but they are really good and should be sought out and enjoyed at every opportunity.

Don't expect the sort of 'Mexican' food in a restaurant in Mexico that you get in a US 'Mexican Restaurant'. The latter serve what is basically Tex-Mex food, about as much relation to the real thing as chop suey bears to Mandarin cooking.

The cooking in the expensive restaurants and deluxe hotels is very seldom Mexican at all. The Mexicans themselves call this cuisine 'International' and it is about the same as you might reasonably expect to find in establishments of like quality anywhere in the world, except that in Mexico the standard of cooking is somewhat lower than in London, Paris, Nice or Barcelona.

The most economical — and often the best — food is to be found either in the town market itself or somewhere close by. Another place for inexpensive, reasonably well-cooked meals is in the little restaurants that tend to spring up around the central bus terminals. The terminals always have their own restaurants, usually cafeteria-style, but most local travellers regard these as too expensive and/or their food as inferior, so these little restaurants have come into being. Some are so small that only the actual kitchen is under the roof, and the customers either stand around outside eating out of their hands, or the patrona has brought a couple of tables from her home for her customers' convenience.

Dishes from other parts of the world are working their way onto the native menus. *Hamburguesas* (hamburgers) and pizza are two examples that come to mind, but there are others. The first-named is now a staple in almost every hole-in-the-wall beanery in Mexico, although here too the Mexican penchant for non-standardization comes into play, and what a tourist receives who has ordered a hamburguesa often comes as a complete surprise!

Vegetarians are in paradise when they visit Mexico. The markets are chock-a-block with organically-grown fruits and vegies just as they come from the fields. There are many fruits and vegetables unknown outside Mexico that are deserving of wider distribution. And street-corner vendors peddle sliced and chopped produce ready to eat so you are saved the necessity of strolling down to the market!

Beer

Mexicans are justifiably proud of their beer, which perfectly complements the food. It is customarily served very cold, as befits a warm country. There are around 30 different brands, many of which have a limited, local distribution. 'Leon Negro' for example is a local beer, brewed in Merida, but seldom seen outside of Yucatan. In my opinion 'Superior' is the best nationally-distributed beer in Mexico. It is brewed at various locations and is available in almost every town in the country. My second choice is always 'Bohemia', which, though called an ale now and then, to me is an out-and-out lager.

Among the other beers, 'Corona de Barril' is my third choice. It is not a draft beer and gets its name from the shape of its bottle. 'Dos Equis' is a dark beer and is extremely popular with Americans, but it has a slight apple flavour which in my opinion is completely out of place in a beer. 'India', is another dark beer apparently intended to compete with Dos Equis — not very good, but at least there is no apple flavour. 'Carta Blanca' is made in the image of the weak, tasteless beers of the US.

'Tres Equis' comes in two varieties, clara (light) and oscuro (dark). A canned beer, it is not universally distributed. Theoretically the clara should resemble Superior (they're made by the same company) but to me it doesn't, nor does the oscura taste too much like Dos Equis to me, but it may well be due to the packaging — I detest canned beer. 'Modelo' and 'Tecate' are two other canned beers.

Mexican beers can run a bit higher in alcoholic content than US beers, which with the enhancing effect of Mexico's high altitudes can cause acute embarrassment if you over-estimate your capacity.

Wine & Spirits

Wine is not too popular in Mexico as it doesn't really go too well with local food, but there are some excellent wines made in Mexico, although this statement will stir up a lot of argument from people who have spent time in the Republic! The problem is that Mexicans are pretty well adjusted to beer and treat wine the same way! Wine should be stored on its side or with the cork down, kept at temperatures lower than convenient for most stores and restaurants in Mexico, and be drunk before it has an opportunity to over-age. Instead in Mexico it tends to be grossly mishandled all along the line, so it is wise not to order wine unless you are absolutely certain of the vendor's ability to provide unspoilt wine. Don't assume that because you are dining in a fancy restaurant on 'international food' that it follows the wine will be up to standard. I've been served so much bad wine in Mexico that I very rarely order it any more.

If you are served a bad bottle of wine in a restaurant, treat it just as you would in London, Stockholm or San Francisco — send it back! Don't accept a bottle of wine unless it is opened at table. Mexicans, not knowing much about wine, are prone to shove the cork back in a returned bottle and try it on the next customer.

Be that as it may, the wine is often good when it leaves the winery, and occasionally excellent, no matter how it may be when it winds up on the table. A fairly reliable way to buy wine in Mexico is from the large super-markets that are springing up and do a huge volume of business. Because they have a rapid turn-over, their table wines are rarely on the shelf long enough to spoil. Mexican cities generally have lots of parks which are ideal for picnics, and what is a picnic without wine? I buy a bottle of 'Urbino', 'Vergel', 'Domeq', or 'Cotillon' at the local supermercado, along with the other ingredients, and have a meal that beats any restaurant. Mexico is the home of tequila and its close relative, mescal, either of which is liable to come with a worm in the bottom of the bottle. The advantage of these two beverages from the standpoint of the local is that they can be had dirt cheap. The average Mexican is totally unable to understand their popularity with foreigners. And in an ordinary bar that doesn't have much tourist business you will completely confuse the bartender if you order a 'Margarita'. If you feel you can't live without one of these concoctions you should locate a saloon catering to the tourist trade, usually to be found in or near an expensive hotel, and with prices to match.

Brandy is now very popular in Mexico, with a fair number of brands from which to choose. My favourite is 'Viejo Vergel'; some others are 'Gran Vergel', 'Presidente' and 'San Marcos'.

Soft Drinks
Coca-Cola (called *coca* by the locals) and Pepsi-Cola are universally available, usually at very low prices. Fruit-flavoured carbonated drinks are also extremely popular, and they come in a plethora of flavours. Would you believe apricot and apple, for instance? Mexicans dote on sweets, and their soft drinks, including Coca and Pepsi are loaded with sugar. If, like me, you dislike excessive sweetness, you can order *agua mineral* (mineral water), *con gas* (carbonated) or *sin gas*.

REST ROOMS
Public rest rooms in Mexico are located in railroad stations, bus terminals, markets, airports and ferry terminals, although the railroad stations are generally accessible only around train time. Unfortunately these facilities are rarely right downtown, which is the focal point of the towns and cities, so feel free to use those of the large tourist hotels which have rest rooms for the public operated as an adjunct of the bar operation. Another safe bet is the franchised quick-food emporiums, such as Denny's and VIP. They, like the tourist hotels, make it a point to keep their rest rooms spic and span.

The central bus terminals vary widely in cleanliness. Some are surgically clean, others would gag a maggot, but they have one great, compelling advantage over some other facilities — they never close.

For a man, the friendly corner bar is a good bet, but in many towns women are not permitted on the premises. Period. Not that most women would want to use the facilities even if they were admitted because as often as not the urinal is just a trough at one end of the room. Or the wall itself.

Uniformly of low sanitary standards are the rest room facilities at the public markets. These are accessible during ordinary market hours, which may be from 4 am to as late as 10 pm. These are really intended for the market people, but outsiders are never turned away. And almost always the way is barred by an elderly person requesting money. For those urgently seeking relief that *tostón* or peso is a small price to pay for a piece of toilet paper and an opportunity!

Toilets in Mexico are about the same as in the US, except that in public places, such as low-price hotels, bus terminals and public markets, many of them are not made to accept seats or else have their seats missing entirely. The reason usually given is that the people steal toilet seats, making it a waste of time to instal them.

Papel higiénico (toilet paper) — if available at all — is manufactured strictly as a fill-in during slack times at the sandpaper works, so it is a good idea always to carry a small packet of Kleenex tissues. The locals make do in markets and some other public places with ordinary newspaper. Among other serious technical disadvantages newspaper has a tendency to plug drains, which is why so many toilets have a wastebasket standing alongside for used toilet paper. Be prepared for abuse if you are responsible for stopping up the toilet by failing to make use of the basket.

TOBACCO

The cigarette industry is alive and thriving in Mexico, using home-produced tobacco. *Cigarros* (cigarettes) are available in domestic brands as well as in locally-manufactured foreign brands. Cigarettes are fast-moving items and they are generally in fairly good condition when purchased. The same cannot be said of *puros* (cigars) and/or pipe tobacco which are usually allowed to dry out in the shop and become unusable.

Sandborn's big store in Guadalajara keeps its cigars in a humidity-controlled showcase, but when I tried one it was dry as bailed alfalfa and with about as much aroma. The clerks had neglected to add water to the humidifier.

HEALTH

Diarrhea has been a severe problem with foreigners in Mexico since at least 1519. It is variously called the 'Toltec Two-step' and 'Montezuma's Revenge' or just *turista*, and is the complaint known as 'Delhi Belly' or 'Malta Dog' and other appelations that affects travellers all over the world. It has been the subject of a great deal of study over the years, both within and without Mexico, and at various times I have heard it attributed to 'the water', the change in diet by people unaccustomed to the lard used in Mexican cooking, local spices, blown dust, high altitude, and a goodly number of other things. It is my guess that at various times and with different people it may be all of these, or none. Some travellers escape unscathed, and others fold up immediately like a Swiss Army knife.

I've read books and magazine articles that recommend — quite seriously — dipping all green vegetables in a disinfectant solution before eating, boiling all water and taking all sorts of inconvenient precautions to ward off the evil complaint. And I have on several occasions travelled with people who followed these recommendations to the letter, and in most cases they wound up deathly sick!

My preferred remedy for this complaint is a liquid called Kaomycin, available from every drug store. It is a mixture of antibiotic and Kaopectate tasting pretty much the same as the latter. The trick is to take a big swig, say about 15-25 ml, at the first sign of the trots, followed by another in two or three hours. If it doesn't cure the complaint it will at least mitigate the problem, and if the internal difficulties get out of hand to the point where cramping begins Kaomycin will still alleviate the misery. This is a specific that treats both the disease and the symptoms.

Lomotil is also popular. Again available at every chemist's shop, it treats the symptoms more than the disease, but many travellers swear by it. Entero-vioform is still found in a few drug stores, and many older travel books recommend it. This compound is actually a vermifuge and not a diarrhea medicine. Some years back the Japanese found that Entiro-vioform affected the optical nerves and was actually causing blindness. Since then it has been barred from most markets in the civilised world, but it is still available occasionally in Mexico.

Turista should not last longer than about three days. If it persists you may have something more serious which should be treated by a doctor.

Aside from the Revenge, which by no means bothers most visitors, Mexico is a relatively healthy place. For the rare medical complaint more serious than the turista Mexico offers excellent facilities. The government makes a concerted effort to see that every village has a physician and at least a small hospital. To this end medical students are assigned to remote towns for a year before they are licensed to practise. In effect this means that a little no-plaza town way out in the boonies might take better care of a patient than a physician in one of the more affluent cities who hasn't cracked a textbook in 33 years. (Medical schools in Mexico are good enough to attract a large number of students from the US, and there are so many English-speaking medical students that there is even a 'Students' Wives Club' in Guadalajara.)

Nearly all medicines available in Europe, Canada and the US are available in Mexico, usually under the same names, although the Spanish pronunciation will sometimes cause confusion. The safest bet is to take your medicine bottle to the *farmacia* for a refill if the label has a typewritten list of the contents. A prescription is unnecessary for almost anything you can possibly need. Pharmaceutical items are price-controlled by the government and are generally cheaper than in the US.

For eyeglass wearers it is a good idea to carry a copy of your optical prescription — optometrists are thick on the ground in Mexico. Lacking a prescription, if you have the misfortune to break a lens gather up the pieces very carefully. The optician will usually be able to deduce the prescription by working from the shards. Optical shops, by the way, usually have their own in-house lens-grinder, and thus are able to offer very rapid service. All types of lenses are available, including photo-grey.

BOOKS

There have been dozens of excellent books published on Mexico over the years. The following are a few I have used.

The War with Mexico, Justin H Smith (published by Peter Smith). This is the definitive book on the Mexican-American war, the most important war ever fought by either of the countries.

Terry's Guide to Mexico, updated by James Norman (Doubleday 1962). This is the best guidebook ever written on the Republic, although by now it is some 20 years outdated.

Peoples' Guide to Mexico, Carl Franz (John Muir Publishing). An excellent book by a writer who really knows the country. More a set of suggestions for getting along and staying out of jail than a guidebook, and it is very popular with the younger travellers who tend to use VW vans in their travels. Recommended for entertainment value as well as its practical advice.

Mexico, a General Sketch, Pan American Union, 1911. Much information about the country at the end of the Diaz regime.

Six Faces of Mexico edited by Russel C Ewing (University of Arizona Press). The best book I know for getting an overview of the country. Intended as a text-book, but available in many libraries.

The Easy Guides to Mexico City, Guadalajara, Acapulco, etc, by Richard Bloomgarden (Editur SA, Lago Silverio No 224, Mexico 17, DF). At last count there were 20 of the Easy Guides, all specialising in a small region, city, or even a church. Priced in US currency (presently US$1.95 to US$3.95). Available in Sanborn's in most cities and any place US citizens may be expected to accumulate. Some have gone through a dozen revisions, and all are quite up-to-date. Definitely recommended.

COMMUNICATIONS

Mexico has door-to-door mail service in all but the tiniest towns, and there is no reason why you can't have your mail sent to your hotel. 'Poste Restante' or 'General Delivery' is *Lista de Correros* in Mexico, literally 'Mail List'. In many places people receiving letters have their names inscribed on a public list. This saves having to wait in line some minutes to find out if there is mail today. Mexico uses the Spanish system of personal nomenclature, in which the mother's name is listed last, preceeded by the father's name. This means that a Mexican clerk will automatically file a letter for 'John Wesley Noble' under 'W' and not 'N'. If you use only two names it can eliminate a bit of confusion now and then.

Both air mail and surface mail are slow, either in or out, but by and large air mail is the least slow of the two, although it wouldn't be wise to bet on it. In fact, Mexican mail service is so inferior to that of the US (which in turn is far worse than that of Great Britain) that Mexican businesses in border towns habitually receive their mail at the post office on the American side of the line. The slight nuisance involved in crossing the border to pick up their daily mail is far outweighed by the rapid service.

Packages, either in or out of Mexico are a nuisance. Coming in, the mail is slow, the risk is high, and you may have to go to the Customs to pick up a package. Going out is almost as bad, and a package sent to a foreign destination must be inspected by the Customs before it can be accepted by the post office. If for some odd reason somebody sends valuables to Mexico they should be sent by Registered Mail to prevent pilferage — good luck!

There is a story about the mail man going around and collecting letters from pillar boxes who always started out on the morning's rounds with a pocketful of small rocks. As he came to each box he would drop a pebble in through the slot and by careful listening he could tell whether there was enough mail inside to make it worthwhile in opening the box. I have never seen this with my own eyes, but I've been told about it so many times that I'm convinced it happened somewhere, and to anyone knowing Mexico at all it sounds perfectly logical!

Telegraphs and Telephones

Mexican telegraph service is excellent, with none of that 'Mailgram' crap that prevails in the US. In Mexico a telegram is delivered the way a telegram is meant to be delivered, by a young man on a bicycle or small motorcycle. There are telegraph offices, using the old clickety-clack system, in almost every town in the country, regardless of how remote or isolated.

Telephone service is another kettle of fish entirely. Long-distance calls originating in Mexico are usually made in a telephone 'store' which is either a business devoted entirely to telephones, or an area in a store or restaurant set aside for this specific use. Establishments offering this service have a blue and white telephone sign outside with the words *Larga Distancia* (Long Distance) prominently displayed. There are special international operators who are supposed to speak English, but the easiest way to place an international call seems to be to write the country, state, city, area code and telephone number on a piece of paper and hand it to the attendant. Once the call is made, the quality of the transmission is surprisingly good, travelling as they do over a modern Japanese-built microwave relay system. International calls placed in Mexico cost an arm and a leg, and it makes no difference at which end they are paid. If possible, it's usually more economical to arrange for international calls to be made from the other end.

SHOPPING

Whole books have been written advising the affluent traveller on 'How to Shop in Mexico', as if anyone needs a guidebook on how to spend money. But shopping seems to be a major preoccupation for some travellers so here are some of my expensively-won thoughts on the subject.

There are areas in the country famous for certain products that are almost exclusively sold to tourists. Taxco is a prime example. At one time it was a wealthy silver-mining camp, but with the exhaustion of the mines it fell on evil times and almost became a ghost town. This condition persisted until an American, Bill Spratling, came along and developed a silver handicraft industry. As the market for sterling silverware is severely limited in Mexico, Spratling aimed the local output square at the tourist market, and in order to provide a source of supply encouraged the rehabilitation and conversion to hotels of many of the beautiful old mansions. What with one thing and another, Taxco has become a mecca for the wealthy traveller, and generally the prices are a reflection of this. Not that Taxco is necessarily a rip-off but be aware that the silverware is sold by the troy ounce and the price works out very dear indeed. Aside from the silver racket, Taxco is an interesting and charming place and well worth visiting for itself.

There is a thriving commerce in 'pre-Columbian' artifacts, centred around the various ruins such as Palenque and Chitzen-Itza. You may be approached by a swarthy little man who looks fearfully over his shoulder before pulling an earth-stained figurine out of his side pocket and shyly offering it for sale, together with the information — in English, yet! — that he dug it up yesterday while plowing the maize field. This is probably true, but he may omit to tell you how he buried the artifact the previous spring in order to impart the authentic aged appearance. And even if the Chac-mool or whatever happens to be authentic — which is unlikely to say the least — both the US and Mexico take an extremely dim view of people other than accredited scholars and museums owning pre-Columbian art.

Querétero is famous world-wide for its opals, and invariably anyone who looks like a foreigner will be offered a selection of stones, all done up in a grubby handkerchief. They will appear to be quite cheap to the uninitiated, but not when you remember that making opals out of old bottles has developed into a folk art around Querètero!

A major cottage industry in Mexico is making forged 'designer labels', and there are fancy stores in Mexico City selling goods with the trademarks of Cartier and Gucci that bear absolutely no relation to their famous namesakes. (These stores have been sued for trademark infringement but to little avail.)

There are lots of things for sale in Mexico that are both economical and practical, but they are seldom sold in the places likely to be frequented by the average tourist. An exception to this are the blankets, ponchos and serapes peddled off people's backs around the zocolos of Oaxaca, although this is rather a poor place to buy because the vendors know only too well that most foreigners aren't aware of the local price structure or don't know how to bargain, or both.

One last thought on shopping. Remember that certain items are both fragile and bulky, such as the very practical clay *cazuelas* (cooking pots), and the beautiful lacquerware for which Pátzcuaro is justly renowned. Transportation should be considered prior to purchasing. If you do buy something too big to pack in your bag, do as the locals do: pack your purchases in a corrugated box with lots of newspaper padding and tie them securely, so that the rope becomes a handle. Take them to the bus station and check them on your ticket. At layover points simply check the box at the left luggage counter while you are sightseeing.

Other shopping suggestions are scattered throughout this book under the headings of the various towns.

WHAT TO TAKE

First, avoid taking huge, heavy, ungainly suitcases. I have travelled for months at a time with my only luggage a shoulder tote bag which easily qualifies as cabin luggage on planes, and stows easily on the overhead baggage shelf on intercity buses. This avoids the twin bugaboos of airline travel — lost bags and long delays in recovering the checked items that didn't get lost — and also saves it from destructive cargo handlers.

A few travellers still persist in using unnecessarily huge framed packs which from the rear make them look like walking pagodas and are too big to be carried aboard aircraft. Another serious disadvantage in Mexico and Latin America generally is that because of the huge influx of *jipis* (hippies) during the late '60s and early '70s, these contraptions are still associated with people who tended to be unwashed and objectionable to the locals in other ways. This discrimination can be rather subtle, such as being informed that a hotel is full when in fact rooms are immediately available for other travellers.

Drip-dry clothes are great for minimising your luggage. My total travelling kit seldom weighs more than 6½ kg, usually less. In addition to basic toiletries and a couple of changes of shirts and underwear, I recommend taking 'Chapstick' lip balm (sometimes hard to find in Mexico), an emergency flashlight with a spare bulb, a box of wax matches, a dozen purse-size packets of Kleenex, half a dozen Band-aids and a small traveller's clothes line. A thick paperback book helps to pass the time if you get stuck in an uninteresting town.

I also expect to buy odds and ends as I need them along the way, such as a wool sweater if it were to turn cold, or a small cheap umbrella if it rains (but I would look for one that I would feel free to discard later). My tote bag is not full when I leave home so there is plenty of room for the jacket which I start out wearing, and also for odd things bought along the way. I keep my tourist permit and Mexican currency in my wallet, a small Spanish/English dictionary in my pocket, and my foreign money in the concealed pocket of my money belt.

WHAT TO WEAR

Clothing worn in Mexico is predominantly casual and much the same as worn in comparable climates all over the world. For both men and women this usually means blue jeans or slacks, with a sweater or shirt. A coat or jacket may be useful as the climate demands. Mexican women always wear bras and rejoice in stiletto heels, but low-heeled shoes are best, especially for the rough and broken sidewalks. Beach wear is never worn on the street away from the beach. A head covering is advised for women visiting churches. Mexican business men are conservative in their dress, and a dark suit, white shirt and non-spectacular necktie is the badge of the executive.

The *Guayabara* shirt rates a special paragraph. It is a man's shirt, although now and then you may see a woman wearing one. It is square-bottomed, and always worn outside the pants. But the thing that makes a guayabara a guayabara is its fancy embroidered or appliqueed design. It can be worn anywhere, any time, but it really comes into its own at night when it doubles as a jacket at all but the most formal occasions.

It is considered a breach of good manners for anyone, male or female, to go barefoot on the street, unless desperately and obviously impoverished. The extremely practical *guarache* (also spelled *huarache*) a sandal with a sole made out of a piece of retired tire and with a top made of woven leather strips, is regarded as the footwear of the lower classes and is not too often encountered these days in the cities, but they are cheap, cool and comfortable, and a well-made pair of guaraches will wear like a bottle of tabasco sauce. In the US they cost around US$30, but in Mexico they cost about a fifth of that.

Getting There

BY AIR

Mexico City is the hub for a number of international airlines, and direct flights are available to Europe, the United States, Canada, Central and South America. There are also flights to Guadalajara and Yucatán. Flying direct to Mexico is the fastest way, but also the most expensive. From Europe it is usually cheaper to fly to Los Angeles which is only 175 km from the border.

From Los Angeles and San Francisco, Mexicana operates a popular one-class night flight, nicknamed 'El Tecolote' (The Owl), to Guadalajara and Mexico City. This is usually the cheapest way from the west coast of the United States and it is extremely popular with Mexicans themselves, but check around because occasionally other airlines offer cut-price promotional fares on this route. Because air fares are usually in a state of flux, try a good travel agent who is familiar with Mexican flights, or better yet, try several because it is far from uncommon to get a different fare with each inquiry.

BY LAND

Bus service in the US and Canada is nowhere near as good as Mexico's, but it does offer a low-priced alternative to flying. All the US border cities of any size are served by one or both of the two major US bus companies, and their stations are generally close to the border. Greyhound, for example, will actually haul you to the bus station in Tijuana from either San Diego or Los Angeles, but from there on you have to travel by Mexican carrier. (See 'Getting Around' for details.)

From San Diego airport there is city bus service to the border town of San Ysidro. This is an extremely economical way to get to the border.

From San Ysidro you simply follow the signs to cross the international border into Mexico. Bear right until the causeway is reached, cross the street, walk across the causeway, and at the other end keep a sharp eye out for the Tres Estrellas de Oro bus station. There is another bus station serving the Pacifico line, but it doesn't handle very many buses. In addition to buses to mainland Mexico, buses running down the Baja Peninsula to La Paz leave from the Tres Estrellas station.

For practical purposes there is no rail passenger service in the United States, so I will omit any remarks, except to say that Amtrak, the US passenger train operator, is run by the government and not especially interested in hauling people to the border so they can spend their money in a foreign country!

Another method of transport from San Diego is by tram (also called a streetcar in many places). A recently-completed 20-km line runs from downtown San Diego to San Ysidro, and it is such a success that it is being extended. It originates at the Amtrak station.

Getting Around

Of all the countries I've had the pleasure of visiting, Third World included, Mexico has far and away the best public transport system. Some of it, such as the railroads and the ferry system, is government owned and operated, while the inter-city buses, some airlines and the taxicabs, are in private hands. Oddly enough, it all works fairly well, and parts of it give excellent service, far exceeding what one ordinarily encounters in the USA and Europe, and generally it is quite cheap.

TRANSPORT PRICES
Bus fares took a 30-50% hike in 1981, but compared to the US and Europe they are still downright cheap. Currently 2nd-class fares in Mexico average around 43 centavos per km anywhere in the country. For example, from Tijuana to Mexicali (189 km) the fare is M$87; Merida to Campeche (176 km) is M$86, and Queretaro to Mexico City (220 km) is M$92. The 1st class bus fares vary more, but average 51 ctvo per km, or about 20% more than 2nd class.

Long-distance rail fares are lower than bus fares, except for pullman with berth, which works out at around 80 ctvo per km. Ordinary 1st class comes out at around 30 ctvo and 2nd class gets down to 16 ctvo per km, calculated on the basis of equivalent highway miles, which can vary considerably from actual distances.

Internal air fares run from six to ten times bus fares over the same routes.

BY AIR
Because the distances are so great and surface travel fairly slow, Mexico has developed an extremely efficient network of air routes, with services to almost every city of over 50,000 inhabitants. Equipment is modern and well-maintained and — wonder of wonders! — the airlines stick pretty close to schedule. However, air travel in Mexico has the disadvantages of being vastly more expensive than surface travel, and it is no way to see the sights — clouds and mountain peaks look much the same in Mexico as the rest of the world.

BY ROAD
Taking an automobile to Mexico can be disconcertingly expensive, and an almighty nuisance.

To begin with, only 'Mexican Auto Insurance', issued by local underwriters, is recognized in the Republic. This specialized variety of extortion is sold at all US-Mexico border crossings and by Sandborn's, of McAllen, Texas. All types of coverage are available, including collision, but the important one is Public Liability and Property Damage in amounts in excess of that required by Mexican law. The cost is modest; fortunately increasing the amount of PL & PD doesn't cost too much more than the minimum, and is a good investment if only for the additional peace of mind it provides. This specialised insurance is not a requirement in Mexican law, but the driver must bear in mind that in the Republic automobile accidents are handled under the criminal code and in case of an accident an uninsured driver may languish in jail for six or seven months or longer before his case is heard — and a Mexican jail is no summer cruise! Mexican drivers, many of whom simply can't afford insurance, cope with the problem in a unique way that isn't readily available for the tourist: they depart the scene of an accident with maximum velocity. This ploy is generally impractical for the foreigner.

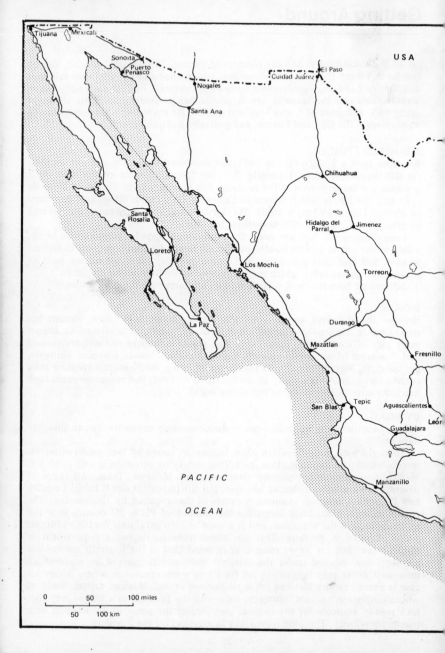

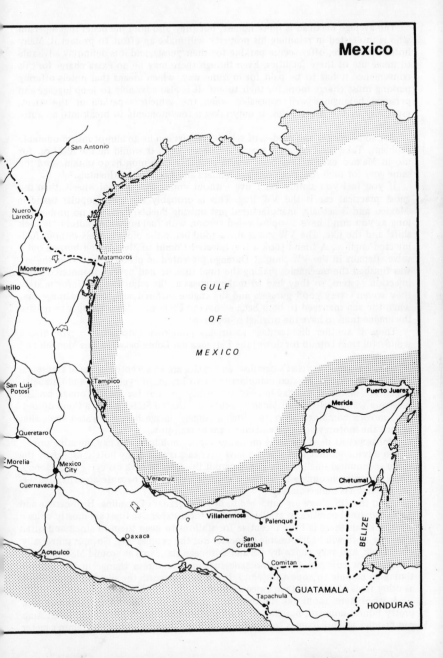

Mexico

The average Mexican is quite honest, but they also hold the belief that a person who is interested in retaining his property will make an effort to protect it. Many hotels, therefore, offer secure parking for their guests, and it is definitely advisable to make use of these facilities. Even though there may be no extra charge for this convenience it has to be paid for in some way, which means that hotels offering parking must charge more for their rooms. It is also advisable to keep luggage and personal belongings well concealed when the vehicle is parked on the street, especially in the larger cities. It only takes a few moments to break into an automobile.

For some makes and models of vehicles repairs can be an almost insurmountable problem. Take the extremely practical Citroen 2CV. It would be the ideal car for use in Mexico except that parts would probably take months to obtain. And the same goes for such American cars as Cadillacs and Lincoln Continentals.

If you feel you simply can't live without your own personal wheels, then the most practical car is the VW Bug. This is probably the most popular brand in Mexico and is actually manufactured just outside Puebla. Parts are no problem so long as you don't have a sophisticated version with fuel injection, 'automatic stick shift' and the like. The VW van is also a good bet in the older models without fuel-injected engines. A friend took a fuel-injected Combi to Mexico and burned out a valve. Repairs in the VW shop at Durango presented no problem, but when the job was finished the mechanics making the final tune-up had never encountered a fuel injection system, so they had to make a guess at the adjustments. Unfortunately they weren't very good guessers and the engine suffered such severe damage that when the van managed to limp back across the US border it was cheaper to replace the engine than to have the original re-repaired!

There is another disadvantage to driving your own automobile — you miss a wonderful train trip up (or down) the Barranca del Cobre between Los Moochis and Chihuahua.

Mexico is a motorcyclist's paradise, and cycles are an accepted mode of transportation for the locals. Mexico manufactures two brands of cycles, Islo and Carabella, which are intended for day-in, day-out utility and not for sport. Foreign cyclists receive a warm welcome in Mexico, unlike the United States where a flood of 'outlaw' movies combined with the 'Hell's Angels' image have mitigated somewhat against the motorcycle as a standard means of transport.

Motorcyclists need the same insurance as automobilists, and pay the same price.

An advantage that motorcycles have over cars is that many hotels, especially the more economical small hotels, gladly permit the rider to park his cycle in the lobby. Some actively encourage it. This is a considerable saving because an expensive security lock-up is unnecessary.

As in the US, there are supposed to be three grades of gasoline. High-octane and unleaded are theoretically available, but as these expensive fuels are mostly unused by the locals there is little incentive for stations to keep them in stock and often either or both will be impossible to locate. But the peoples' gas, Nova, is universally obtainable, and very cheap by US and European standards at around M$7 per litre. Automobiles adjusted for high-octane fuel may require a change in the ignition timing to be able to cope with Nova, but it is well worth the slight effort involved as other fuels cost better than twice as much.

A word here about gas stations. As I pointed out, Mexico averages out as a pretty honest country, but the gas station attendants could give lessons to an Arab rug peddler when it comes to fraud and trickery. Failing to roll the pump's meter back after serving the previous customer and chronic short-changing of customers unfamiliar with Mexican money are commonplace, and most foreign motorists — including myself — have been stung at one time or another by a Mexican gas-pump jockey. For some reason these tricks are seldom used against motorcycle riders, another slight plus for the bikes.

When you bring a vehicle into Mexico the Government demands that you take it back out. Period. There are many sad tales of motorists who were involved in serious wrecks and had to put their junk on a truck and haul it to the border.

BICYCLES

A very few extremely hardy souls ride their bicycles to Mexico, but it is by no means a popular means of travel for foreigners, although locals use bicycles extensively for going to and from work. When riding the highway the cyclist who desires a long life and happiness keeps a wary eye over his shoulder for traffic, and gets off the pavement in advance. To do otherwise is to invite death and destruction, for the trucks and automobiles pay a license fee for the use of the roads, and are bloody well going to use them.

TAXIS

Taxis are available in even the smallest and most remote villages, including those that don't appear on the very best of highway maps. In most instances taxis in Mexico are a rare bargain compared to Europe or the rest of North America. But riding a cab in Mexico is not quite the same as riding one in London, Paris, Barcelona or even San Francisco. Some taxis are metered, some are metered but add a more-or-less fixed surcharge, some add a percentage of the meter reading to the total fare, and some are totally unmetered. This last includes taxis that have cloth hoods over the meters. These are mostly found in Mexico City and are intended strictly for the tourist trade. Needless to say they are expensive by any standard, triply so by local custom.

Taking the unmetered first, you should agree on the fare before entering the cab, otherwise there is no practical limit to what the driver will feel free to charge. Tourists wax highly indignant about this, but it is a custom of the country requiring only an inquiry to avoid. With an agreed price the driver ordinarily keeps to his end of the bargain, even if it actually costs him money out of his pocket.

I once caught a cab from downtown Mexico City to the International Airport, normally a 15-20 minute trip, but we got trapped in a gigantic traffic jam and wound up taking an hour and a half. Nevertheless the driver only asked for the fare which we had fixed beforehand, but obviously he was losing his shirt on the deal, so I thought it only right and just to triple his fare.

Where there is a surcharge to the metered fare there will usually be a sign — occasionally it will even be in both English and Spanish — to that effect. A taxi with an inoperative meter — not all that uncommon! — should be treated as an unmetered taxi and the usual haggling should take place prior to boarding, if possible.

In some places, notably Mexico City, taxis come in several sizes, and one would logically assume that a VW Bug would command a lower fare than a huge Ford Fairlane. In fact they charge about the same, but for reasons of speed and agility the VW is the hands-down favourite for one or two people with little baggage — these little cabs have no front passenger seats and are technically licensed for two people, and of course they aren't with it with the big Fords, Dodges and Chevvies when it comes to baggage space.

Some of the larger bus stations have a kiosk that sells coupons good for one taxi ride. These are handy and eliminate a lot of misunderstandings and should be instituted throughout the country. They are located in the concourse and are highly visible. You just go up and tell the lady your destination and she immediately fills out the ticket and assesses the fare. Then go out to the taxi rank and pick a cab. It is best to tell the driver if there is no hurry, because ride-sharing is the rule rather than the exception, and the last passenger out often gets a guided tour of parts of the city he would ordinarily never lay eyes on.

INTERCITY BUSES

Foreign travellers in Mexico seldom ride intercity buses, and in so doing are depriving themselves of a great deal of enjoyment and also passing up the opportunity to save a considerable amount of money over driving, renting a car, flying or whatever. Travelling by bus is an unrivalled way to get the feeling of the real, non-tourist Mexico and is probably the greatest bargain around. The 1st-class fare is around 30 centavos a km, and second class is slightly less.

Travellers from north of the border and Europe may ignore the advantages of bus travel because they've been told Mexican buses are clapped-out converted school buses with small livestock mixed in with the paying customers. Or else because they can't figure out how to cope with the multiplicity of operating companies and routes, together with the universal absence of printed timetables.

To begin with, Mexico has a very progressive bus-building industry that exports to the rest of Latin America, and the 'Made in Mexico' intercity bus is at the very least the equal of the best equipment used in this service anywhere in the world. Most of the coaches have three axles, and a few of the deluxe models are equipped with four axles. This means that the 'ride' of a Mexican bus is vastly superior to that of an automobile over the country's oft-bumpy highways.

I'm talking here specifically about the equipment used on long-distance runs, as from Juárez to Mexico City, or from Tijuana to Guadalajara, and not of the short-haul runs that trickle out over the countryside from every city of any size in the Republic. These long-distance buses, either 1st or 2nd class, definitely do not haul pigs and chickens in the passenger compartment, although most operate on a no-holds-barred concept when it comes to the things stowed in the possum-belly baggage compartments beneath the floor.

All 1st class buses, and some 2nd class as well, operate on a reserved-seat basis so it is advisable to purchase your ticket well ahead of time at originating points, rather than waiting until the very last moment, and there are a couple of definite advantages in doing this. First, the earlier you buy and make your reservations the greater your selection of seats and the less chance of getting sandwiched in one of the first two seats opposite the driver, which are extremely deficient in leg-stretching room. Secondly, you have the greatest chance of getting on a bus when you want to, for buses are sometimes filled many hours prior to departure time, especially true around Christmas/New Year. I was quoted a one-week waiting period from Oaxaca to Vera Cruz one Christmas Day. Delays can be even more annoying during Easter Holy Week which the Mexicans take much more seriously than Christmas or New Year.

Advance reservations are not so important at towns on the US-Mexican border because they are the originating point for so many runs into the interior. As an example, I once had no difficulty in obtaining the seat of my choice on a coach out of Nogales, Sonora for Mazatlán a couple of days before Good Friday, but the bus was completely filled at Magdalena, 80 km to the south, and took on no more passengers until my companion and I disembarked and made room for two replacements.

As recently as 15 years ago central bus stations were extremely rare; instead down-at-heel restaurants, ratty cantinas and desolate,weary grocery stores doubled as 'bus stations' where the coaches simply pulled up and loaded and unloaded passengers in the mud in the middle of the street. This situation still exists in a few places, but during the last decade there has been an intensive construction program aimed at providing modern central bus terminals for almost every large city — plus many small ones. These new *Centros de Autobuses* look more like international airports than conventional US-style bus stations. They have long lines of ticket counters lined up along one side of the concourse, and shops selling everything a traveller can logically be expected to buy on the opposite side. These shops routinely deal in anything from office machine repairs to saddles, with an emphasis on local products. For instance, in Celaya there are several shops that dispense nothing but cajeta, a syrupy, caramel-flavoured confection for which the area is justly famous. Meal stops on the long-distance buses are nearly always at these terminals with their (mostly) clean restrooms and ample and economical eating facilities.

One feature of most central bus stations that may disconcert the stranger is the person stationed at the entrance to the restrooms soliciting contributions and/or selling toilet paper. He or she is not a begger in any remote sense of the word, and anyone taking advantage of the facilities should not begrudge a 50 centavo or even a peso donation. These people have the job of keeping the place clean, and most of the time they do an excellent — or at least a fair — job of it. Sanitarios operated in this fashion are generally much cleaner than 'free' installations.

With the exception of Mexico City, most of the central bus terminals are within easy walking distance of the Zócolo, making them ideal for the traveller who doesn't object to a 15 or 20-minute walk through colourful streets.

With so many competing lines at the big *Centros* it is generally easy to pick a departure time that exactly suits you. Or if one line is full it is usually a simple matter to make a connection with one of the others. Unlike the old-time makeshift bus stations, the modern terminals almost always boast baggage-checking facilities so you can check your luggage and then stroll around.

Bus tickets are for a specific company, and usually cannot be used on a competing line. However the people at the ticket counters often work with an informal agreement of cooperation. If one company is fully booked, the clerk is likely to ask the competitor at the next counter if they have any seats. In this way you will often get a seat at short notice with very little trouble.

Most of the new central terminals handle all classes of buses in the same part of the terminal, which can be a terrific advantage. If the 1st-class seats are all taken you will usually get a seat on one of the more numerous 2nd-class coaches. For example, at Querétero I have often arrived on a 1st-class bus and have seldom spent over half an hour waiting for a bus out to San Miguel de Allende.

This brings me to what, for foreigners, can be the most confusing part of travelling on Mexican buses: buying tickets. The most important item in a traveller's kit in Mexico is a good road map. Unfortunately, most road maps are woefully short of detailed information, omitting smaller towns along the main highways and fairly large ones off to the side. My qualifying test for a Mexican road map is to see if it shows Choix (north-east of Los Mochis), Tequila (about 30 km out of Guadalajara on CN-15) and Comonfort (between San Miguel Allende and Celaya). If some or all of these are missing I assume lots of others are too, and start looking for another map.

A road map really comes into its own at the larger bus stations where there may be lots of bus lines, each using a different route to arrive at the same destination. The exact routes are shown by listing towns along the way, so with a map you can choose the most suitable route. Another use for the road map is in the actual ticket buying. Instead of struggling with place names you simply point to your destination and indicate with your fingers the total number of boletos' (tickets) you want. Stopovers are not ordinarly permitted, so if you want to take a break in your journey simply buy a ticket to the intermediate destination and plan on purchasing another ticket on a later bus for the next leg of your journey.

In addition to knowing where the towns are that the bus will touch it helps to be able to read the station signs. Listed below are some of the more common words you can expect to read or use:

asiento	seat
boleto	ticket (not *billete!*)
caballeros	gentlemen
cada	each
corto	short route, about the same as *directo*
cuota	Literally 'quota', but it means 'by toll road', always the fastest route because in this instance it means freeway or motorway.
damas	ladies
directo	direct
equipaje, guarda or *guarda equipaje*	baggage check room
hombres	men
llegada	arrivals
mujeres	women
puntos intermidios	intermediate points
regresso	return
sale de espera	waiting room — can also be translated as 'hoping room'.
salida	departure or exit
sanitarios	toilets. *Bano* usually means a place to bathe.
senores	men
senoras	women
1^a	1st, as in 'first class'
2^a	2nd, as in 'second class'

CAR RENTALS

So far I have made no mention of renting a car. This is because I've had poor luck going this route in the Republic, and I've talked to many people who have had similar problems. There are a number of car rental firms doing business in Mexico, both international and local, but their efficiency seems to fall by the wayside under the Mexican sun, and it is common to encounter lost reservations, no cars available as promised and a host of other petty annoyances. And to put the frosting on the cake, if one does succeed in finally renting a car, and it actually doesn't break down, it will prove to be an extremely expensive proposition when compared to other means of land transport available to the traveller!

BY RAIL

Contrary to the usual practice in most countries, railroad fares are even lower than bus fares, and trains connect all major cities in Mexico, although they miss a number of tourist spots such as Puerto Vallerta and Cancún. Mexico City is the hub for railroads, as with the highway system. Due to the extremely low fares, and also because so many travellers are railfans, trains are fairly popular with foreigners. Most of Mexico's railroads were constructed in the latter part of the 19th century under the Díaz regime. British-built, they have served the Republic well, but as almost all of them are strictly single-track operations, lacking modern train-control equipment, under today's conditions they are tremendously overloaded.

As the cost of rail travel is subsidized for the benefit of the poor, the 2nd class coaches are usually crowded, hot, smelly and uncomfortable, with small children whooping and hollering and dashing up and down the aisles at all hours of the day and night. But 1st class costs only a little more than 2nd, and in most instances you can even obtain reserved seating. As there are no standees — theoretically! — you are usually spared the horrible overcrowding that is common on 2nd class cars. Most 1st class coaches are supposed to be air conditioned, but don't take air conditioning too seriously in Mexico. Even lacking air conditioning, 1st class is a great improvement in every way over 2nd. There are also sleeping cars, mostly ex-US Pullmans, with the conventional US-style upper and lower berths, roomettes and so on, but when you go Pullman the price advantage is lost!

Trains are much slower than buses, even if they manage to stick to their schedules, which doesn't happen all that often. Mexican trains are much given to mysterious pauses out in the midst of nowhere, and running on time is more the exception than the rule. It is by no means uncommon for a train from Mexicali to pull into Guadalajara 10 hours or more behind schedule.

Very few Mexican trains can be relied on to carry dining cars, although quite a few have lunch counters, so the experienced rail traveller packs a bountiful picnic hamper at the market before embarking. An alternative to the picnic hamper is to depend on buying food from the hawkers who swarm aboard the train at almost every station, peddling tamales, tacos, tortas and other Mexican-style quick foods, including cold beer and soft drinks.

There would be more tourist travel on Mexican railroads from the US border if the American passenger service, Amtrak, made better connections with its southern counterpart. During the heyday of US rail travel it was possible and enjoyable to climb aboard a Pullman car in Chicago and get off in Mexico City, but with the deterioration of rail passenger service in the USA this is now a practical impossibility.

FERRIES

A government-owned ferry system connects Baja California Sur with the mainland. Ferries cross between Puerto Vallerta and Cabo San Lucas; Mazatlán and La Paz, and Guaymas and Santa Rosalia. As befits the considerable distances involved, these are full-fledged ocean-going vessels, equipped to carry vehicles up to and including large trucks and semi-trailers. Because they are intended more for internal commerce than the tourist trade, it is not uncommon for several private automobiles to be left languishing on the dock to make room for a truckload of agricultural products. Normally they each operate three trips a week in each direction, with one day off for restocking, repairs and R&R for the crew. They are quite reliable when it comes to leaving on the advertised time and stick pretty close to their schedules, although they often arrive a little late at their destinations on account of weather conditions, fouled bottoms or engine-room problems.

Most passengers, domestic and foreign, elect to travel as deck passengers in the spacious lounges, but stateroom service, purported to be air-conditioned, is available for a slight surcharge. When I tried a stateroom several years back, my cabin was on the port, or sunny, side so I thanked my lucky stars for the air-conditioning. However the air-conditioning packed it in at about the same time the lines were cast off, and my comfortable stateroom soon got hot enough to bake scones, so I spent the remainder of the trip in the lounge where I am sure I was the highest-paying passenger.

Baja California

TIJUANA

Tijuana, Baja California (population ca 1.2 million), is one of the most popular international border crossings in the world, with millions of people going through each year. It is a free port for both individuals and merchandise, and formalities are at an absolute minimum for people and motor vehicles who are going no farther south than Ensenada or farther east than Mexacali. Travellers going beyond Ensenada down the peninsula can pick up their immigration documents either at the border or at the little town of Maneadera, 14 km beyond Ensenada. Those bound for Mexico's mainland must get papers at Tijuana.

Tijuana is no longer the booze and broad centre it once was, and it will be difficult if not impossible to find one of the famous donkey acts that attracted the sailors from Dago and Pedro of yore. Today it is a thriving commercial centre, deriving much of its income from trading, importing and exporting, and small-part assembly work contracted by American manufacturers. As with almost all border towns, it is rather more expensive than the average Mexican city, and about as charming as Erie, Pennsylvania.

Avenida Revolución, the main tourist shopping street of Tijuana, is living proof of the old adage that nobody ever went broke catering to the poor taste of the American public. Chartered buses bring loads of blue-haired ladies across the border for a day's shopping as a regular occurrence. And the shopkeepers on Revolución are masters of the hard sell that would put a Phoenician rug peddler to shame.

Places to Stay

There is little necessity for overnighting in Tijuana, but for those forced to do so there are three small laborers' hotels to the left as you leave the Tres Estrellas bus station, and in the same block. There is little to choose between them; all are inexpensive. If you leave by the front door of the Tres Estrellas station and turn right, then left at the next corner the *Hotel Nelson* is straight ahead and about a block away. The Nelson is a commercial travellers' hotel and is nowhere near as new as it looks; expensive.

Places to Eat

Tijuana is not too bad for eating. As you swing around the igloo by the border there are usually taco wagons, fruit stalls, etc. These are very inexpensive. For a good Mexican sit-down meal it is hard to beat the restaurant in the *Hotel Nelson*. As with all Mexican home-style restaurants a foreigner ordering 'bifstek' under the impression he will get North American beefsteak will be bitterly disappointed, but stick to the standard fare, such as encheladas and carna asada and you will do OK. Prices are moderate.

Up Revolución is the *Hotel Cesar* and the restaurant of the same name, where the Cesar salad is popularly supposed to have originated. Whether or not there is any truth to the legend, the Cesar is a good place for a snack, a Cesar salad or a beer and is very popular with the local merchants, but it's expensive.

Getting There & Away

Most travellers enter Tijuana on their way to or from the US. How to get there from the US is described in the 'Getting There' chapter.

To get to the bus station for the south-bound buses, or to catch a Mexican bus out to the new central bus station on the eastern outskirts of town,

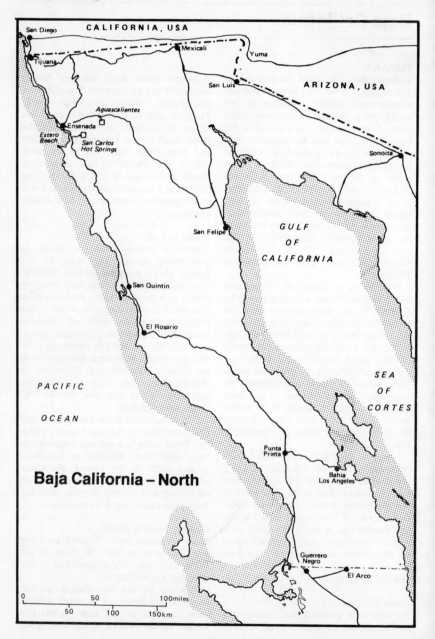

Baja California – North

go to the old Tres Estrellas de Oro ('Three Gold Stars') downtown. Cross the border and bear right around the concrete igloo. Walk across the Tijuana River on the pedestrian causeway signed 'Centro'. The bus station is short distance straight ahead from the end of the causeway; look for a large electric sign with three gold stars.

ENSENADA

Ensenada (population 125,000) is slightly over 100 km via the new toll road from Tijuana. It is very popular as a resort for residents of San Diego and Los Angeles, and as a result has a thriving tourist-oriented business. The tourists who visit Ensenada are, generally, more knowledgeable than those who take the package tours and 'Love Boats' to other resorts in Mexico. As a result the majority of the shops price-mark their merchandise, having found that Americans won't take the time to haggle, and as the competition is on a dog-eat-dog basis, the prices for Saltillo serapes, Taxco silver and Oaxaca pottery are about the best in the Republic.

A sort of general store of indigenous artifacts is located at the northern edge of Ensenada. It's called 'El Nuevo Nopal', and carries everything from Taxco Silver to 'murals' made of tiles that are assembled something like a jigsaw puzzle to create a long-lasting indoor/outdoor decoration. The latter are seen all over Mexico, often on very old buildings, but very seldom are available in stores nowadays. And best of all, the prices are right. It is on the main road about one km from the tourist street. Even if you don't buy it is worth a look if only because the New Nopal will give you a good line on current prices and quality. Recommended.

The summer climate is about the same as the part of San Diego nearest the ocean, although winters can get a mite raw at times. In my opinion

Ensenada beats the other Mexican resorts hollow when it comes to weather, with little of the oppressive heat and high humidity so prevalent elsewhere.

There are two main shopping streets. Avenida Juarez is the one for locals and is where to buy picnic supplies, work clothes, auto parts, good mountain-grown coffee and so on. Mateos is the tourist street closer to the waterfront. It has the majority of the hotels and motels and is where you can buy 'souvenirs' (some of which come from Hong Kong!), belts, buckles and pottery.

Ensenada is located on the shore of Bahia de Todos Santos and fishing, both sport and commercial, is superb. Many of the weekenders in Ensenada come down for the fishing, and sport-fishing boats of all sizes are available for charter, along with the requisite gear.

Like Acapulco, Ensenada doesn't really make its money from tourism. It is a busy seaport, especially for agricultural products from the Colorado River Valley, and there is a thriving modern boat-building industry turning out commercial fishing boats. There is a great deal of commercial fishing, and several fish canneries and a number of freezing and chilling plants.

The best beach is the Playa Estero, about 9½ km south down Highway 1. The turn-off is signed.

About 3½ km south of the turn-off for Estero Beach there is an unpaved road leading left into the hills 19 km to San Carlos Hot Springs. This is a rather primitive area with a bathing pool made by damming the little creek that is fed by a number of hot springs strung out along a fault line. It is relatively unknown and you bring your own food and fuel and camp for a weekend. There is a small charge for admission to the hot springs.

Another, fancier hot spring is reached by going up the road from Ensenada toward Ojos Negros for about 26 km to the turn-off marked 'Hotel Aguascalientes'. The hot springs and hotel are 8½ km from the main road over an unpaved track that is perfectly navigable for ordinary cars. Intrepid hikers can wander down the arroyo to San Carlos Hot Springs, about 10 rough km. There is a restaurant, swimming pools heated by the hot springs, and a fairly large hotel. One of the oddities of the Hotel Aguascalientes is that the toilets flush with hot water.

Another 'must see' is La Bufadora, a geological oddity in which water and air are compressed by wave action in a small cave. There is a vent in the top of the cave, and a pillar of water periodically jets into the air, like old Faithful. This can really be spectacular, although the degree of action varies considerably, depending on the wind and the state of the tide. La Bufadora is at the end of a 22-km paved road that branches west at Maneadero, south of Ensenada.

Places to Stay

Ensenada entertains hundreds of thousands of tourists every year and is gradually tilting toward the expensive, deluxe side in the way of hotels, but there remain a number of low-priced establishments.

Back in the days before the Transpeninsular Highway — Numero Uno — was built, many of the back-country travellers made their headquarters at the *Rancho Motel* on Alvarado and Calle Secunda. It was cheap and there was adequate enclosed parking. Now a new addition is being constructed and so the parking is somewhat congested as a result, but the prices are still moderate in the original structure. The Rancho is a block off the tourist street, Mateos, so it is reasonably quiet. To get there go south on Mateos to the Pemex gas station and turn left down the hill — the Rancho is on the next corner.

The *Hotel Royal* on Castelum above Mateos has a bath house as part of the operation, so the clients are reasonably assured of getting a hot bath, one way or another. Enclosed parking. Moderate.

The biggest and oldest out-and-out hotel in Ensenada is the *Hotel Plaza* on Mateos at Castelum. Ideal for those without automobiles. Moderate.

At the upper end of Mateos, near Ryerson, is a sign that simply says 'Hotel'. Actually it is the *Hotel Ramirez* and the cheapest place in town, which is about the best that can be said for it. Inexpensive.

The *Hotel Aguascalientes* at the hot springs seems largely unknown to gringos but is popular with well-to-do Mexicans; expensive. Campsites are also available. Inexpensive, but you pay extra for a hot tub, which is gratis for hotel guests.

Places to Eat

Ensenada is one of the best eating towns in Mexico, with bitter competition between the various restaurants. It is the only city in Mexico that I know of where restaurants are continually going broke.

Being a major fishing port naturally the emphasis is on seafood, and one of the best is the *Costa Baja* at the foot of Riveroll across the street from the monument to Hidalgo, Carranza and Juarez. It is one of the better places for a late dinner. Expensive.

Another seafood restaurant is the *Casamar* at the foot of Macheros near the rental area for sport-fishing boats. This one is a bit more expensive than the Costa Baja but the food is excellent. Expensive.

Up the street on Mateos near the Pemex station is the *Bahía*. This is more of an all-around restaurant where you can sit at a table by the street-side windows and inspect the passers-by. Opens early for breakfast. Moderate.

Victor's Cafe on Mateos between Riveroll and Miramar is an old standby, extremely popular for breakfast with early-rising fishermen, both amateur and professional. Inexpensive.

Hussong's Cantina is easily the best-known establishment in the various Californias, and their T-shirts — which they sell — are seen all over the world. This is an ordinary Mexican bar distinguished from all the others only in that they permit women on the premises, and by its antiquity — it dates back to 1892. On Ruiz above Mateos.

Getting There & Getting Around

The Central Bus Station is on Riveroll between Calle Decima and Calle 11. To get downtown go out the front door and turn right. Mateos is the tenth cross street and at one time was called Calle Primera.

SAN QUINTIN

San Quintin is a new, unremarkable town about 187 km south of Ensenada and the last place for automobile drivers to stock up on picnic supplies.

About a hundred years ago Bahia San Quintin was the site of a couple of ill-starred attempts at colonization by British and Americans. A flour mill was built and a narrow-gauge railroad was constructed some 32 km north toward San Diego, its intended destination. After a number of lives and fortunes were lost the promoters gave up the game and today all that remains to show for all the work, money and human misery is an old Turner steeple-type compound steam engine from London and the remnants of the graveyard. The village and pier established by the colonists is slightly over 4 km south of the mill, and another 3½ km will bring you to the old graveyard. A dam was constructed across an arm of the bay in front of the mill, but when and for what purpose I have been unable to ascertain — the sense of history among the locals is somewhat lacking.

Places to Stay

There are two motels side by side at Bahia San Quintin, *Ernesto's* and *El Molino Viejo*. Both have restaurants and boat rentals; both are expensive. The signed turn-off is about 2 km south of San Quintin, but the rest of the 7½-km route isn't very well marked, so it is inadvisable to attempt the trip after dark — there is a maze of roads in the area and even during the day they look pretty much alike. In wet weather it is inadvisable to make the trip in an ordinary vehicle as the dirt roads turn to greasy mud.

BAHIA LOS ANGELES

A thriving community on the Sea of Cortés, this is almost entirely the result of the efforts of Antero Díaz to wrest a living from what was originally a barren wilderness. The nearby mine of San Juan and the associated mill at Las Flores are about 10 km from the settlement. Señor Díaz early established an airstrip, on the sound theory that not enough fishermen and back-country loafers would come down the old road to make his operation pay. Today there is a paved road to his door, but Bahia Los Angeles is still popular with fliers and offers fishing, hiking and swimming.

Places to Stay & Eat

There is a motel/hotel and restaurant (both expensive), and a store for general supplies. Because of the isolation, supplies are somewhat more expensive than elsewhere, but not exorbitantly so. Camping on the beach is perfectly acceptable.

GUERRERO NEGRO

This town has sprung up near one of the largest salt evaporation works in the world. Guerrero Negro was for many years almost the only source of steady employment in Central Baja California and a magnet for the young people of the economically depressed towns. Today it is a fairly large community offering all services, including hotels, restaurants, automobile repair shops, and so on. It is about two km west of the Transpeninsular Highway, measuring from grotesque 28th Parallel Monument. And as with the rest of the Republic's new cities, Guerrero Negro is singularly unattractive.

EL ARCO
When the new highway was paved in the early '70s it missed El Arco by about 40 km, and so a new road was built and paved. The new branch is a long way from the original which came out by Rancho Los Angeles. Unfortunately the new paving job is by far the worst part of the government's efforts and a side trip to El Arco is definitely not recommended.

There isn't much there anyway. It is a sort of ghost town. Originally there was a mine there developed by North American interests about 50 years ago. The mine soon closed down due to a combination of labour unrest and scarcity of gold, and since then El Arco has survived by acting as a small supply centre for the outlying ranches and even smaller towns. Construction of the new road put the final nail in El Arco's economic coffin by eliminating the through traffic and also by making it relatively easy for local residents to do their shopping in Guerrero Negro. A place of profound drabness and not worth a visit, especially over the lousy road.

SAN IGNACIO
San Ignacio is a true oasis and I doubt there is a sight in the world as welcome as the first view of the date palms as one comes south over the burning-hot desert during the summer months. It was named after San Ignacio de Loyola, the founder of the Society of Jesus, and contrary to what one reads here and there, it was founded by the diligent Jesuits — can you imagine a Dominican or a Franciscan naming anything 'San Ignacio?'

There have been people living on the site since long before recorded history. There were an estimated 5000 Indians living in the vicinity when the Spaniards arrived. Originally the town was called Cadacaaman and the official name of the place is San Ignacio de Cadacaaman, but nobody calls it anything but 'San Ignacio'. The Jesuits established their mission in 1728 (although it is known that Father Piccolo visited the site as early as 1716) and during the following 25 years San Ignacio served as a base for the exploration of the wild and desolate area. Disease reduced the number of Indians to around 100 but San Ignacio, unlike most of the old missions, was never abandoned. The present residents are largely descendents of immigrants from Sonora and Jalisco who began to arrive there in the 1830s.

The date palms that contribute so much to the beauty of the town are another legacy from the Jesuits, and were probably introduced sometime around 1760-65.

The town itself was built to the standard Spanish design for the New World settlements, with a functional, tree-shaded plaza fronting the church and its attendant outbuildings. The church itself is an exquisite example of frontier construction, built out of hewn lava blocks with walls 1½ metres thick. The buildings surrounding the plaza are mostly over two hundred years old, although many have been repeatedly rebuilt and only the original stone facades preserved.

Today the population is around 1500 and has been essentially static for many years. There is virtually no opportunity for employment and for many years San Ignacio's principal export has been its young people. Guerrero Negro probably has more people from San Ignacio than

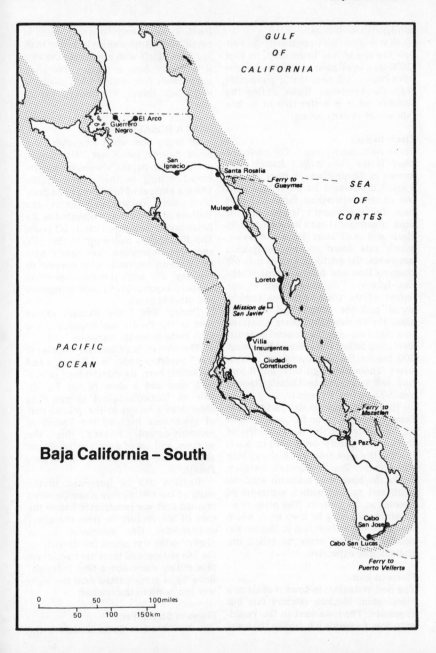

GULF
OF
CALIFORNIA

El Arco
Guerrero
Negro

San
Ignacio

Santa Rosalia

Ferry to
Guaymas

SEA
OF
CORTES

Mulege

PACIFIC
OCEAN

Loreto

Mission de
San Javier

Villa
Insurgentes

Ciudad
Constiucion

Baja California – South

Ferry to
Mazatlan

La Paz

Cabo
San Jose

Cabo San Lucas

Ferry to
Puerto Vellerta

0   50   100 miles

50   100   150km

San Ignacio itself does!

If you have the opportunity to visit one town, and one town only, in Baja California, by all means make San Ignacio your choice. But note that it gets hotter than the hinges of Hades during the summer, so it is better to visit in late fall, winter or early spring.

Places to Stay

There isn't much choice. The preferred place is the *Posada San Ignacio* also known as 'Oscar Fischer's Place'. This is a small motel built by Oscar beside his late father's repair shop, famous all over Baja for the world's largest pile of broken springs. Oscar's is immaculately clean and well away from the water, which cuts down on the mosquitoes somewhat. To get to La Posada turn off Numero Uno and follow the signs into San Ignacio. You enter town at one corner of the plaza; continue straight ahead past the church and turn left along the far side of the plaza. Continue to a sign that says 'La Posada' or equivalent, and follow the arrow. After about 200 metres the street ends at a cross street. There is no sign here, but if you turn left you come to Oscar's Place in about 75 metres. Expensive.

The other place to stay, just in case Oscar's happens to be full, is the *Hotel El Presidente*, but this is the saddest of the lot and grossly overpriced to boot. It is on the road from the highway into San Ignacio. The Presidente's designer, unlike the Spaniards, made his windows small and square, with a minimum of opening at the bottom. The place relies on air-conditioning to keep cool, which would be fine except that in Mexico air-conditioning can never be relied on. Ridiculously expensive.

Places to Eat

The best restaurant in town is at *Oscar's Place:* plain Mexican country fare but expensive. The restaurant in the Presidente does a capable job, unlike the hotel itself. It runs heavy to steak, which is cut in North American style, rather than just hacked off with a machete the way it is usually done in Mexico. The cook understands fish, which when available is the best choice. Ridiculously expensive.

SANTA ROSALÍA

It all began here when a rancher from Santa Agueda, one Rosas Villavicencio, made a rich copper discovery and initiated mining in the region. In the 1880s a number of local mines and prospects were consolidated under the Rothschild's banner and operated as the Boleo mines for almost exactly 50 years. The Rothschilds pulled out in the '50s, and their operation was taken over by Mexican interests, who operate to this day. The original copper operation has been expanded to include manganese and other minerals.

During WW I the German sailing fleet in the Pacific was interned in the little harbour for the duration.

The church is of interest because it was prefabricated in Europe and assembled here. Its exterior is of galvanised steel and a close runner for the title of Mexico's ugliest church. The older frame houses in the central part of town were built by the French as company-owned housing for the workers, and are of a pattern familiar to anyone who has visited the South Pacific.

Railfans will be interested in the relics of the metre-gauge steam-powered railroad that was constructed before the turn of the century to serve the mines and smelter. One locomotive is on display at the wye across the street from the bus station, and there are two others plus rolling stock and a tiny Industrial Brownhoist crane parked near the highway just north of the smelter.

Places to Stay & Eat

The best hotel in Santa Rosalía is the

venerable *Central*, across the street from the church. To reach it go out of the bus station and angle left by the wye and follow the traffic up the valley about three blocks. Moderate.

There is another small hotel to your left about a block from the station. Last time I saw it there was only a small sign saying 'Hotel' because they hadn't gotten around to naming it as yet. Inexpensive.

The all-out best restaurant in town is the one in the *Hotel Central*, surprisingly good for such an out-of-the-way place, probably as a result of the years of French influence.

Of course you can always grab a snack at the little hole-in-the-wall restaurants around the bus station.

Getting There & Away
There is a regular ferry service from Santa Rosalía to Guaymas, with three round trips a week. This is the shortest crossing to the mainland and also the cheapest. The ferries leave at night and arrive in Guaymas early in the morning.

This route from Tijuana to Guaymas is about 150 km shorter (in land distance) than going around the northern end of the Sea of Cortés. The cost is about the same, but the trip down through Baja is much more interesting and with the chance to visit Ensenada and San Ignacio, whereas the route around the north end and down through Hermosillo is essentially boring and with no towns of any particular interest.

If you miss a boat to Guaymas the hotel rooms are cheaper in Santa Rosalia than anywhere up and down the Peninsula, so waiting for the next boat isn't too costly. Also, in case of a lengthy stopover, one can easily catch a bus to Mulegé or Loreto to break up the monotony.

Getting Around
To get downtown from the bus station, go out the front door and angle left to the one-way street and follow it uphill.

Santa Rosalía doesn't have much of a plaza as it was laid out by the French and not the Spanish, and downtown sort of meanders with residences and stores all mixed in.

To get from the bus station to the ferry terminal, turn right as you leave thé station and follow the road south along the shore. The terminal is less than five minutes walk.

MULEGÉ
About 60 km down the road from Santa Rosalía, Mulegé is drier and cooler, ever so much more attractive than its near neighbour which, after all, is only a rather unattractive raw mining town.

Located near the mouth of the Arroyo Santa Rosalía, which provides water for crops, Mulege occupies the site of a former Indian community called Caamanc-ca-galeja. Its modern history begins with the construction of a mission, Santa Rosalía de Mulegé, in 1705, by the Jesuits. The present mission church was built in 1766 by another Jesuit, Father Escalante. This was one of the last Jesuit constructions prior to their expulsion by the Spanish crown.

Today Mulegé is a pleasant little town of around 4000 population. Because of the availability of a small amount of fresh water, there are date palms dating from the days of the Jesuits, along with some truck farming. There is also excellent fishing, and the Club Aereo was built so that foreigners could fly in to wet their lines. There is a cute little palm-shaded Plaza, which in its present form only dates back to about 1956. You will also find a supermercado, Pemex gas station, hotels and several general stores.

Places to Stay and Eat
The *Hotel Hacienda* is located on the plaza and is distinguished by the sign 'Broken English spoken' (in fact Sr Alfonso Cuesta Real, el patrón, handles English quite well). There is a recently-

built swimming pool in the patio, much appreciated during the summer. Moderate.

There are a number of restaurants, none of which deserve any prizes. The best restaurants are not in town, but up at the wye for the benefit of the customers driving large trucks. I prefer to stock up at the Supermercado and eat at my leisure on the mini-zócolo.

Getting There & Getting Around
The highway misses Mulegé. To get into town stop at the wye where the big trucks park and follow the signs left. The Pemex gas station is on the right going into town, and the Supermercado is about 25 metres farther on.

The plaza is about 75 metres to the right of the Supermercado, but if you are driving you will have to go to the next corner and turn right and come back around past the Hacienda — little Mulegé is full of one-way streets.

LORETO
This is probably the oldest settlement in the three Californias, but it was pretty much abandoned for a number of years. It was established by the Jesuit Superior Juan María Salvatierra during the days when California was a theocracy so absolute that even the Spanish soldiers sent out to garrison the country were individually vetted by the Order. Over the door of the church is carved (in Spanish) 'The Head and Mother of Missions in Upper and Lower California', and for over a hundred years this building was the de facto capital of California. When the Jesuits were expelled in 1768 their operation was taken over by the Franciscans, and it was from here that Padre Junipero Serra left to begin his life's work of establishing missions in Alta California (better known today as simply California).

Considering the ancient history, Loreto today doesn't amount to much, aside from the old church.

Places to Stay & Eat
There are several very expensive hotels but very little point in overnighting.

Best place to eat, especially for breakfast, is the *Hotel Presidente*. Breakfasts there are moderate but otherwise it is ridiculously expensive. I prefer to picnic.

Getting There
Loreto is 135 km south of Mulegé on the main highway. Apart from road transport there is also a scheduled air service, and lots of fishermen fly their own planes in from the US and stay at the Flying Sportsman Lodge.

MISIÓN DE SAN JAVIER
From just south of the turn-off to Loreto there is a signed branch road leading inland 35 km to the old Misión de San Javier. This is the best example of Jesuit stone construction in Baja California. It was built for the ages in an arid location, and stands today just as the good fathers finished it, with almost no deterioration even though there has been no maintenance or restoration work in the intervening years.

The old mission sits at the end of a double row of houses, complete with non-operating fountains, a sort of enlongated zócolo. It is the scene of a pilgrimage each year on 6 December that draws (mostly) back-country people for about a week of socializing and drinking. If you are in the area around this time it is definitely worth a visit.

LA PAZ
Up until WW II, La Paz was a pearl-fishing centre, but for some unknown reason the pearls played out about the time of Pearl Harbour, and I can remember the day when a stroll around town took one past patio after patio decorated with complete hard-hat diving outfits deteriorating in the blazing sun.

With the sudden expiration of the

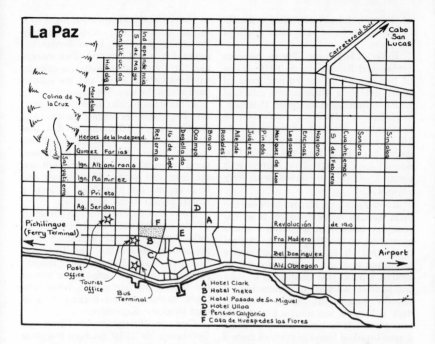

A Hotel Clark
B Hotel Yneka
C Hotel Posada de Sn. Miguel
D Hotel Ulloa
E Pension California
F Casa de Huéspedes las Flores

pearl fishing La Paz lost population and was saved only by being the territorial capital and by some desultory shipping. The road down the peninsula was all but impossible for the average tourist, and the few motorcycle riders and other intrepid types that did manage to cope with the 1500 km of desert trail were not big spenders.

The current boom really started with the advent of a regular ferry service to and from Mazatlan, on the mainland, in the '60s. The airport was improved and scheduled services to the US began at about the same time, bringing in a flood of tourists, and for the first time in memory 'full' signs began to appear in the hotel lobbies. Then in 1973 the paving of the Transpeninsular Highway was completed at last, making it practical for families in softly-sprung automobiles to drive through Baja from end to end. New hotels were constructed up

and down the highway by the Presidente chain, and La Paz began a hotel building spree that continues unabated to this very day.

Unlike most plazas that are dimly illuminated by the penny-pinching town fathers, the zocolo in La Paz is brilliantly lit by dozens of high-intensity discharge bulbs concealed in the old pebbled-glass globes. It is a rare sight, especially if you arrive in La Paz at night.

Places to Stay

Even with all the new rooms that have been added over the past decade La Paz still fills up and sometimes travellers have to accept rooms that they would not normally have chosen. Low-priced places are concentrated pretty much around the plaza, and the economy hotels are all within ten minutes' walk of the zócolo. There are quite a number of viajero hotels, mostly clustered within a few blocks of each other south of the plaza.

Hotel Clark, on Bravo between Serdan and Revolución de 1910, is one of the newest of the current crop of small hotels, a three-storey structure with non-functional balconiés. Moderate.

Hotel la Purisima, on 16 de Septiembre between Revolución de 1910 and Serdan. An older house, dating back to at least the 1960s, that doesn't look its age. Four storeys with elevator. Close to downtown. Very expensive.

Hotel Yneka, on Madero between the plaza and 16 de Septiembre, is an old economy hotel that sheltered a whole generation of travellers over the original truck trail. It has recently suffered a facelifting and now is two storeys built around a patio that doubles as a lobby and parlour. All sorts of gimcracks now line the walls of the zaguan where the desk is located, including a breast drill, lots of antlers not necessarily in pairs, a wood-spoked iron-tired wheel from a child's goat cart, a small collection of padlocks together with a large assortment of non-matching keys, and much, much more. Otherwise it is the same old Yneka except the price has gone up. Moderate.

Hotel Posada de Sn Miguel is on Belesario Dominguez near 16 de Septiembre, across from the army barracks and hard by the old market which is now a shopping arcade. View this one from across the street to get the full Arabic effect of the handsome tiled facade. Moderate.

Hotel Cristine is on 16 de Septiembre between Madero and Revolución de 1910. Built in 1971, it looks much older. It is a two-storey family-style hotel and considerably larger than it appears from the sidewalk. To get a fix on its true size head back through the zaguan past the desk to the patio. It was previously the *Hotel Mouron*. Moderate.

Hotel Ulloa is identified at night by a bright electric sign reading 'Brandy Presidente Hotel'. It is on Serdan between Bravo and Ocampo. Two storeys and the front rooms include a balcony overlooking the street and the schoolyard across the way. Moderate.

Pensión California Casa de Huespedes, on Degollado between Madero and Revolucion de 1910, has a sign that states 'This is not a hotel. It is a home for our guests'. Fairly quiet neighbourhood, especially at night, and not too far from the plaza. Single-storey and built around the plant-filled patio of a former private home. Moderate.

Hotel San Carlos is on the corner of 16 de Septiembre and Revolución de 1910, but you actually enter on 16 de Septiembre under the sign that says 'Relojeria Jaz-vic. Reparacion de relojes'. Although the San Carlos is on one of the busiest intersections in town it is likely to have rooms because it is so hard to locate. Expensive.

Casa de Huespedes las Flores, on Revolución de 1910 between the plaza and 16 de Septiembre is a typical no-frills casa de huespedes. It also doubles as a bath house, so hot water should be no problem. Moderate.

Librado Gonzalez' *Hotel Prado* is at the corner of Bravo and Verdad (both streets are named for lawyers, believe it or not!). During the '60s it was way out in the country among the windmills; now it's an ongoing construction and ten times larger (and a great deal more expensive) than when I stayed there the first time. For drivers it offers secure, enclosed parking. Very expensive.

A much better deal is the newer and somewhat cheaper *Hotel Santana*, on Revolución de 1910 between Juarez and Pineda. The Santana is housed in a three-storey building with a clean appearance due to the bright white paint, orange rejas and beige trim. As usual, it is built around the patio. The neighbourhood is fairly quiet by day, dead quiet at night. The Santana is far enough from the zócolo so it takes a bit longer than most to fill, and against all reason it is cheaper than the Prado. In my opinion a much better deal, but still it's very expensive.

Places to Eat

As with any boom town, La Paz is a fairly expensive place in which to eat — even the market is expensive. The following places used to be cheap; recently their prices have gone up a lot but they are still less than the better-publicised places down on the Malacon.

Restaurant Ceilo Azul, on Bravo between Ramirez and Altamirano has been face-lifted by the addition of some cheap pine-finish plywood panelling, but at the rear it is still the same old Ceilo Azul of yore! One of the waiters used to be a wrestler called El Jipi Sucio (the dirty hippy!) who was full of stories about his nomadic life. The Ceilo Azul does very well these days with higado Mexicana, and generally gives excellent value for the peso. Moderate.

One of the new markets, at Degollado and Revolución de 1910, has rather more elaborate restaurant facilities than most of its kind, but is inexpensive. There is another new market on Bravo between Prieto and Ramirez. It is mostly a meat market, but also has restaurant facilities, again inexpensive. The new markets, by the way, are the result of the destruction of the original market, the one with all the character, to make way for a min-iscule shopping arcade, complete with operating fountain in the middle.

Cafe Olimpia is across the street from the La Purisima Hotel and is the best place to eat near the plaza. The bakery next door is actually a part of the cafe. The locals are well aware of the Olimpia's merits and at times it is a bit difficult to get a seat, either at the counter or at one of the tables on the sidewalk. Inexpensive.

By contrast, restaurants opposite the side of the church on Independencia are without exception poorly operated and the help is ignorant and incompetent. Definitely not recommended.

Antojitos El Mexicano, on 16 de Septiembre near Serdan, specialises in menudo, burritos and other home-cooked specialities, and makes a big thing of its comida corrida. Moderate.

Restaurant de la Rosa is another Mexican-style restaurant that I can recommend. It's a little place next door to the Ceilo Azul, selling Machaca, pozole, and so on. Moderate.

Getting There

La Paz is the transport hub of Baja California Sur. It has scheduled air services to mainland Mexico and the US. Roads lead north to the US and south to Todos Santos and Cabo San Lucas.

The bus station in La Paz is one of the most conveniently located in Mexico and is about five minutes' walk from the plaza. Turn either right or left as you leave the front door of the station on the ocean side, and turn uphill away from the water at the first inter-section. The zócolo is three blocks away.

There is a ferry service from La Paz to Mazatlan. The terminal is at Pichil-ingui, about 14 km along the northern shore of Bahia de La Paz, but there is a ticket office for the government ferries in downtown La Paz at Victoria and La Paz. Look for the sign that says 'Caminos and Puentes Federales de Ingresos y Servicios Conexos.'

From time to time there is a ferry to Topolobampo, the seaport for Los Mochis, Sinaloa, but the route suffers from lack of patronage which causes service to be discontinued until some other optimist takes over.

CABO SAN LUCAS & CABO SAN JOSE

Cabo San Lucas is the southernmost tip of Baja California. It has received a good deal of tourist-oriented publicity not long back because it is the site of several high-priced hotels. Originally it was visited by big game fishermen such as the late Bing Crosby and his sidekick Phil Harris, but there aren't enough fishermen to make a large hotel complex worthwhile, and now the publicity is aimed at everyone with the price of an airplane ticket whose idea of a vacation is to sit around a pool and drink margaritas and touch up their tans. Not a town worthy of the name.

Cabo San Jose is not a popular tourist destination, and its hotels cost about half as much as the ones at Cabo San Lucas. San Jose is a town of about 3000 and has all the services of an isolated community, including liquor stores, bank, gas station and so on.

Getting There

There is a frequent bus service from La Paz by paved road. Cabo San Jose is 185 km, Cabo San Lucas 215 km.

There is a ferry service from Cabo San Lucas to Puerto Vallerta, but it is more convenient, even for those actually going to Puerto Vallerta, to take the ferry from La Paz to Mazatlan. There are more ferries for one thing, and for another the ferry terminal at Cabo San Lucas is difficult to reach. If a ferry is missed the hotels at Los Cabos are more expensive than staying in La Paz.

The West Coast

The West Coast route, via Baja California, Mexicali and Nogales is the preferred land route for travellers visiting Central Mexico and beyond.

Most tourists begin at Tijuana. The new bus station on the eastern outskirts of Tijuana can be reached by local bus from the Tres Estrellas station downtown (see 'Tijuana' in the previous chapter), or by Greyhound from the US, which is somewhat more expensive but an awful lot less trouble.

It is vitally important to get your Mexican tourist permit at the border. Mexico has *Migración* check points along the roads leading down from the border and if the mood of the inspectors happens to be bad they are perfectly capable of sending a foreigner back to the border to pick up a tourist permit.

MEXICALI, Baja California

In summer this is one of the hottest places in North America. It is the capital of the state of Baja California but is included in this chapter because it is the terminal of the railroad running along the west coast to Mexico City. At one time there was a connecting railroad, the San Diego and Arizona Eastern, that ran to Tijuana, but a number of washouts caused by a severe storm gave its owner, Southern Pacific, an excuse to discontinue the service. The tracks are still in place, however, and I suspect it may be repaired because Tijuana is getting so large and generates so much business.

Trains generally depart around noon for Guadalajara and Mexico City. First class is somewhat cheaper than bus, and the 2nd class fare is about half the price of a bus ticket, but I definitely don't recommend Mexican 2nd-class trains to any but the most poverty-stricken foreigners. Second-class travel is like making a trip in the cargo compartment of a garbage truck with the denizens of a home for disadvantaged infants; 1st class is better, and reserved-seat 1st class not bad at all, but be warned that Mexican air-conditioning in general is unreliable, and that on trains is especially prone to breakdowns. Travelling by train in Mexico is only recommended for dyed-in-the-wool rail-fans; I don't really feel it does much for the casual traveller!

For the most up-to-date information on train service write to: Ferrocarril Sonora Baja California, POB 231, Calexico, California 92231, USA. (The railroad maintains this box in the US because getting mail this way is much more efficient than receiving it via the Mexican postal system!)

SONOITA, Sonora

Sonoita is 266 km east of Mexicali and almost due south of Gila Bend, Arizona. It is where the road branches off to Puerto Peñasco. All buses stop here, but more important to the traveller heading south, at the eastern edge of town there are customs and immigration inspection stations. Although the immigration people are empowered to issue tourist permits at the Sonoita station they have been known to refuse to do so for one reason or another, which means that the foreigner caught short will have to retrace his trip — and forfeit his bus ticket — to a station closer to the border.

The customs station is there primarily to check the belongings of Mexican citizens for such contraband as transistor radios, tape recorders, TV sets and other prohibited items, and the check on the foreigner is perfunctory, to say the least. But be prepared — both customs and immigration have it in their power to make it extremely uncomfortable for the traveller of any nationality without

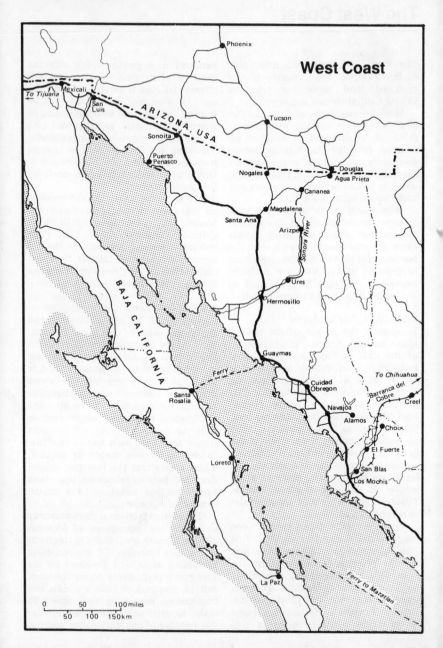

West Coast

ARIZONA, USA

To Tijuana
Mexicali
San Luis
Sonoita
Puerto Penasco
Phoenix
Tucson
Nogales
Douglas
Agua Prieta
Cananea
Magdalena
Santa Ana
Arizpe
Sonora River
Ures
Hermosillo
Guaymas
Ferry
Santa Rosalia
Cuidad Obregon
To Chihuahua
Barranca del Cobre
Creel
Navajoa
Alamos
Choix
El Fuerte
San Blas
Los Mochis
Loreto
La Paz
Ferry to Mazatlan

BAJA CALIFORNIA

0   50   100 miles
  50   100   150km

a tourist permit or with an undeclared tape recorder, etc. There is even a notice to this effect, in both Spanish and English, back at the Mexicali bus terminal but time and time again travellers ignore the warning and wind up in an embarassing position!

PUERTO PEÑASCO, Baja California

For some unknown reason, this is known to English-speaking North Americans as Rocky Point, although this is nowhere near an exact translation of the Spanish!

Peñasco attracts a considerable number of tourists, mostly people with an interest in salt-water fishing, shell collecting or like pursuits, plus the usual sun-worshippers who like to loll about the beach and cultivate their tans. (Along this line, four couples from Arizona were peacefully sunbathing in the nude when they were arrested and marched back through town in the altogether to the jail. It took them several days to effect their releases during which time they had no clothing.)

Puerto Peñasco is a small, prosperous town sprawled over a large sandy area and its principal income comes from fishing, shrimping, boat-building and repairing, and selling ice-cold beer in case lots during the summer. It is a new community and as such has no interesting old colonial buildings suitable for conversion to viajero hotels, and no plaza to form a focal point for the community. Many Americans come to Peñasco for the sportfishing; they drive down in huge motor homes, towing their boats behind them.

Places to Stay & Eat

The closest hotel to the bus station is the *Villa Granada Hotel*. It is about 1½ km south on Benito Juarez, the street the bus station is on, and a block to the left of the CFE office. Very expensive and cursed with a large noisy bar that goes until the wee small hours.

There is also the *Motel Señorial*. Continue along Juárez past Villa Granada and turn right at the stop light and go four more blocks. The Señorial is about the same calibre as the Granada and also very expensive.

There is a trailer camp, marked with a big sign, about six blocks beyond the stop light on Juárez.

The restaurant situation is murder. The only place I would care to mention is the restaurant in the Señorial.

Getting There

Peñasco is at the end of a 100-km paved road from Sonoita. Buses mostly originate in Mexacali, and stop at Sonoita. If coming from the east buy a ticket to Sonoita and catch the Peñasco bus at the junction. The bus station is at the northern edge of town.

Rarely, an adventurous soul will take a train down from Mexicali, or up from Central Mexico, but that's doing it the hard way!

SANTA ANA, Sonora

This is a nothing sort of town whose only excuse for existence is that it is situated at the junction of the main west coast routes from Nogales and Tijuana, probably the busiest highway intersection in Mexico north of Mexico City.

NOGALES, Sonora

Nogales is about 100 km south of Tucson, Arizona, and is one of the most popular border crossings for travellers. It is also the export gateway for much of the produce grown on the industrialized farms in the states of Sonora, Sinaloa and Jalisco.

Getting There

The sister city, Nogales, Arizona, is reached by Citizen's Stage Lines bus from Tucson, Arizona, about an hour's ride. The bus lets passengers off at the Citizen's station a stone's throw from the border. Walk across the border and the Tres Estrellas and Transportes Norte de Sonora (TNS) and Transportes de Sonora (TS) stations are to the right. Be sure to get your tourist permit or passport stamped!

Nogales, Sonora, is a transportation hub. Buses go to Tijuana, Agua Prieta, or Central Mexico. If you are heading south, it is not advisable to take the Tijuana bus to Santa Ana and expect to change to another bus going south — buses very often run full and will accept no more passengers.

MAGDALENA, Sonora

Magdalena is the only town of any interest north of Guaymas. It has a pretty colonial church, and the great Jesuit founder of missions, Father Eusebio Kino, is buried in a glass-topped grave in a little building on the plaza. No kidding — you can see his skeleton!

There is a good restaurant right on the plaza, El Tecolote, with huge cages containing every kind of bird imaginable with one notable exception — there are no owls! Moderate.

SONORA RIVER VALLEY

An alternative route south to Hermosillo is via the new paved road running south from Cananea along the Sonora River to Ures, and then west to Hermosillo. This road is so new that it doesn't appear on many maps yet, and as yet there is very little traffic, with very few big trucks and buses to dodge, a situation that will change with time. This route is more interesting than the desolate CN-15 highway, and for people coming from Douglas, Arizona, it is also somewhat shorter.

The towns here, more than almost anywhere in Mexico have Indian names, and the accent falls on the third syllable from the last, rather than the next-to-last syllable as per the usual Spaniard practice. Watch the accent marks. Examples: Bácoachi, Bácanora.

Of all the little towns along the Sonora River Valley, Arizpe is far and away the most interesting. Originally a mission, it developed into a full-fledged church centre when mines where established in the area.

In 1776 a Spanish officer named de Anza led several hundred Mexican families, including women, children, poultry and livestock, to establish what is now known as San Francisco, California. Contrary to many published reports, the expedition did not start from Arizpe, but Arizpe received de Anza's bones and they rest today in a glass-topped grave in the church on the plaza.

Arizpe is the most progressive of any of the old towns along the river, due mostly to a new, young mayor. The streets are paved, the various businesses are required to put up signs — most of the towns in the region look more like ranches than towns! — and there is even an animal control officer whose job it is to arrest loose livestock daring to crop the plants on the plaza.

There are three hotels, which should soon have names and signs, a number of restaurants, a gas station, grocery stores, and a stated population of around 3500, probably counted on a Saturday night!

HERMOSILLO, Sonora

Hermosillo has nothing much going for it but its good fortune of being the capital of the state of Sonora. It is rather an uninteresting town, blisteringly hot in the summer, and the only people who can be expected to overnight there are the adventurers who come down via the scenic route through Arizpe and Ures.

The new Central de Autobuses is on the outskirts of town with nothing in view but a few hills pretty well covered with mud shacks. The station has post office and telegraph facilities, restaurant and the usual amenities.

Places to Stay

Hotel Monte Carlo, Sonora at Juárez,

at one corner of the plaza, occupies the second floor of the corner building. A well-run establishment. Expensive, but worth it.

Hotel Lourdes, Oaxaca near Juárez, towards the avenue, is unprepossessing but economical. Mexican Miracle Modern. Inexpensive.

Hotel San Andres, Oaxaca near Juárez is another low-price hotel, older than the Lourdes and not as well maintained. Inexpensive.

Places to Eat

There are any number of country-style restaurants in this neighbourhood, but the hands-down best, and my favourite in Hermosillo, is the *Restaurant Monte Carlo* in the hotel of the same name. Well-run by knowledgeable people who know their business thoroughly. For instance, if you order a bottle of Agua Tehuacan, it will be ice-cold, served with a glass of ice cubes with a twist of lime!

And while you are in the neighbourhood, note the shining white teeth of the locals in the neighbourhood, not all that common in Mexico.

Getting Around

To reach the plaza near the low-priced hotels, cross the street in front of the bus station and catch a city bus marked Ranchito. It turns right onto a broad avenue which is eventually joined by railroad tracks which run down the centre divider. After the railroad tracks end, the bus turns left onto a narrow, one-way street called Juárez. Get off at the little plaza a couple of blocks along Juárez and pay the driver a couple of pesos on leaving. Just toss the coins onto the rug on the dashboard.

To return to the bus station, go back out Juárez to the avenue and catch a bus going from left to right, again marked Ranchito. Or you can walk it in about 20 minutes.

GUAYMAS, Sonora

Guaymas, 135 km south of Hermosillo, is the first town you hit coming south down the west coast that can be called a destination in any remote sense of the word. It is primarily a fishing port, with a fine harbour, and also has the usual boat-building and repair businesses. It has been trying to build up its tourist business, but having no beaches to offer the sun bunnies, hasn't had much luck.

Guaymas is a relatively new town, having been founded as Guaymas de Zaragoza in 1769. Because of the fine harbour it prospered early on, and was the shipping port for the ranches and rich mines in the interior of Sonora. The town has had many masters. In the beginning, of course, it was Spanish and so rich that it attracted the attentions of one Count Gaston Raousset de Boulbon who twice tried to sack the town. On the second attempt the Count was captured and suffered the usual end — he was executed by the local commander, General Yañaz. The French were back again during Maximilian's short reign, and during the Civil War, Guaymas served as a trans-shipment point for supplies for the Union forces in Arizona Territory. With the Revolution of 1910 and the accompanying anarchy, Guaymas fell into the financial doldrums from which it took decades to recover.

Places to Stay

As Guaymas itself is not popular with tourists it should follow that there are lots of economical hotels around, but it doesn't quite work that way.

The old *Hotel Rubi*, at Serdán and Calle 29 is a good example. It is definitely overpriced, but when the old Hotel Malema closed there wasn't a lot of choice left. The Rubi has been accumulated rather than built, and you practically need a guide to find your way around. Very expensive. The bar serves little 200-ml bottles of Bohemia beer, a

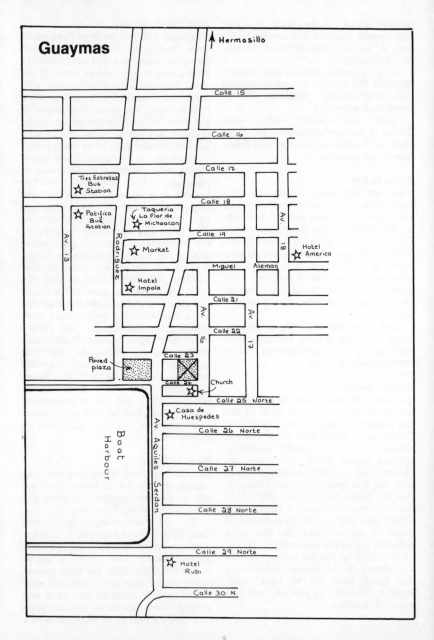

Guaymas

↑ Hermosillo

Calle 15

Calle 16

Calle 17

Tres Estrellas
Bus
Station

Calle 18

Pacifico
Bus
Station

Taqueria
La Flor de
Michoacan

Calle 19

Market

Hotel
America

Miguel   Aleman

Hotel
Impala

Calle 21

Calle 22

Av. 16

Calle 23

Paved
plaza

Calle 24

Church

Calle 25 Norte

Casa de
Huespedes

Calle 26 Norte

Calle 27 Norte

Boat
Harbour

Av. Aquiles Serdan

Calle 28 Norte

Calle 29 Norte

Hotel
Rubi

Calle 30 N.

Av. 13

Rodriguez

Av. 18

Av. 17

total insult to a thirsty person in a hot region.

The *Hotel Ana*, near the plaza may be a good, reasonably-priced hotel, but I have yet to find anybody in attendance, so maybe it is always full.

The *Hotel Impala* (née *Malema*) is on Rodriguez and Calle 29, four blocks from the bus station. The best place in town and the air-conditioning works, as well it should for the price is ridiculously expensive.

Hotel America is up the hill on Aleman (if the street numbering were consistent Aleman would be Calle 20) three blocks on the corner of Avenida 18. As you approach from Serdán there is no sign visible, but the sign can be seen from the other side, and the odd-looking building is painted a pastel blue so it's hard to miss. Expensive.

Casa de Huespedes, on Serdán between Calles 25 and 26, is the best bet of all in the way of economy. In Europe it would be a pension, but don't expect European standards of quality. Inexpensive.

Places to Eat

Guaymas has been long noted as a seafood town, but in recent years the quality has dropped as prices have risen.

The old standby has long been the *Chichén Itzá*, now on the Malecón near the Rubi, but even this old reliable has suffered some deterioration in recent years. Expensive, like all the other fish restaurants in Guaymas.

When the *Impala* (hotel) was the Malema it had the best restaurant in the state and served the best *Pescado Veracruzana* in Mexico. Apparently the original crew scattered while the hotel was closed down during the battle between the heirs. Now that it has been recycled into the Impala it isn't quite as good as it used to be, but it still ranks well in the forefront of Guaymas' restaurants, and getting better all the time. Expensive.

La Flor de Michoacán, on Calle 19 across the street from the market, is a little tacoria that does a better than average job of taco building. Inexpensive.

Unfortunately Guaymas doesn't run heavy to markets, but there are several ample ladies who serve meals in the market at rock-bottom prices. The little market is on Calle 19 at Rodriguez.

Another place for a hearty and economical snack is *Las 1000 Tortas*, on Serdán between Calle 19 and Aleman.

Directly across the street from the Pacifico bus station is a lunch room and fruit stand, both of which receive a good play from the locals. Inexpensive.

For do-it-yourselfers in the eating department, there is a good supermarket at the corner of Calle 18 and Serdán; enter through the liquor store.

Getting Around

There are two bus stations, right across the street from each other on Calle 18. To get downtown, turn left from the Tres Estrellas, TNS and TS station, or turn right from the Pacifico station. In two blocks you will come to Serdán, the main street; turn right and you are in the business section.

CUIDAD OBREGÓN, Sonora

This must be the nothing town of Mexico, or one of them, at least. About 114 km south-east of Guaymas in the midst of thousands of hectares of irrigated fields, the city was built on the agricultural boom caused by damming the Rio Yaqui and using the water for power and for irrigating the fertile plane between the Sierras and the Sea of Cortés. It was named after the one-armed general and president of Mexico who got along well with the Yaquis and who successfully grew chick-peas in the neighbourhood. In fact, Obregon was called 'The Garabanzo King' at the time. Nowadays Cuidad Obregón sells farm machinery, mills and stores grain, packs vegetables and becomes larger and more prosperous year by year.

Places to Stay

In case you have the misfortune to get stuck here, I suggest you take a cab from the bus station to the *Hotel Kuraica* (moderate) on Calle 5 de Febrero Sur. This isn't all that much of a hotel, but it is about the handiest and cheapest in Obregón, which runs heavy to expensive hotels. Make sure the air-conditioning works if you are there during the hot months.

NAVAJOA, Sonora

Navajoa isn't much of a place but it is a vast improvement over Obregón as a stopping place on the long trek south. It is about 67 km down the road south-east of Obregon. The reason most people stop here is that it is the jumping-off place for Alamos, 53 km by paved road to the east in the foothills of the Sierra Madre Occidental.

Places to Stay

Navajoa has a number of hotels, some of them up in the M$400 a night range, but it also has the *Hotel America*. It is about six blocks back toward Guaymas from the bus stations on Calzada de Revolución, the street the Pacifico bus station is on. Except for the noise of the buses, which continues 24 hours a day, the America is a safe bet as an inexpensive hotel.

To reach the *Hotel Aduana* go out the front door of the Tres Estrellas station and turn right on Ignacio Allende. The Aduana is in the next block. Those who stayed in the old Aduana years ago wouldn't recognize the place. The old place has been completely recycled into a new and modern viajero hotel, a vast improvement over the original structure, but I miss the mural of the old town and smelter of Aduana, Sonora, that used to grace the lobby.

Places to Eat

The best place to eat in Navajoa is at one of the stands across from the TNS station. (This is actually another bus station for the many long-nosed buses that serve the outlying small towns over dirt roads.) My favourite among these stands is the one with the sign that says simply 'Birria de Cabro', probably because I like birria, but they are all good, and very inexpensive.

A cheap place for a cooling beer on a summer afternoon is across the street in front of the Tres Estrellas station on Allende at the place with the 'Carta Blanca' sign. The name of the establishment is *Mariscos a la Jojarrita*, but I've never seen anything but cerveza sold.

Avoid as the plague the joint to your left as you leave the TNS station — a not-too-cold bottle of beer will set you back M$26!

ALAMOS, Sonora

Alamos is a rather interesting place. A falling-down ruin only a few years ago, it has been repaired and restored by wealthy Americans who buy old buildings for the proverbial song, and then spend thousands of dollars restoring them to their former glory. Being one of Mexico's National Monuments, the town does not and cannot suffer from the tawdry, plastic schlock construction that has defaced so many once-beautiful Mexican cities.

A few km back toward Navajoa, and just south of the road, is La Aduana (from whence the hotel in Navajoa takes its name), the site of the smelter that separated the silver from the ore from the mines around Alamos for some hundreds of years. If you are interested in industrial archaeology, a visit to La Aduana and an observant eye will give you considerable insight into the art of ore-dressing and its changes over the centuries. As improvements in smelting techniques required different physical structures the old ones were simply abandoned. The last operation took place around 50 years ago, and there is still a complete power house dating from that time, and with the original Fairbanks-Morse C-O engine in place and looking as if it could be started again any day.

La Aduana has a church with a large cactus growing out of the wall, and there is a story about an apparition of the Virgin manifesting on the site and pointing out a large silver vein. The town is also the scene of an important fiesta of the region's Mayo (not Maya) Indians. This is held each year on 20 November and during the fiesta the old ghost town returns to life with a vengeance!

Places to Stay
Unless you happen to have friends in Alamos I suggest you skip this particular national treasure. Hotels are mighty expensive, and the only one that can be wholly depended upon is the *Tesoro* and that will set you back about M$1500 a day!

The guidebooks all list the *Portales*, but last time I was there the *Portales* had 'temporarily' closed its doors and nobody had the least idea when, if ever, it would reopen. And before that it was always full!

Getting There
There is a bus service from Navajoa, but the Alamos bus doesn't use the same facilities as any of the other bus companies, including the long-nosed suburban buses. The Alamos bus has left from several different corners, so ask the people at the Tres Estrellas where the current bus stop is — they will be glad to share their knowledge.

LOS MOCHIS, Sinaloa
BARRANCA DEL COBRE
Most foreigners stop in Los Mochis to transfer to the train or railcar that goes up through the Barranca del Cobre to

Chihuahua. The Barranca is considerably larger than the Grand Canyon of Arizona, although by no means as spectacular. The railroad, Chihuahua al Pacifico, was originally conceived as the shortest freight route between the American heartland and the Pacific. Today it mostly hauls Mexican products to and from the little seaport of Topolobampo, 22 km west of Los Mochis. At the other end, the CHP terminates at the border town of Ojinaga, across the Rio Grande (Rio Bravo to Mexicans) from Presidio, Texas.

The trip is exceeding popular with both the ordinary run of tourist and the out-and-out railfans who make the 650-km trip between Mochis and Chihuahua in large numbers, for this is truly one of the great train rides in the world. The railbed is blasted from the side of the mountain for hundreds of km, and there are over 30 tunnels. The passenger equipment is either standard USA (retired) or Fiat diesel-propelled railcars called Autovias. Some of the standard cars are equipped with observation domes, and such trains are called Vista Trens.

Some railfans have loud and impassioned arguments as to which is superior, a Vista Tren, Autovia or regular passenger train; I've ridden all three at one time or another, and enjoyed them all.

At the upper end of the canyon is the little town of Creel, unusual for a Mexican community in that it is mostly built of log cabins. Many experienced Barranca fans take the train only to Creel and return the next day, claiming there is little to be gained by taking the train on into Chihuahua through the flat and uninteresting farming country.

The trains stop at Divisadero for the benefit of photographers and viewenjoyers. From Divisadero you can look across the canyon into the mouths of three major canyons, equally deep. The one on the northern side is La Barranca del Cobre; the middle one is La Santa

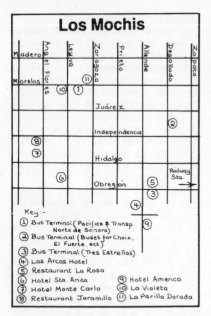

Los Mochis

Key:-
1. Bus Terminal (Pacífico & Transp. Norte de Sonora)
2. Bus Terminal (Buses for Choix, El Fuerte, ect.)
3. Bus Terminal (Tres Estrellas)
4. Los Arcos Hotel
5. Restaurant La Rosa
6. Hotel Sta. Anita
7. Hotel Monte Carlo
8. Restaurant Jaramillo
9. Hotel America
10. La Violeta
11. La Parilla Dorada

Streets (from map): Madero, Morelos, Angel Flores, Leyva, Zaragoza, Prieto, Allende, Degollado, Zapata, Juárez, Independencia, Hidalgo, Obregón, Railway Sta.

monumental foul-ups by people who attempted this. It is important to remember in Mochis that 'railroad time' is an hour ahead of local time. Many disappointed would-be passengers have stood at the station with tickets in their hands looking at the empty tracks an hour after the train has been and gone!

As with all schedules, the CHP feels perfectly free to change train times at will, but generally speaking a morning train from either Chihuahua or Mochis is the way to sight-see, and an evening train is for those who for one reason or another are interested in transport more than scenery.

The CHP station in Los Mochis is way out from the centre of town. A cab costs about M$75, or there is a bus available. Catch it near the Tres Estrellas station on Obregón; it's green, and the fare is around M$4.

Places to Stay

The cheapest place I know in Los Mochis is the *Casa de Huespedes* (not otherwise identified by name) reached by going out the back of the TNS station, past the bus stalls, and across the alley. Inexpensive.

Coming up a little in price and a great deal in quality is the *Los Arcos Hotel*, around the corner on Allende from the Tres Estrellas bus station. The blue-fronted Los Arcos represents excellent value for money and tends to fill up early on, so check in as soon as possible. Moderate.

Down Allende past the Los Arcos is the *Hotel America*, long a favourite with automobilists because of the lock-up parking lot around in back. Expensive.

Hotel Monte Carlo, on Angel Flores between Independencia and Hidalgo, is a big, older hotel that looks as if it should be inexpensive but it isn't; however it makes quite a point of having air-conditioning that works! Expensive.

Hotel Santa Anita, on Leyva

Sinforosa and the most southerly is El Canon de Balojaque, known to some English-speakers as 'Urique', God knows why.

The CHP is not operated solely for the benefit of the tourist business. Its primary purpose is to provide access to an extremely large, otherwise inaccessible area, rich in minerals and forest products, and to allow ocean freight to move into the interior of the northern part of the country from the Pacific side. Passengers are hauled as a convenience to the traveling public and the railroad doesn't put itself too far out of its way for their benefit, Mexican or foreign. The CHP also transports automobiles, but it usually takes an extra day or two at each end for loading and unloading, and it's an expensive service.

The best way to get tickets for the Copper Canyon trip is to go out to the railroad station in Los Mochis. Theoretically they are available from local travel agents, but I've been told of between Hidalgo and Obregón, gets more of its business from the tour packagers who always offer 'first class accommodations', which translates that it is overpriced and that at least one employee speaks a language that sounds something like English. Included here because it stands out like a sore thumb and makes an excellent landmark. Ridiculously expensive.

In Creel a number of hotels have been established to cope with the train passengers who do not want to continue on to Chihuahua. Most of them, including the new *Parador* are in the M$700 a day class, or even higher.

An exception to this sweeping statement is the tiny *Hotel Korachi*, near the station. Because it is small and low-priced it is often full of penny-wise travellers, and if you intend to overnight there I suggest you wire a reservation from Mochis stating the day and train on which you expect to arrive. Moderate.

There is also a fancy hotel at Divisadero, for the benefit of people who take package tours, apparently. Ridiculously expensive.

Places to Eat

There are lots of economy-model restaurants around the Tres Estrellas de Oro bus station in Los Mochis. My favourite is the *Rio Rosa*, across Obregón from the station. Hearty meals for country people featuring such Central Mexican items as chiliquiles, cocida de rez, picadillo, flan and a fantastic rico pozolo. Moderate.

Those using Pacifico or TNS buses aren't quite so fortunate. The best way they can go is *La Parilla Dorada*, which contrary to the name is painted lavender. It is almost as good as La Parilla up the hill in Chihuahua. Expensive.

The *Madrid*, on Obregón at Leyva, has been good for many years. Despite the name, it's really mostly Mexican, rather than Spanish. Moderate.

There is a tiny public market in Los Mochis, on Independencia between Degollado and Zapata. There are several good little restaurants intended primarily for the market people but all comers with money are welcome, making this the cheapest place to eat in town. Very inexpensive.

SAN BLAS, EL FUERTE & CHOIX, Sinaloa

The north-south railroad station serving Los Mochis is at San Blas, some 40 km east. Aside from this, San Blas doesn't have much to offer. If you find yourself there waiting for a train the wait can be trying. The station lunch room doesn't amount to very much, and eating is definitely better in the little town of San Blas, which is about one km away.

El Fuerte, on the other hand, is worthy of a visit in its own right. It is 78 km inland from Los Mochis at an altitude of 400 metres.

El Fuerte is the charming and unpublicized 'sister city' of Alamos that never did become a ghost town and have its buildings abandoned, nor did it become an Americanized 'National Monument', although most of the buildings date from colonial days. There is a large grassy plaza with the usual ornate bandstand and an unusual pair of fountains that both work. El Fuerte gets no play at all from the usual run of tourists but is well-known among the bass-fishing brotherhood perpetually seeking world-record fish.

About 50 km beyond El Fuerte, on the same black-topped road, is the only town with a French name, to my knowledge, in Mexico. Choix is nestled up against the foot of the Sierra Madre Occidentales, and serves as a supply and outfitting point for the ranchers, miners, and prospectors of the region. A busy place, it has several small hotels and a multitude of shops selling everything it takes to run a ranch or mine. About 3000 people, an altitude of about 600 metres, and a much better climate than Alamos. Some good marijuana is grown in the area.

Places to Stay & Eat

El Fuerte has a good viajero-type hotel, the *San Fransisco*. It is easy to find — the bus stops at the front door. It is built around the patio of a former great house. Moderate.

The restaurant in the San Francisco serves Mexican dishes and is as good as any in town. Also moderate.

Another hotel and restaurant combination is the vastly more expensive *Hotel Hidalgo*. It is definitely worth a look because of the excellent conversion job that was done to an old mansion. Enter via the ramp that used to carry the diligencias up into the grandee's courtyard. Ridiculously expensive.

Getting There

All three towns are customarily reached by bus from Los Mochis. The buses leave from a little station near the market on Degollado between Juárez and Independencia. Not all buses make all three towns, so always check to see if the Choix bus, for instance, will stop at El Fuerte.

The main north-south railroad stops at San Blas, and the Chihuahua al Pacifico Railroad also serves all three, but the stations are not actually in, nor very near, the towns themselves. Shuttle buses normally meet all trains, so getting to any of the three by rail is not a problem.

MAZATLAN, Sinaloa

Mazatlán is the northernmost destination along what the publicity people are pleased to miscall the 'Mexican Riviera', but as with most Mexican resorts it has a lot more going for it than the vagaries of the tourist business. In addition to the highly-visible tourist hotels along the Malecón, there are coffee roasters, breweries, fishing, boat-building and repair, shipping, canning and a host of other enterprises to contribute to the economic base.

As with all resorts, the tourist business is concentrated on the beaches. Mazatlán has a couple of the beaches very close to the downtown area, and it is a common sight to see people in bathing suits, robes and zoris carrying their sun-tan oil, books, umbrellas, beach chairs and so on past the plaza. As with any town in Mexico, women are expected not to traipse around in bikinis, and people naturally wear robes, or skirts and tops, when away from the beach. As I said, it is by no means an equivalent of the Riviera!

Many of the town's buildings look ancient, but actually Mazatlán is a relatively new town. About the time of Maximilian some Germans made Mazatlán their base for selling agricultural machinery and the town as it now is really dates from then.

For some years a hermit has lived in the towers of the Mazatlán Cathedral. Separated from his wife, Pablo Vargas wandered into the church one day and asked Monsignor Trinidad if he could sweep the floor in return for something to eat. The regular bell-ringer had recently died, so the monsignor asked

A Mexico's traffic laws are frequently disregarded, as shown by the cart on the road beyond this sign.
B Dancers at a local fiesta near Actopan, Hidalgo.
C Baja California has been called the world's biggest cactus garden.

A
B C

him if he would accept the job of campanillero. Vargas climbed the tower then and there and has stayed there ever since, never coming down. He is a salaried employee of the cathedral and is fed by the church; his pay is sent to his children and grandchildren because living in the towers he has no need or use for the money. High in the towers he escapes much of the town's oppressive summer heat, and when it rains he simply retreats into a tiny stone shelter. He has rigged ropes so he can ring the four bells from inside without venturing out into the rain.

On 21 de Marzo 904, near Serdan, across the street from the Vista del Mar Hotel, is a beautiful, well-maintained Buddhist temple, striking in its brilliance. It is a reminder of the days when the Chinese were a well-heeled minority. Mexico once had a sizeable Chinese population, but the Chinese had the unfortunate habit of working hard and investing with foresight, a combination of traits which allowed them to become very successful, and the Republic in its wisdom expelled most of them about 50 years ago.

Places to Stay

As with most of the older resort/commercial towns, Mazatlán has a number of inexpensive hotels located downtown and fairly distant from the beach.

The *Hotel Vialta*, on Azueta between Hidalgo and Estrada, is built around a patio in Mexican Modern style. Moderate.

The *Hotel Victoria*, Azueta at Estrada, on the other hand, is built around its parking lot. Far from palatial, but inexpensive.

Casa Familiar Aurora is on Azueta between Estrada and Ocampo. Family-style Mexican hotel that is better for groups of two or more, in which case it is inexpensive.

The *Hotel San Lorenzo* is on 21 de Marzo between Serdan and Azueta. Because it is on a seldom-used side street it is one of the last economical hotels in Mazatlán to put up the 'completo' sign. Moderate.

From the bus station on Rio Tamazula, there are three hotels in sight, plus a number of concrete-built food stalls. Across the street is the *Hotel Economica*, slightly misnamed because it is expensive. It is a new house, built to take advantage of the flow of customers from the almost equally new bus station.

The *Hotel Fiesta*, along the same street at 306 Rio Tamazula, is also new. Slightly cheaper than the Economica, but still expensive.

The best bet in the neighbourhood is the *Hotel Esperanza*, on the hill above the station on Carretera Internacional. Go out the front door of the Central Camionera bus station and you'll be on Rio Tamazula. Turn left and go up to the stop light and you will be on Carretera International. The Hotel Esperanza is now to your left and across the street. During daylight the Esperanza stands out because its brick-trimmed facade is painted bile green. Moderate.

Places to Eat

Mazatlán being a minor fishing port, the

A Mules and donkeys are still Mexico's basic form of transport in the country.
B In Merida horse-drawn carriages are still popular, and not just for tourists.

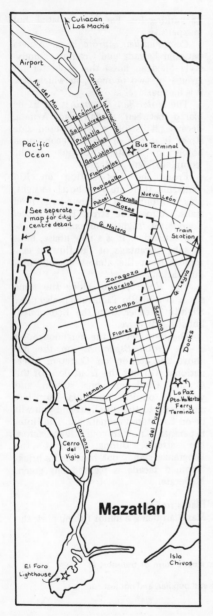

Culiacan
Los Mochis

Airport

Av del Mar

Carretera Internacional

Pacific
Ocean

T. de Canaler
San Lorenzo
Pinolatla
Albatros
Gaviiotas
Flamingos
Papagallo
Patos
Peralta
Rosas

Bus Terminal

Nuevo León

See seperate
map for city
centre detail

G. Najera

Train
Station

Zaragoza
Morelos

Ocampo

Flores

G. Leyva
Serrano

M. Aleman

Docks

La Paz
Pto.Vallarta
Ferry
Terminal

Av. del Puerto

Carranza

Cerro
del
Vigia

Mazatlán

Isla
Chivos

El Faro
Lighthouse

seafood situation is good, but for some reason seafood in Mexico runs expensive, and in Mazatlán M$100-150 for a shrimp cocktail, and M$50 for an octopus ceviche, are by no means unusual along the beaches, and only slightly less downtown.

My unqualified recommendation for a good and dependable restaurant is the *Restaurant Dony*, previously at Canizales and 5 de Mayo but soon to move to 5 de Mayo and Escobedo. This is an old favourite of Mazatlán regulars and is very efficiently operated. Good service, excellent food and the prices are, surprisingly, moderate.

The *Cafe Oriental* ('specializing in Chop Suey') is on Serdán between Estrada and Ocampo. The chop suey notwithstanding, the Oriental has provided a welcome change of pace from standard Mexican fare for many years. Moderate.

El Shrimp Bucket, on the Malecón (Olas Atlas) at Flores, in the Hotel La Fiesta, is part of a chain. Some people like it, but it is ridiculously expensive, and has such menu listings as moo for beef and oink for pork. But they have music for dancing and there will be lots and lots of people there for you to practice your English on.

As usual the cheapest eats in town — and almost the cheapest in Mexico — are served by the market ladies. Go into the market on the Ocampo side at the entrace across the street from the Banco Provincial and turn left up the stairs immediately, before you get into the market proper. There are several restaurants on a balcony overlooking the street. They are a bit difficult to find and thus attract very little foreign custom. Unfortunately they are on a west-facing balcony and are thus extremely hot during the afternoon. Very inexpensive.

Skip the restaurant in the bus station if the stands outside along Rio Tamazula are open. These are permanent concrete

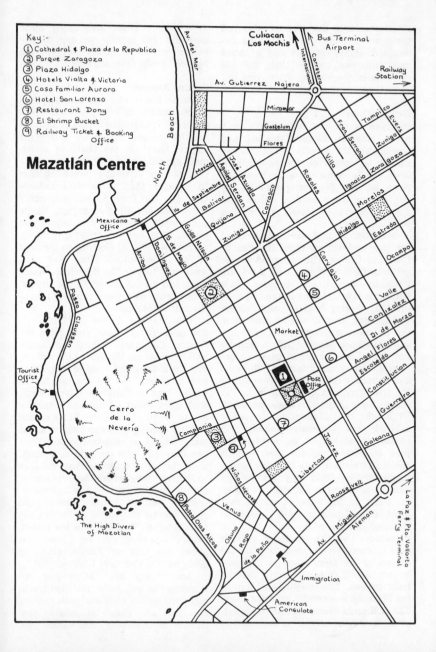

Key:-
1. Cathedral & Plaza de la Republica
2. Parque Zaragoza
3. Plaza Hidalgo
4. Hotels Vialta & Victoria
5. Casa Familiar Aurora
6. Hotel San Lorenzo
7. Restaurant Dony
8. El Shrimp Bucket
9. Railway Ticket & Booking Office

Mazatlán Centre

structures, and the women who run them are fiercely proud of their undoubted ability to put out a better meal for less money than the big cafeteria in the station. Prices vary but at most are inexpensive.

Getting There
Mazatlán is on the main north-south route between Nogales/Mexicali and Guadalajara/Mexico City. The railway station is located on the east side of town, quite some distance from the plaza, but very few foreigners arrive by rail, barring the occasional railfan who doesn't object to travelling the hard way.

Mazatlán is the mainland terminal for the ferries that cross the Sea of Cortés to La Paz. This is a good way to get to or from California USA if you are travelling by land because Baja California is much more interesting than the long, boring haul through Sinaloa and Sonora. During the summer there can be more passengers than capacity, and sometimes people wind up camping out for a day or so in order to get tickets. The crossing takes 15-20 hours and is usually calm. Ferries leave during the late afternoon and arrive in La Paz the next day in time for a late breakfast. Or lunch. The information number is 1-24-54, but probably nobody will trouble to answer, so go down to the foot of Serdán and ask there — it is about a 10-minute walk from the plaza.

Bus service, both long distance and local, is excellent at Mazatlán. It has all the buses on the heavily-travelled west coast routes plus a route inland to Durango (see below).

Because of the booming package tour business, plus a continuing barrage of special low fares, more people come by air, mostly from California, than by train or bus. The international airport for Mazatlán is 30 km from town. The taxi costs about M$250, but lower-price 'limousine service' is supposed to

be available. Those arriving by plane generally go directly to one of the expensive 'beach' hotels that line the Malecón across from the ocean.

Getting Around
Mazatlán has regular taxi service, plus a unique vehicle called a *pulmonia* which translates 'pneumonia'. This is a three-wheeled vehicle driven by a tiny gas engine, based on the Cushman metermaid special. It can carry three passengers and is obviously much cheaper to operate than a standard full-size taxi, but the fares do not necessarily reflect the operating advantage. Haggle and bargain about the fare before you get in, otherwise the driver is perfectly within his rights in charging to the limit of his imagination. These toy taxis work only within the downtown beach areas and do not go out to the airport; I have even seen them refuse a fare to the railroad station!

The city bus service in Mazatlán is first-rate. To get downtown from the Central Camionera (about an hour's walk) just go out the side of the station, pass the lunch stands onto Rio Tamazula and turn left. Go up the hill to the traffic light at Carretera Internacional, walk right about a block and catch the bus in front of the bank. Buses should pick up passengers at Rio Tamazula, but many drivers are reluctant to stop for a lone fare and miss the light as a result, so it's better to walk the short distance to the next stop where there are almost always people waiting. The bus downtown is marked 'Centro-Morelos' and goes down by the market on Serdán, the main drag of Mazatlán. For the return, catch it one block over on Azueta. Just about any bus on Azueta winds up going out the Carretera Internacional.

Around the bus station you will probably notice little pick-up trucks equipped with a couple of seats running fore and aft. These are *peseros* that shuttle between the bus station and downtown and, unlike the buses, adhere to no fixed schedule. But if you're going downtown and one happens to be available, then by all means grab it — it will be quite a bit quicker than fiddling around with the bus.

Side Trip to Durango
It is 318 km from Mazatlán to Durango, and the road is one of the most spectacular in Mexico. Branching off the coast road at Villa Union, about 25 km south of Mazatlán, at sea level, it climbs about 1625 metres through rugged mountains. At times the road winds along a ridge with not even room for shoulders and with hundreds of metres of sheer nothing on each side. If you happen to have a fear of heights, then make the trip at night. The trip takes around seven hours, and there are lots of buses originating in both Mazatlán and Durango, so it is not ordinarily a

problem to get a seat.

Cutting up to Durango is a good bet any time you are fed up with the coastal route, and it is a short-cut to the interesting colonial cities of the high mesa, such as Sombrerete and Zacatecas, although Durango doesn't have much to offer unless you are making a horse opera.

TEPIC, Nayarit
There is only one reason to stop in Tepic — to get somewhere else! It is the place to abandon the main north-south coastal route for branch-line trips to Puerto Vallerta or San Blas, Nayarit.

It is best to arrive in Tepic in the morning, but if you have to overnight the *Hotel Tepic*, which can be seen from the back of the bus station, is not a bad house, and the rates are moderate. The restaurant in the hotel is on the inferior side.

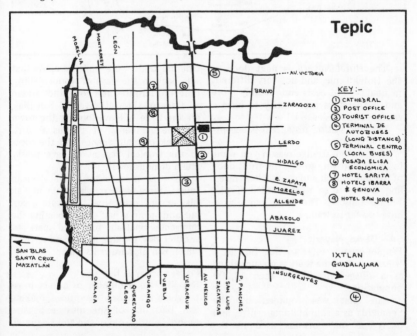

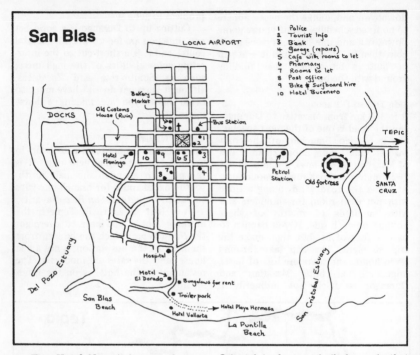

San Blas

LOCAL AIRPORT

1 Police
2 Tourist Info
3 Bank
4 Garage (repairs)
5 Café with rooms to let
6 Pharmacy
7 Rooms to let
8 Post office
9 Bike & Surfboard hire
10 Hotel Bucenero

DOCKS

Old Customs House (Ruin)

Bakery Market

Bus Station

TEPIC →

Hotel Flamingo

Petrol Station

Old fortress

SANTA CRUZ ↓

Del Pozo Estuary

San Cristobal Estuary

Hospital

Motel El Dorado →

● Bungalows for rent

···· Trailer park

San Blas Beach

→ Hotel Playa Hermosa

Hotel Vallarta

La Puntilla Beach

The *Hotel Nayarit* is next door to the Hotel Tepic, and not very different in quality, but costs considerably more and is therefore more likely to have a vacancy. Expensive.

The bus station restaurant is acceptable. Moderate.

If for some strange reason you want to go downtown, go out the front door of the bus station and catch a bus travelling from left to right marked 'Tepic-Fresno-Xalisco'. The town centre is a mite too far to walk.

SAN BLAS, Nayarit
People usually refer to San Blas as a 'village' but to me there is no such thing as a village with better than 40,000 population.

San Blas was founded by the Spaniards as a ship-building centre, and many of the bottoms used in the

Oriental trade were built here. As that was back in the days of wooden ships, time and termites have long since erased all trace of this activity. Old San Blas, on the little hill overlooking the town has the remnants of the usual fort, but lack of maintenance and the roots of the tropical vegetation have pretty much demolished it.

As with most other small Mexican towns, there isn't much to do in San Blas except swim, loaf, cultivate a sun tan and spend a half-day inspecting the miniscule Spanish fort and part of another day looking at the spring from which San Blas draws its water.

Places to Stay & Eat
San Blas has a number of hotels, most of which are grossly overpriced, making San Blas one of the most expensive 'resorts' outside of Cancun and Cozumel.

The *Hotel San Blas* is reasonably priced. The famous *Bungalows Economicos* are anything but. Behind the restaurant Alteno, they are grossly misnamed and very expensive.

A viable alternative is to take a tent and camp on the beach, of which San Blas has a more than adequate supply. A tent is necessary because the little mosquitoes on Mexico's West Coast are persistent, voracious and very, very itchy.

Eating in San Blas can be difficult if you don't favour seafood. There is *McDonald's* which is totally unrelated to Ronald and the Arches. It is near the plaza and is essentially a seafood joint. Moderate. Or you can try the nearby *Diligencias*. Similar menu but very slightly higher prices. Also moderate.

For those who want a total change of dietary pace, there is the Berkeley-ish *La Tumbra d'Yaho* which combines granola and honey with (mostly non-local) handicrafts. Expensive.

For the cheapest eating in San Blas, and in many ways the best, head south from the plaza to the beach where enterprising locals have set up little restaurants and sell fresh-caught fish for very reasonable prices. San Blas doesn't really have much of a market area, and these stands take the place of market eating. Inexpensive.

Getting There
Most people arriving in San Blas come by way of Tepic, 75 km away. Some people apply logic to the transport situation and decide that there is no point in continuing an extra 35 km to Tepic on the Coastal Route when they could get off at the turn-off to San Blas and catch a bus there. But after they have been passed by several buses they realise that the only wise thing to do is to catch a bus into Tepic and double back to San Blas.

There is also direct bus service to San Blas from Guadalajara, but most buses originate in Tepic.

GUADALAJARA, Jalisco
Guadalajara is one of my favourite cities of the world. It advertises itself as the City of Eternal Spring and for once the Chamber of Commerce hyperbole is fully justified. Although it is in the tropics and as far south as Saudi Arabia the considerable altitude ensures cool nights and makes an air conditioner more a status symbol than a practical necessity. There are wide boulevards reserved for walkers, elegant shops, a gigantic public market, a fairly efficient public transport system and restaurants of every calibre, from street-corner barrows to sophisticated, white-tablecloth establishments the equal of any in the Republic.

The **University of Guadalajara** is at Juárez at Tolsa. Housed in a former Jesuit monastery it is of interest to the non-student mainly for the mural by Jose Clemente Orozco in the lantern of the lecture hall of the main building. In addition, there are some excellent, though little-known, murals by Siquerios and Cuevas in the chapel. Guadalajara is very much a university town, with numbers of Americans enrolled in the medical school, so many that there is even an American Students' Wives Club providing social outlet for the mostly non-Spanish speaking ladies.

The **Templo Expiatorio**, at Madero at Tolsa is across the street from the University. It is often miscalled a cathedral by Americans labouring under the impression that any large, imposing ecclesiastical structure is a cathedral. One of the finest buildings erected in Mexico since colonial times, it is built of hand-hewn reddish stone using old-world techniques. It is well worth visiting for the stained-glass windows alone.

The **Instituto Cultural Mexico Norte America**, Tolsa at Miguel Blanco, close to the Templo, is a language and

Guadalajara

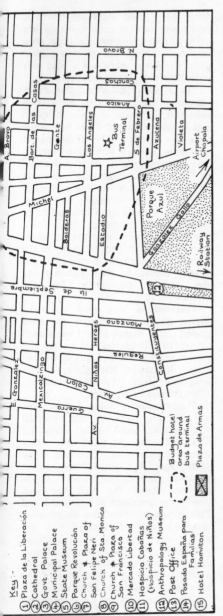

Key:-
1. Plaza de la Liberación
2. Cathedral
3. Govt. Palace
4. Municipal Palace
5. State Museum
6. Parque Revolución
7. Church & Plaza of San Felipe Neri
8. Church of Sta. Monica
9. Church & Plaza of San Francisco
10. Mercado Libertad
11. Hospicio Cabañas (Hospicio de Niños)
12. Anthropology Museum
13. Post Office
14. Posada España para Familias
15. Hotel Hamilton

art school that teaches English, among other cultural services, but at the back of the extensive patio is an inexpensive snack bar and tables open to all comers. A fine place to practice English or Spanish (or Spanglish!) with the students.

The **American Consulate** is on Progreso between Libertad and Lopez Cotillo. The Ben Franklin Library is on Libertad in the same building, and it carries a catholic selection of periodicals plus the usual run of fiction and non-fiction. A home away from home for the more literate expatriate Americans.

French-speaking sojourners hungry for the sound of their own language will appreciate the **Alliance Francaise**, out on Lopez Cotillo between Robles Gil and Athena. The Alliance is housed in a handsome, tasteful and unusual building.

The **Teatro Degollado**, on Degollado between Hidalgo and Morelos, is a European-style opera house and one of the architectural gems of Guadalajara. The School of Theatrical Arts of the University usually presents a folklorico each Sunday at the unlikely hour of 10 am — a must-see for any visitor. The programs are changed from time to time and I've had the pleasure of attending four performances with no two alike. Most tourists buy the most expensive main-floor seats, but the next-cheaper ticket gives me a choice of boxes above the heads of the main-floor audience. Recommended enthusiastically.

The **Plaza de la Liberacion** in front of the Degollado is being excavated for an underground parking lot, but when this is completed the plaza will be restored to its former charm, as has already been done with some of the other plazas.

The **Museo Regional de Guadalajara**, occupies an old seminary on Liceo between Calles (not Calzada) Independencia and Hidalgo. As with most Mexican museums it leans heavily toward dark oil paintings of former bishops, government officials, just plain ordinary wealthy men, and determined-looking women. But aside from this personal carping, the museum is one of its kind. Especially interesting is the building itself, a magnificent example of Spanish ecclesiastical construction of the late 1600s.

The **Mercado Libertad** on the Calzada Independencia at the foot of Juárez, is a Guadalajara don't-miss. It is huge as only the public market of a very large city can be, bigger than the market in Mexico City which is broken up into a number of smaller, more manageable units. On first seeing Libertad anyone would justifiably assume it is a very old market, but in truth it only dates back to 1959, although there has been a market at the site since before the Spaniards arrived.

The Libertad is so big that it encloses several patios, on different levels, and the variety of merchandise on offer must be seen to be believed. There is a whole section devoted to huaraches and shoes, another devoted to candy, and meat markets where you can purchase all or any part of a bull, steer, pig or sheep — or even the difference between a bull and a steer. You can buy a hat or a reata, a diamond ring or a crucifix, or have anything from cuticle scissors to a planer blade sharpened. One of the more unusual offerings is found among the medicinal herb stands — a herb that restores virginity. This is why you will occasionally hear a young lady referred to, cattily, as 'Señorita Hierba'.

On the side of the Mercado Libertad is the small, triangular Plaza Tapatio. It is also known as La Plaza de las Mariachis because the various mariachi bands meet here of an afternoon while getting ready for their nightly round of music-making. Mariachi music originated in Guadalajara in the middle of the 19th century. Originally the bands played for weddings, and the word 'mariachi' is a pochismo derived

from the French word for marriage. Now they play for anyone with a few pesos to spend, and most of them do it very well indeed. The plaza is a good place to have a snack and a cold beer while listening to the bands practising.

The **Hospicio de Ninos**, also called Hospicio Cabañas after its founder, is also near Libertad, at Calle Hospicio and Avenida Cabañas. It can be reached from the rear left side of the market and across the new pedestrian overpass. The Hospicio was supposedly designed by Tolsa and is a huge place with about 25 patios. It is a working orphanage and interesting in itself, but most visitors see it to view the famous Orozco murals, among the master's best efforts. The boisterous children of the orphanage wore the bottom part off many of the murals, and Orozco repainted them shortly before he died. Cabanas was the bishop responsible for the orphanage.

Tlaquepaque is a must on most tourist itineraries, including the all-in guided tours. At one time it was a small suburb of Guadalajara, but as the city grew it reached out and surrounded the place. It has a fine plaza, and is altogether worth the slight time and effort it takes to get there.

Tlaquepaque is noted for its glass and ceramics 'factories', and potential customers are urged to visit them. But note that some 25 years ago, writer James Norman said, 'Not too many years ago this one-industry town produced charmingly-decorated, fragile pottery. Today the craft has been largely industrialized and debased and Tlaquepaque is now the chamber-of-ceramic-horrors of Mexico'. It is the same today, and just about anything you see in one of the shops in Tlaquepaque can be purchased cheaper — with a bit of dickering — from one of the vendors at the Mercado Libertad.

To get there, go over on Sanchez and catch a city bus marked 'Tlaquepaque'.

As destination signs aren't always too reliable in Mexico, I suggest you ask, 'A Tlaquepaque?' before boarding. The fare is four pesos.

Alternatively, on Federalisimo (about a ten-minute walk from 16 de Septiembre) you can board a trackless trolley (known as the metro) which will take you to the Tlaquepaque plaza with less fuss than the crowded city bus, and for the same fare.

Shopping

Shopping in Guadalajara is probably the best in Mexico, and that includes Mexico City. There are large department stores off Juárez, right downtown, plus specialized leather-goods shops, charro outfitters and even a few guayaberas-only stores in Juarez itself. A number of downtown streets have been closed to vehicles and the Juarez sidewalks have been widened about a metre at the expense of the street.

There are a large number of bookstores in Guadalajara. Liberias Gonvill is a chain of bookstores with outlets all over the city, including one on Juárez between Martinez and Guerra which is good for the latest English-language paperbacks. For those who read Spanish, a good bet is El Libro Barato, on Guerra between Juárez and Lopez Cotillo.

A good place to find flown-in US newspapers and *Time*, *Newsweek* and other US magazines, plus some paperbacks, is the newsstand in the lobby of the Hotel Fenix at 16° de Septiembre and Lopez Costillo. This is also a good place to pick up a copy of the local English-language weekly, the *Colony Reporter*, which gives many an amusing insight into the trials and tribulations of people living in a foreign country who are mostly too indolent to learn the language and customs of the millions of people who surround them.

The Casa Montero liquor store, on Galeana between Morelos and Moreno,

is worth browsing if you are interested in Mexico's thriving beverage industry. It has about the best assortment in the country.

Places to Stay

The Guadalajara Yellow Pages has about 20 pages of hotel listings.

The *Hotel Hamilton*, Madero 381 between Ocampo and Galeana, has been my favourite for years. It is downtown where the activity is, and though the rent has jumped recently it is still moderate.

If you have an automobile, the *Motel Isabel* on Montenegro between Tolsa and Belgicia is within walking distance of downtown. But for the non-motorist I wouldn't recommend it because it is ridiculously expensive.

Travellers with families anticipating a fairly lengthy stay in Guadalajara should look over the *Posada España para Familias*, on Lopez Cotilla at the corner of 8 de Julio. Hard to miss with its brilliant green facade. Often full, but inexpensive.

On the opposite side of the Mercado Libertad and across the street is the *Hotel Imperio*, about a block away from the Plaza de las Mariachis. It is still reasonably-priced (moderate) but probably not for too long.

All along the Calzada Independencia toward the Central de Camiones there are small hotels. A year or two back they were all inexpensive, but what with inflation they are now mostly expensive, with a few moderate and a few very expensive. Some people swear by one or another of these places, but I dislike them because Calzada Independencia carries a heavy load of smoking diesel buses.

The *Hotel Sonora-Sinaloa*, on Dr R Michel at Gante is near the bus station, but not visible from it. A dive, admittedly, but inexpensive.

There are nine hotels visible from the front steps of the Central de Camiones, mostly moderate but tending to expensive. If there are plenty of vacancies, shop around until you find one that suits, but if not check into the first one you find with a vacancy and use it as a base until you find more suitable quarters.

Places to Eat

Guadalajara is a first-rate eating town, and sometimes seems to have restaurants on every corner. These are some of my favourites.

Right downtown is the Mercado Corona, the small market on Hidalgo between Sta Monica and Zaragoza, and occupying a stand within the market is a large restaurant as market restaurants go, the *Carnes Asadas en su Jugo*. Instead of the carne asada, with or without juice, I have their tacos al pastor which they do remarkably well. Very inexpensive.

A plaque on the old balustrade in front of the Corona says (in Spanish) 'Don Antonio Flores was hung, drawn and quartered here by the despotic Spanish in 1812'.

Out toward Tolsa and the university there is the *Nuevo Leon*, on Libertad near Tolsa and the branch post office. A really good Mexican-style restaurant serving such hard-to-find northern specialties as Cabrito al Horno, the best south of Chihuahua and Sonora. Expensive.

At the *Instituto Cultural Mexico*, Tolsa at Miguel Blanco, the snack bar is open to all comers and inexpensive.

The local *YWCA* called 'Associacion Cristiana Femenina', is on Montenegro between Belgicia and Argentina, near the Motel Isabel. It doesn't run a hotel, but it offers an economical restaurant and welcomes both male and female customers. It has a soda fountain, too. Inexpensive.

Back toward the city centre a good place for lunch is the *El Greco* restaurant, Lopez Cotilla at the corner of Penitenciaria. This is a family operation, popular with business types from the many neighbourhood offices. Despite the name, El Greco serves Mexican, not Greek, fare. Moderate.

For vegetarians, the *Gran Comedor Vegeterano*, down the street at Lopez Cotilla between 8 de Julio and Martinez is good news. Cream front with red rejas, but not very conspicuous and easy to overlook because it is not well signed. Good food and inexpensive.

Mexico is noted for its fine baked goods and *Postres de Mexico*, on Guerra between Cotilla and Madero, is one of the best around. Moderate.

The *Cafe Latino*, next door to the Hamilton Hotel on Madero between Ocampo and Galeana, is that rarity that makes café con leche the way it should be done, with espresso coffee and hot steamed milk, served separately in individual containers so you can mix your own. And beer comes sweating-cold with a frosted mug, and not the usual warm glass. Moderate.

Next to the telegraph office (located in a recycled church at Colón and Moreno) is an open-air cafe that is definitely the place for afternoon people-watching over a refreshment or two. Suggest you do your eating elsewhere, though. Moderate.

There is a *Denny's* on Juárez at 16 de Septiembre if you're feeling homesick. Standard fare including hotcakes, hamburgers, pie and some out-and-out Mexican dishes, such as chilaquiles. The waitresses here are inclined to huddle around the coffee machine and giggle while their hapless customers are perishing from coffee deprivation. Expensive.

For a more economical alternative to Denny's, go around to the back of Denny's on 16 de Septiembre and into the shopping gallery by Gonvill books, then upstairs to the *Fuente de Sodas los Locos* which serves about the same sort of food as Denny's in an open-fronted restaurant overlooking one of the busiest intersections in town. A good place to read the Sunday papers over breakfast. Moderate.

La Cava restaurant on Priciliano Sanchez at Galeana is probably the best-kept secret in town so far as travellers are concerned because the entrance on Sanchez is through the boutique Cachee, and the side entrance on Galeana is somewhat out of the way.

La Cava is located in a certified historical monument and has considerable ambience; very popular for upper-echelon business meetings and luncheons. I've never had a bad bottle of wine there and the food is first rate. Expensive.

For a hangover remedy I can recommend a bowl of La Cava's tortilla soup, washed down by a half-bottle of the red; the caldo de tortilla is made with a rich meat stock, unlike the usual insipid product.

Another place in the same neighbourhood that rarely, if ever, sees a foreigner, is *El Palomar* restaurant on Sanchez between Ocampo and Guerra. A plain restaurant for people that match. Small and usually very busy. Good and inexpensive.

The cheapest restaurant in any town is almost always at the market, and at Guadalajara the *Mercado Libertad*, Juárez and Calzada Independencia, has dozens and dozens of them. They are mostly along the second floor/balcony, but my favourite is on the first floor more or less hidden among the vegetables. There may be a sign saying 'Gorditas' which is the restaurant's specialty. They are made from a thick corn tortilla, fried, slit open and stuffed with goodies of the customer's choice. Two gorditas and a bottle of Coca — beer is no longer sold in the market — make a very inexpensive and very filling meal.

To really pinch pesos, it is hard to beat shopping at the *Gigante* super-

market on Juárez at Martinez for picnic ingredients. Everything, meat, bread, mayonnaise and even a wide selection of domestic and imported wines are available at quite reasonable prices. After shopping, a good place for a picnic is at the park just beyond Federalisimo, about three blocks out along Juárez.

Getting There

Guadalajara's transport situation is excellent with a railroad passenger service and hundreds of buses a day with direct service to most larger cities in Northern Mexico — buses in Mexico go to, but not through, Mexico City. There is also a direct air service from the International Airport in all directions.

The most popular way of getting to Guadalajara from outside Mexico is by air. There are many scheduled flights each day and a number of cut-rate promotional fares. The cheapest and most popular regular flight is Mexicana's flight, called 'El Tecolote' (the owl) by the Spanish-speaking, from San Francisco and Los Angeles; it arrives in Guadalajara at about 6.30 am, on its way to Mexico City, just in time to begin a day's activities.

Airport baggage-handling techniques in Mexico are generally inefficient, and in Guadalajara they are a total disaster. Luggage is hauled to the terminal on little cars and tossed through a long hole in the side of the building onto iron-covered shelves.

Guadalajara International Airport is about 20 km from the city centre and the taxi fare will take your break away — around M$250. A more economical alternative is offered by the VW van service, called 'colectivos', that take passengers downtown for a mere M$50.

Better still, for passengers who are not overburdened with luggage, is to go out the front of the terminal, turn right and walk about 500 metres to the Guadalajara-Chapala highway. Cross the highway and catch a north-bound bus.

The road is travelled by both local and long-distance buses, and there is frequent bus service.

Getting Around

At the front door of the railroad station, the street that runs slightly to the left is 16 de Septiembre, called 'Revolución' by the locals; and it will take you to Juárez and the Zona Centro. The street that goes beside the park on the right is Calzada Independencia; it leads to the Mercado Libertad.

To get downtown from the bus station, go out the front and through the parking lot. Turn right onto Dr R Michel. Continue north in a direct line after passing the circle and monument at Calzada Independencia and you will be on Corona which in turn will take you to Juárez and downtown.

Walking time from either the bus or railroad station to downtown is about 15 minutes.

CHAPALA, Jalisco

There are about 20-30,000 Americans living in the vicinity of Guadalajara — there are no hard figures — and a large percentage of them live in and around Chapala, some 50 km south of Guadalajara.

Originally Chapala was a sleepy little town of agricultural workers and fishermen, but more and more it is becoming the home-away-from-home for retirees from the US and Canada, mostly retired military types and salesmen. The attractions are good year-around climate and cheap living, though inflation is rapidly eroding the latter advantage.

It has the usual US-style amenities, including an American Legion post, and constitutes an English-speaking colony, hence the name of the English-language weekly, the *Colony Reporter*. The majority do not trouble themselves to learn the national language, and one of the best selling English-language books

locally is one that purports to explain to housewives how to communicate with 'your Spanish-speaking maid'; the book explains such vital operations as how to toast bread and prepare typical mid-western meals.

But Chapala is basically a pleasant little town, although so boring for most people that they typically settle here when they retire and then move back to Canada or the States when the monotony becomes unbearable!

Almost close enough to Chapala to be considered a part of it is Ajijic and its neighbour, Jocotepec, about 17 km farther along the lake shore. Although Chapala is known as a retiree centre, these two towns actually have a few working writers and painters in residence, but it is the same old story, the artists discover a place and then the non-producing squares move in and pretty soon the prices are too high for the original residents.

For the casual traveller, I recommend making a day trip of Chapala and environs from Guadalajara. You can come down on one of the early buses and return the same night.

The bus service between Chapala and Guadalajara is excellent, with never more than half an hour's wait.

Places to Stay & Eat

The *Hotel El Nido* is my choice if you want to stay overnight. It is a small hotel with comfortably large rooms. Moderate.

There are lots of restaurants in town, but one of the better places to eat is the cafeteria in the bus station. This is a small leisurely place stuck off in one corner, perfectly complementing a community of retirees who have lots and lots of time on their hands. Moderate.

SAN JUAN DE LOS LAGOS, Jalisco

San Juan de los Lagos is about 150 km east of Guadalajara and is another place that should be visited on a daytrip basis, not because it is uninteresting or overly expensive, but because while it is just another easy-going town most of the time, it has occasional spurts of frenetic activity which make it intensely interesting and fill the hotels to the rafters.

San Juan de los Lagos makes its living primarily from the Image of the Virgin of San Juan de los Lagos, housed in the big Parroquia on the plaza. The image is said to have miraculous powers and is the motivation for several pilgrimages each year, the most important of which brings people in large groups on foot for hundreds of miles. They camp along the way in an atmosphere reminiscent of the great pilgrimages to Santiago Campostela during the middle ages, or the pilgrimage to Mecca. This fiesta culminates on 5 January and is the major event of San Juan's year. But there is a lesser fiesta 1-16 August, and a sort of quasi-commercial festival that lasts about a month around 20 November. This one has cockfights, bullfights and all sorts of hucksters working out of tents and peddling everything from cheap gimcracks for charm bracelets to quite high quality serapes. The last formal fiesta starts on November 28 and lasts until December 8. Oh, yes — there is a minor celebration around Christmas time!

During the various fiestas there isn't a prayer of obtaining a hotel room; they're all taken by families who come back year after year and occupy the same rooms.

It isn't too practical to commute from Guadalajara, but it is practical from every standpoint to stay down the road in Lagos de Moreno and commute the 50 km or so. There are lots of buses.

To get to the plaza from the bus station, go left out of the waiting room and then turn left again at the highway. Go downhill to the Posada de la Plata sign on the right, and turn right and head for the spires of the Parroquia.

Walking time is under 20 minutes. Taxi fare is about M$50, so walking is definitely worthwhile.

LAGOS DE MORENO, Jalisco
Lagos de Moreno is located 200 km east of Guadalajara at the intersection of two highways that have always been among Mexico's busiest — the east-west road between Guadalajara and San Luis Potosi, and the north-south road between Juárez and Mexico City. In the days of the stagecoach it was an important stop, and even today it derives much of its income from the services it provides for the highway traffic. To augment the traditional income from transportation Lagos also has a number of plants processing agricultural products, mostly milk, and is a supply centre for the surrounding farmers and cattle ranchers.

Note that the highways completely miss the town, except for the outskirts, and because of this few but the locals know about Lagos de Moreno. A great pity.

Although Zacatecas advertises itself as the 'most colonial city in Mexico', I'd give the title to Lagos. Most of the buildings in Lagos date from colonial times, and there has been almost no building since in the central part of town, except for the market which is off to one side and out of general view. With the exception of the market building itself, any construction that has taken place since the exodus of the Spanish has been designed to blend into the overall motif. There is the usual handsome pink stone church on the attractive plaza, and the plaza itself has lots of bright green trees trimmed to cylindrical shapes, a topiary design that complements perfectly the angularity of the church and other buildings surrounding the plaza.

Recently the well-planned Calzada Pedro Moreno and Paseo Ribera — essentially the same thing — along the river have been refurbished and restored

to their 1880s elegance. And at the end of the overhaul job the high-squirting fountain worked!

Places to Stay

In addition to being a charming place for a honeymoon or writing a book, Lagos has a number of inexpensive hotels.

As you come in from the bus station along Calzada Pedro Moreno, just after you pass the fountain you will notice a green neon sign that says *Hotel* and nothing else. This hotel is inexpensive and comfortable and good value for the money, but I prefer to stay at one of the two places on the plaza simply because the plaza is the centre of activity.

The *Hotel Paris*, on the zócolo opposite the church, is actually a huge ex-private home, and what a home it must have been! The lobby measures a full 50 metres from the front door to the back, and as you come through the entrance you are struck by a fancy split staircase leading up to the second floor that looks like a set left over from an old Busby Berkeley musical. Most of the rooms are large, even after the modern bathrooms are installed. The Paris doesn't survive on its hotel business — most of its money is derived from the little bar in front. There is also a restaurant on the premises, but the less said about this the better. The hotel is inexpensive.

On the left side of the plaza as one faces the church is the much plainer *Hotel Plaza*, also a converted private home, but one that was nowhere near as grand as the Paris. The Plaza is much better managed than the Paris. Inexpensive.

Going up in ambience and price we have the *Hotel Colonial*, also in an old mansion, on Hidalgo, the street running in front of the church in the next block.

The Colonial is owned by the local veterinary who has spent a good deal of money and thought on it. It is far and away the best hotel in town, but very expensive.

If you turn right at the fountain on the Paseo Ribera before you reach the 'Hotel' you will see the *Hotel Victoria*, a horrible concrete-and-steel-window-frame building. Fortunately it is far enough away from the plaza that it doesn't have a deleterious effect on Lagos's charm. Popular with truck drivers. Moderate.

Places to Eat

The best place in town to eat, and the most popular, is the *Restaurant Pastor*, on Hidalgo to the left of the church as you face it. It is the gathering place for the lanky men with rope-burned hands and big cowboy hats who do not look anything at all like the general conception of Mexicans. Photo-murals on the walls are worth a trip to the Pastor in their own right. They were made by a local photographer, and are of local scenes. The Pastor has a diversified menu, including fish, which is almost always available. Moderate.

The restaurant *La Troje* on the plaza serves good food, and I've eaten there several times, but it is more expensive than the Pastor and not all that much better. Expensive.

There is a restaurant in the *Hotel Colonial* which is the largest in town in terms of seating capacity, and does a pretty good job of cooking, but is not always consistent. It is still better than most Mexican restaurants, but very expensive.

As usual, the cheapest place in town for a good meal is at one of the stands in the market, up on Rivera.

Getting Around

To get to the plaza from the bus terminal, turn left as you leave the front door and cross the bridge over the Rio Lagos.

At the far end of the bridge on the left there is a narrow ramp leading down to a paved walkway along the river bank — the Paseo de Ribera. In time this becomes the Calzada Pedro Moreno and a sort of long park. At the far end of the Alameda keep on the right side of the Calzada and it becomes Hidalgo and goes past the Hotel Colonial to the plaza. Walking time is under 15 minutes.

QUERÉTARO, Querétaro

This is one of Mexico's most beguiling larger colonial cities, head and shoulders better than San Luis Potosi, and they're about the same size.

The main street of Querétaro is Corregidor which runs beside the Alameda and near the bus terminal. The museum (Museo Regional de Querétaro) is on Corregidor across from the little Plaza de la Constitucion with its statues of Mexican heroes. (The Constitucion, by the way, used to be the city market until the market was moved a number of blocks west of downtown.)

The museum is housed in the former Convento de San Francisco de Assisi and the authorities had the good taste to leave the old building pretty much as it was in 1700 when it was only a hundred or so years of age. The building itself is a fine example of Spanish design and construction, and is of more interest to me than the many paintings of important colonial personages. Of general interest is the material relating to the ill-fated Maximilian, including his coffin, a diligencia and the usual assortment of objects dating from colonial days. The original name of the museum was the 'Museo Pio Mariano', and it still appears that way on a few maps.

The lovely little Plaza Independencia, a couple of blocks east of the museum, contains a statue of one Don Juan de Urrutia, the man responsible for bringing potable water to Queretaro back in the 1730s. The plinth bears a plaque stating that the statue was knocked down by a cannon ball in 1867. It was rebuilt in 1892. In recognition of his achievements Don Juan was created the Marques de Villa del Villar del Aguila. Also on the plaza is the Palacio Municipal, once the home of La Corregidora, the heroine of the 1810 revolt. Doña Josefa was the wife of the Spanish Corregidor (similar to mayor) and learned that the conspiracy had been discovered and immediately sent word to Allende and Hidalgo. This occurred on 15 September 1810 and effectively touched off the revolution. She is the one referred to on obsolete Mexican money and around Querétaro as 'La Corregidora' without additional identification.

And this is why Querétaro refers to itself as 'La Cuña de la Independencia' — the 'Cradle of Independence'.

Querétaro is the closest large city to the opal workings at Tequisquiapan, about 20 km from San Juan del Rio, to the south. There are always people wandering around the streets with handfuls of 'opals' done up in old bandanas and looking for a moneyed stranger. If you are interested in buying — and occasionally bargains are to be found — I suggest you first go up Calle Libertad to the 'Union de Artesanos Orfebrers y Lapidarios Querétaro.' This mostly opal and mineral shop has a couple of non-functional suits of armour in the doorway so it's hard to miss. All kinds of opals are on display, both cut and uncut, and a close study of the prices will give you a good idea of current values and might even keep you from investing in a chunk of heat-treated Coke bottle down in one of the plazas!

Maxmiliano and the Hill of Bells

Those with a macabre and/or historical turn of mind may wish to visit the Templo do la Cruz, and the attached convent which served as Maximilian's prison while he was awaiting Juárez'

signature on the execution orders. Conducted tours are run each half hour with lectures — in Spanish — on the history of the old convent. If you don't understand Spanish it is still interesting for the opportunity to view the old buildings.

To reach the Templo go out Independencia about seven blocks from Corregidor.

The more bloody-minded may even wish to go out to the west edge of town to the Cerro de la Campana where the luckless Maxmilian, a romantic to the very last, met an inglorious end with his two faithful generals, Mejia and Miramón. Today the spot is marked by a small brown-stone chapel, the Templo de Expiacion, built by Austria many years after the sanguinary event. Its interior is lined with pictures of Maximilian and his dotty wife, Carlotta. Many locals call it 'La Capilla de Maxmiliano' — Maximilian's Chapel.

To reach the Cerro de la Campana, go out Corregidor to Morelos, the third street north of the Plaza Principal, and turn left. Follow Morelos about 12 (long) blocks, crossing a glorieta near the end. At the end of Morelos turn right, then left at the next street and follow it uphill to the Templo. Walking time is about 35 minutes.

Places to Stay

The hotel situation in Querétaro is fairly good, and not weighed too heavily in favour of the high end of the scale as are so many Mexican cities nowadays.

As you walk up Corregidor from the bus station you will see the big new *Hotel Impala* on the left side opposite the Alameda. The conventional rooms are expensive, but not as much as you might expect from appearances as the hotel was built long enough ago to have pretty well paid for itself by now.

The *Hotel Corregidora* on Corregidor in the middle of the next block past the Impala is smaller, older and cheaper.

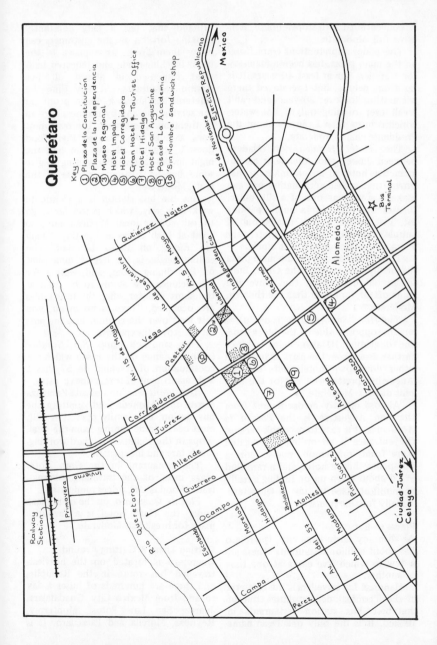

Querétaro

Key:-
① Plaza de la Constitución
② Plaza de la Independencia
③ Museo Regional
④ Hotel Impala
⑤ Hotel Corregidora
⑥ Gran Hotel + Tourist Office
⑦ Hotel Hidalgo
⑧ Hotel San Augustine
⑨ Posada La Academia
⑩ 'Sin Nombre' sandwich shop

A conventional two-storey house, it is often full. Moderate.

The plain, unpretentious *Gran Hotel* on the main plaza, has been a mainstay for travellers for at least 40 years. It is far from deluxe, but I've stayed there off and on for over 20 years and can't recall ever running out of hot water, which is more than I can say about the Presidente chain. Moderate.

The *Hotel Hidalgo*, on Madero between Juárez and Allende is an unattractive hotel in an old mansion that proves that with determination one can make a sow's ear out of a silk purse. It uses the patio for a public parking lot. I've stayed at the Hidalgo out of simple necessity but far prefer the Plaza or the Gran in the next block.

The *Hotel Plaza* is on the main plaza diagonally across from the Gran. Built in an old house, but the conversion came off far, far better than the Hidalgo. Moderate.

The *Hotel San Agustine*, is on Suarez on the opposite side of the block from the disgusting Hidalgo. Being a block farther away from the plaza than several other downtown hotels puts the San Augustine pretty well out of the high rent district. Moderate.

Almost directly across Suarez from the San Augustine is the *Posada la Academia*. It is easy to overlook because the entrance is an ordinary iron-gated store front, one among many. More a huespedes than a hotel, and a rare find — I'd about given up on finding a really economical place to stay in Querétaro. Usually full; inexpensive.

Places to Eat

As with any fairly large city, Querétaro has about a jillion restaurants. These are a few in which I've eaten at one time or another.

Handiest for travellers is the cafeteria in the Terminal de Autobuses, one of the best bus station restaurants in Mexico. It is the only one I can name offhand that has a lady constantly cooking tortillas so the customers can enjoy them fresh, as opposed to the usual machine-made and reheated half-soles dispensed in almost all bus station restaurants. At any time the cafeteria has about a dozen people in the serving line and by no means are all of them bus passengers. The restaurant does a huge business, so their food doesn't languish all day and half the night in the steam table waiting to give some hapless customer a case of the trots. Moderate.

But the bus station is a 15-minute walk each way, which is too far to go to eat conventional Mexican fare, so I eat at such places as the tiny *Fonda Sta Elena*, on Paseo Libertad. The ceiling height is the largest dimension of the dining room, and seating for 18 includes five stools to be used at the short counter when the four tables are occupied. There is no menu, you just look over the counter into the pots on the stove. Inexpensive.

The sandwich shop *Sin Nombre* (with no name) on the Paseo which is a continuation of Avenida de 57, has a wide assortment of tortas. Inexpensive.

Restaurant Izar, on Calzada Zaragoza across the Alameda and opposite the bus station, is a family operation with most of the trade coming from the small shops in the vicinity. Standard working-man's fare and inexpensive.

The restaurant in the *Gran Hotel* snags most of the travelling salesman trade. Food is OK, prices moderate.

Flor de Querétaro, on the main plaza under the Plaza Hotel is a favourite place for breakfast. Moderate.

Getting There & Getting Around

Querétaro is located on the heaviest-travelled bus route in the Republic, and there are hundreds of buses a day to and from Mexico City, Guadalajara, Juárez, San Luis Potosí, Monterrey, Reynosa, Morelia and Patzcuaro. It is also the ideal jumping-off place for San Miguel Allende.

The railroad station is seven or eight blocks from the plaza. To get downtown, go out on the tracks and turn right. Where the tracks cross a heavily-travelled street, turn right for about two blocks. Turn right again and continue on Corregidor until the main plaza is reached. Walking time is about 15 minutes.

To get uptown from the bus station, go out the front and across the pedestrian overpass and turn left, then right at the next street, Corregidor. The main plaza is straight ahead. Walking time is about 15 minutes.

The High Road from Juarez to Mexico City

The road from Juárez spends much of its time following the eastern edge of the Sierra Madre Occidentales. Never dropping below 1130 metres, it is the coolest summer route across Northern Mexico, though in the winter it can get colder than a bartender's heart. It traverses some interesting cities and is the second most popular route into the interior after the West Coast route from Tijuana.

Ciudad Juárez on the border definitely isn't one of Mexico's more interesting cities. About all I can say about it is that it has a good Central de Autobuses and excellent connections to almost anywhere in Northern Mexico.

The first town that catches any tourist traffic is Chihuahua, not so much for itself as because it is some 380 km south of the border, a good day's travel by any means. Instead of taking the main road, an alternative way to get to Chihuahua from Juárez is by bus via Nuevo las Casas Grandes, a town named after the nearby ruins of Las Casas Grandes.

This bus travels through flat, essentially uninteresting countryside to Janos, originally a Spanish presidio established to protect the ranchers of the area from Apache depredation. In later years Janos was the settling place for a number of Mormon families from Utah who migrated in search of greater religious freedom so as to continue their practice of plural marriage. Today their descendants still live in the same vicinity in peace and prosperity, operating their own schools and sending their children north to Brigham Young University.

NUEVO LAS CASAS GRANDES, Chihuahua

This is a thriving city serving as a supply point for the mines and ranches of the area as well as an important shipping point on the railroad. The town isn't at all interesting, but the ruins of Las Casas Grandes are. Last occupied around 1500 AD, they are the farthest-north trace of the Mesoamerican Culture, and the northernmost example of pyramid building. The ruins are about 7½ km south of the town proper, and quite extensive, covering almost 100 hectares. Not very spectacular, but at least as interesting as the 'developed' pyramids to the south that are better publicised.

There are a number of hotels, of which the best seems to be the *Hotel Juárez*, a one-storey brown-brick structure across the street from where the long-haul buses stop. Moderate.

There is not much to choose from among the restaurants.

Nuevo las Casas has no plaza, and is laid out like any midwestern US railroad town. The bus service is excellent, including a line that runs across the continental divide to Agua Prieta, on the border south of Douglas, Arizona, from where you can catch a bus on either side of the border to the West Coast of either country. This is the last highway crossing to the west for 1300 km — the next crossing point is the Durango-Mazatlán road.

CHIHUAHUA, Chihuahua

Chihuahua is the capital of the largest and wealthiest state in the Republic, but more important to the foreigner, it is the first and most logical place to overnight on the road south from Juárez and is a transportation junction. From here you can take the Chihuahua al Pacifico railroad down to Los Mochis through the Copper Canyon. Trout fishermen come here to fish the cold-water streams that gush down the eastern flank of the Sierras.

Chihuahua isn't too long on things to see or do. The Cathedral is worth seeing and unusual for Mexico in that the interior is somewhat more interesting than the exterior. It is a big building, and was far and away the largest structure in the city until the recent spate of high-rise construction. The twin spires loom 45 metres above the Plaza de la Constitucion. The main altar is supported by 16 elaborate columns. The decorations are impressive but one can only imagine what they were like before the wars, revolutions and the Reform Laws of the 1850s took their toll.

Chihuahua is known far and wide for its tiny dogs, the famous *Perros Chihuahuanos*. Today they are very rare in the region of their origin, but a few old street-peddlers still try to foist any mongrel puppy off on tourists.

The Pancho Villa Museum is probably more popular with Americans than with Señor Villa's countrymen. It was a private undertaking operated by the late Señora de Villa and her numerous family, and the sole support of the tribe, displaying memorabilia, including six-shooters and the Dodge touring car in which Villa was assassinated. Since the death of Señora Villa there is some doubt as to whether the museum will continue in operation.

The museum is located in Calle 10, but since this street has mysterious startings and stoppings, the best way to reach the museum from the bus station is to pick up Calle 8 and follow it out until it changes its name to Ocampo. Stay on Ocampo until you come to the triangular Parque Lerdo. At the far side of the Parque is the Paseo Bolivar. Turn left on Bolivar and pick up Calle 10, the next street. The Villa Museum is now five blocks. This sounds like a long way, but it can be walked in half an hour or so from the bus station. Walking is simpler than taking a city bus which still involves walking about 10 blocks, anyway.

Around Chihuahua you will see lots of farmer-looking men dressed in pain bib overalls, together with their women who are dressed in drab long dresses in the style of 1833. These are Mennonites, members of a protestant sect founded in Friesland by Menno Simons about 400 years ago. They accept the New Testament as the sole rule of faith, reject infant baptism, the swearing of oaths, military service and holding public office. They lead simple lives and in Mexico are extremely successful farmers. They are found in numbers as far south as Guadalajara, but thrive in the states of Chihuahua, Durango and Zacatecas.

There is a bathhouse offering both regular and steam baths, with separate men's and women's facilities — no mixed bathing yet. To get there from the bus station, turn left along Articulo 123 to the next block. The showers won't work unless the treadle is trod upon. Public bathhouses are a tradition in Mexico dating back to preconquest times and a hot bath, even in a hot region, is one of the most relaxing things imaginable.

In addition to the usual post and telegraph offices, the Chihuahua camionera has a meat market that sells some groceries, also a public accountant, a cowboy outfitter and a drug store. The drug store stocks some US magazines but be sure to check the date if you don't want back issues.

The 'Guaderia' is only open from 9 am to 8 pm, short hours that have been known to cause considerable bitterness on the part of people who were forced to overnight because they couldn't get their belongings unchecked.

To get to the plaza, turn left on Progresso in front of the bus terminal and follow it until you come to Calle 2. Turn right and in six blocks you will come out on the plaza in front of the

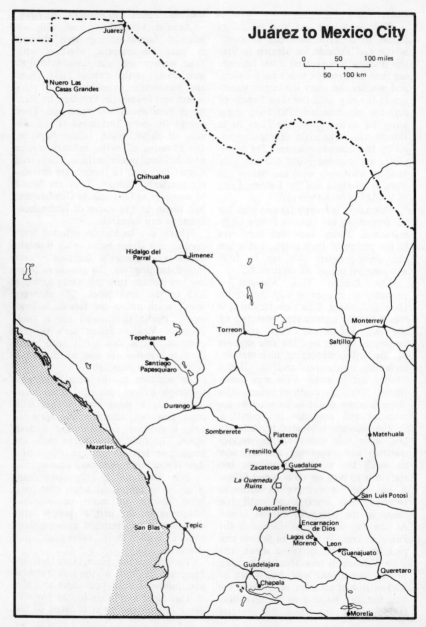

Juárez to Mexico City

0   50   100 miles

50   100 km

Juarez

Nuero Las
Casas Grandes

Chihuahua

Hidalgo del
Parral   Jimenez

Monterrey

Saltillo

Tepehuanes   Torreon

Santiago
Papasquiaro

Durango

Sombrerete   Plateros   Matehuala

Fresnillo

Mazatlan   Zacatecas   Guadalupe

*La Quemeda
Ruins*   San Luis Potosi

Aguascalientes

Encarnacion
de Dios

San Blas   Tepic   Lagos de
Moreno   Leon

Guanajuato

Guadalajara   Queretaro

Chapala

Morelia

Cathedral. 14 mins on foot.

The CHP has its own railroad station in Chihuahua, just as it does in Los Mochis. To get to the station from the Plaza, go out Calle 2 to the Paseo Bolivar which is a road, not a 'walk' as indicated by the name. Turn right and follow Bolivar to Diaz Ordaz and turn left. This is for dedicated walkers only. I'm a dedicated walker myself, but I always take a cab. It is over an hour's walk.

The trains for sightseers leave in the morning around 8 am; the train for travellers-only pulls out for Mochis around 9 pm. Buy your ticket and make reservations at the station and not from a travel agent. This will avoid bodacious foul-ups. And check schedules — it would be inappropriate to set forth departure times in a book of this nature. All schedules are subject to change without notice and in Mexico are sometimes disregarded entirely!

Places to Stay

Chihuahua doesn't get a big play from tourists and as a result there are quite a number of good, economical hotels, most of which are located either near the bus terminal or near the plaza.

Hotel Cayman, Calle 10 at Juárez, is new, modern and expensive.

Casa de Huespedes Libertad, on Libertad between Calle 10 and Ocampo is a small rooming house and is usually full because it is inexpensive.

The *Hotel Plaza*, is easy to locate because it is directly behind the Cathedral and only a block from the plaza. It is newish and about the best value for the pesos in town. Moderate.

Hotel Maceya is on Calle 6 at Doblado and popular with cowpunchers, truck drivers, muckers and itinerant peddlers, buskers and others of like stripe. Inexpensive.

Hotel on Trias between Ocampo and Calle 10 is identified by the red

brick facade and the green neon sign. It's another small house, but with a somewhat higher class of clientele than the Maceya. Inexpensive.

Hotel Carrillo on Calle 14 Vieja between Progresso and Carrillo is very near the bus station, but not very ostentatious and easy to miss. Most travellers overlook it, so it takes a little while to fill up. Moderate.

Hotel El Dorado, on Calle 14 at Progresso, two blocks from the bus station along Progresso on the right. A nice place, but a bit overpriced: very expensive.

Hotel del Cobre is to the left as you leave the bus station. It makes a play for bus passengers and is easily visible from the front door of the terminal. As a result it is one of the first places in Chihuahua to put up the 'lleno' sign despite being very expensive.

Places to Eat

Chihuahua isn't a bad eating town, and there is a healthy number of acceptable reasonably-priced restaurants.

La Parilla is one of my long-time favourites. The sign out front says 'tacos' but it is about as far from a taco joint as one can imagine. Try their barbocoa, the most Mexican of dishes. The Parilla is on Victoria between Ocampo and Calle 4. Moderate.

Hard by the left side of the Central Camionera is the little *Cafeteria Rosevel* — the sign painter ran out of ts — on Calle 10 at Articulo 123. This one is popular with cab drivers and other local workers. Usually good and inexpensive.

Loncheria on Calle 10 between Progresso and Carrillo is a sandwich shop that also serves such old standbys as pozole and rico menudo. Inexpensive.

Go out the front door of the camionera and turn left along Progresso and in a couple of blocks you will come to the wholesale produce market, always a place for cheap, filling food, especially during the early morning hours. Restaurants and push-carts are, at most, inexpensive.

PARRAL, Chihuahua

Hidalgo de Parral, usually called Parral, is another old silver-mining town. In the early 1600s there were over 7000 men working in the local mines. Since that day the mines in Parral have closed down one by one until now there are only three or four working in the town itself. The area is rugged, and some of the small towns in the region are popular with makers of western shoot-em-ups.

The only reason most foreigners ever hear of Parral at all is because a cattle rustler named Doroteo Arango decided to change his name to Pancho (not Francisco) Villa, a course of action which eventually led to his being turned into a colander, an event which took place after he retired in Parral. Last heard, his old home was being used as a grocery store while the Pancho Villa Museum is in Chihuahua (described earlier).

The most interesting building in town is the Palacio de Pedro Alvarado, built by a miner who struck it very rich indeed with the La Palmilla Mine. The outside is stunning, with columns fit for a midwestern Post Office built ca 1890, while inside there is an onyx stairway and even a private chapel.

The church of Nuestra Señora de Fatima is much newer. It incudes ore samples from the various local mines, making it unique in Mexican ecclesiastical construction.

To get downtown from the Estrella Blanca bus station, go out on the street in front and turn left — the plaza is about three blocks along. From the Omnibus de Mexico bus station, turn left along the triangular plaza; The Plaza Principal is about two blocks more.

Places To Stay & Eat

The *Hotel San Jose* is about a block from the plaza and a block from the O de M bus station. An unfortunate Mexican modern design, but then, it's quiet. Moderate.

The *Hotel Turista* is an older and cheaper house facing the O de M bus station across a little plaza. Also moderate.

Because it is essentially a working-man's town, Parral has oodles of low-price restaurants, and one of the better is the white-tablecloth house next door to the Estrella Blanca bus station, but not a part of it. Another good choice, and very popular with the locals, is the restaurant *Turista* in the hotel of the same name by the O de M bus station. Both are moderate.

San Francisco del Oro & Santa Bárbara

These are two ancient mining towns, founded by Spanish prospectors about 50 years before the Pilgrims hit Plymouth Rock. Although Parral's mines have been pretty well exhausted, these two old camps are still going great guns. If you want to see what a real, old-time mining camp looks like, get on a bus in Parral and ride the 40-odd km out to either Santa Bárbara or San Francisco del Oro.

DURANGO, Durango

Over 20 years ago the very knowledgeable writer James Norman described Durango as a fair overnight stop for travellers. The city has almost no other attractions. In the intervening years nothing much has changed.

Although the city of Durango itself has little to offer an awful lot of travellers wind up there today because it is now a transport hub and the starting point for the road that winds down through the Sierras and ends up down in the coastal hot country. It is also a popular place for railfans waiting to begin the once-in-a-lifetime trip into the back-of-beyond.

It seems that either Hollywood or Churubusco is always shooting an oater somewhere, and signs here and there proclaim that Durango is 'the western movie capital of the world'. Actually the signs really refer to the state rather than the city, but the city of Durango, being the only place with enough hotel rooms to house a movie-making company always seems to have a production outfit in residence.

Durango was originally a mining centre, and remains one, but it is a far cry from the usual mining town such as San Francisco del Oro or La Paz, although there is large-scale mining practically within the city limits. If you stand on the track side of the railroad station you will see a large black hill rising abruptly out of the plain. This is the Cerro Mercado, a mountain of iron ore named for an old-time prospector Gines Vasquez de Mercado, who was killed by Indians before attaining his home base in Sombrerete.

Although the Cerro del Mercado has been mined steadily for decades, the real ostentatious wealth of Durango was based on silver mining, of which not a trace remains in the city.

Places to Stay

Considering the size of the town there aren't too many hotels.

The green-fronted *Hotel Ferrocarril* is across Filipe Pescador from the railroad station and caters to railroad employees, campesinos and other workers. Inexpensive.

The *Hotel Central* is next door to the Ferrocarril and is very similar. Also inexpensive.

The *Hotel del Valle* is on Juárez about four blocks from Filipe Pescador. (Juárez abuts Pescador a block from the railroad station on the bus station side.) The hotel is a modern three-storey building with a restaurant and bar on the ground floor. The bar-room has a sign requesting patrons to check their weapons — a not-too-subtle reminder that Durango is still a part of the old wild and woolly north. The Hotel is expensive, the restaurant and bar are moderate.

Continue on Juárez toward the city centre and you come to the *Hotel Posada Duran*, an old-fashioned traditional Mexican viajero hotel complete with open-topped courtyard. It is convenient to the centre of things but expensive.

Places to Eat

When you consider that Durango receives a lot of movie business, the restaurant situation is surprisingly bad — people who work the location jobs usually have well-developed palates, but if they do, Durango ain't the place. I have come to the conclusion that the low-priced places near the railroad station are at least the equal of the uptown joints, price considered.

About the best of the several restaurants near the railroad station is the *Restaurante Rocio*, on Filipe Pescador at Juárez. Strictly a working-man's place and inexpensive.

The *Cafe Central* on the corner across from the railroad station in the hotel of the same name does a competent job of feeding the hungry multitudes, but it sometimes keeps odd hours — when I was hungry the doors often weren't open. Inexpensive.

Another safe bet are the food stands strung out along the traffic circle in front of the bus station — but not the bus station restaurant! They serve a wide assortment of quick foods, with emphasis on such things as gorditas, tacos and tortas.

At the restaurant in the *Hotel Casa Blanca* I got the worst meal I was ever offered in Mexico. The food was poorly prepared, the service matched

the food, and the wine had oxidized from long and improper storage. Very expensive, too.

Getting Around

To get from the Durango bus terminal to the railroad station, go out the front door and along the traffic circle to your right to Filipe Pescador, the street that runs in front of the power house. In the middle of Pescador, about 15 minutes walk from the bus station, is an immense monument and nearby is the tourism department office, one of the best in the country and manned by the drivers and mechanics of the Green . Angel trucks.

To go to the Plaza Principal and the Cathedral, cut across the traffic circle and pick up the heavily-travelled street that angles off slightly to the left. About three blocks from the circle is a motel with a large red-and-white sign. This street is 20 de Noviembre and it leads to the plaza in 40-45 minutes.

To get from the railroad station to the plaza, go to the left one block to Constitución and follow it downtown, a total of about 12 blocks and about 20 minutes walking.

If you want a ride to the railroad station catch a red 'Estacion' bus in front of the bus station on the traffic circle. For downtown, catch a 'Centro' or 'Centro-Camionera', or 'Camionera'. The same markings will bring you back to the bus station along essentially the same routes.

Tepehuanes & other trips

There are a number of branch lines fanning out from the Durango railroad station. The train that leaves for Tepehuanes every Monday, Wednesday and Friday at 7.30 am attracts railfans from all over the world.

Most travellers to Tepehuanes plan on returning via bus to Durango the same evening, but the train is often so late that they miss the last bus. Staying at Tepehuanes is no problem because there are several inexpensive hotels in town, but it can be a confounded nuisance for those with little time to spare. If you are on short time buy a ticket only to Santiago Papasquiaro, about 50 km before Tepehuanes, and catch a bus back to Durango from here. Santiago is a busy town served by several bus lines with many buses to Durango every day, whereas Tepehuanes is essentially an end-of-the-line small town. A local bus meets all trains in Tepehuanes and hauls passengers from the station across the river to town, about 1½ km.

You may hear stories from travellers about the unfriendliness of the people in Tepehuanes but I've always been treated with kindness, consideration and the usual Mexican small-town courtesy.

There are other train trips to be made from Durango. You can catch a turnaround train for Aserraderos at 7.30 am or a train for Rojicio at 6.30 am that will bring you back to Durango the same day. Either of these little-known trains provide more interesting scenery and more track-side activity than the famous Tepehuanes trip which mostly travels through plains country about as interesting as central Kansas.

On any of these trips be sure and pack a lunch. There are so few trains and so little passenger traffic that the ladies along the way don't generally prepare food for sale to travellers, and of course dining cars are unheard-of in these parts.

SOMBRERÉTE, Zacatecas

Years and years ago Sombrerete was a filthy-rich mining town, but although mining never ceased in the area as it did in much of Mexico over the years, the days of past glories have fled forever. The main divided street and a number of quite nice old stone Spanish-built homes and one out-and-out mansion remain as reminders of the bonanza of yesterday.

Many Mexican travellers prefer the small-town ambience of Sombreréte to the hustle and bustle of larger communities, and stop over here on their way to or from Durango.

Sombreréte is also the starting-point for a trip to Chalchihuites, another venerable mining town out in the middle of nowhere which has two current claims to fame: the ruins nearby which are not fully excavated and are closed to visitors from time to time, and the Instituto Fenix. The latter is a language school that uses the immersion method whereby the students hear nothing at all but the language under study. The Instituto has established two separate schools, one in Cuernavaca for absolute beginners, and another in Chalchihuites where the students live with a Mexican family and are almost forced to acquire a working knowledge of Norteño Spanish, in self-defence if nothing else. If you're interested, write to them at: Instituto Fenix, Chalchihuites, Zacatecas, Mexico.

Places to Stay & Eat
The *Hotel Hidalgo* is on the main stem and a block or two uphill from the bus station. It is a converted old two-storey colonial mansion large enough so that the patio is now used for parking guests' automobiles. It is a fine example of 16th-century Spanish architecture, with large rooms and the thick walls that act as heat sinks, keeping cool during the summer and contributing warmth during the cold winter nights. For practical purposes it is the only hotel in town. Moderate.

The Hidalgo doesn't run to a restaurant, and most people take their meals under the portales down the hill from the Hidalgo and the bus stations toward the plaza. It is the only restaurant I have ever seen with a glass partition separating the customers in the dining room from a shoe store. The food is pretty good, prices moderate.

There is another restaurant in Sombreréte. Go up the hill toward the Hidalgo from the bus station and turn left just before you reach the hotel. The *Restaurante Sin Nombre* is in the first block on the right side of the street. I've eaten breakfast there several times when I wanted peace and quiet.

Getting There
Sombreréte is a stop on all the second-class buses running north and south, but if you arrive via first-class bus you just might wind up getting let off on the highway by the turn-off, entailing a walk of about a kilometre to the centre of town.

FRESNILLO, Zacatecas
Not many travellers stop at Fresnillo, and many guidebooks don't even mention it. It is a dead-level city of some 115,000 people, high enough to have cool nights in summer and to be damned cold in winter. It is a pretty good place to break the long journey from Juárez, (1350 km to the north), but as for places of interest, forget it!

The Plaza Principal has a monument giving latitude, longitude, altitude, and other geographical information. Odder still, a plaque on the monument is dedicated to Gral Santa Ana, many times president of Mexico and a monumental foul-up who by dint of poor generalship lost the Mexican-American war in record time.

Places to Stay & Eat
About 12 minutes' walk from the bus terminal is the *Hotel Familiar*, made noteworthy by its sanguine-painted facade and its inexpensive rate. To get there from the bus station, cross the little plaza and turn right in the paved street.

If the Familiar doesn't appeal continue for about five minutes more, past

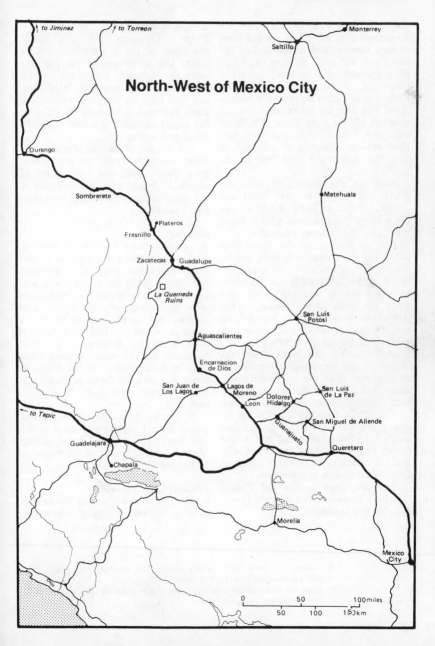

North-West of Mexico City

to Jiminez
to Torreon
Monterrey
Saltillo
Durango
Sombrerete
Matehuala
Plateros
Fresnillo
Zacatecas
Guadalupe
La Quemeda Ruins
San Luis Potosi
Aguascalientes
Encarnacion de Dios
San Juan de Los Lagos
Lagos de Moreno
Leon
Dolores Hidalgo
San Luis de La Paz
to Tepic
Guanajuato
San Miguel de Allende
Guadalajara
Queretaro
Chapala
Morelia
Mexico City

0	50	100 miles
50	100	150 km

the little plaza with the odd hemicycle monument that looks like a reject from ancient Greece, and at the end of the street you will come to three small hotels practically side by side, the *Hotel Cosmolita*, *Hotel Guerrero*, and the *Hotel Maya*. I have no reason to recommend one over the others as they're all chopped off the same block. Whichever you pick, make absolutely sure you have enough blankets if you are in Fresnillo during the cold half of the year!

Back on the little park with the grand monument is the *Hotel del Fresno*, quite a fancy establishment for a town like this, and with a fancy price, too. Ridiculously expensive.

But continuing on the street that passes the del Fresno will bring you to the market. (Not much of a market, but a market. Fresno is too far north to take a market seriously.) Turn right when you come to the market, on the street that chokes down to a pedestrian way too narrow for an automobile, and you will come out on a little plaza by a church. Across the plaza from the church is the inexpensive *Hotel Plaza*; it is quieter than the trio mentioned, above, but also a bit farther away from such activities as Fresnillo offers.

The street fronting the del Fresno also fronts the *Cafe Exelente*, my favourite for a low-priced meal. It is owned by an English-speaking gentleman who made his stake as a bracero in the grape fields of California. Inexpensive.

The restaurant in the *del Fresno Hotel* is a favourite for a US-style breakfast, but it is expensive.

Getting Around

To get to the centre of things, go out of the front of the bus station — don't laugh, lots of people go out the rear entrance directly onto the paved highway! — and cross the little plaza and turn right on the paved street. The Plaza Principal is reached by going to the triplet inexpensive hotels described above and turning right.

The bus station at Fresnillo is a little jewel, complete with sunken dining area, shiny clean, and with a set of murals that sure beat the hell out of the usual institutional paint job on Mexican bus stations.

Plateros

A few km from Fresnillo is Plateros, a small town that started out as a silver camp (the name means silver workers) but after a while the mines pretty well petered out, as mines do, new veins were discovered, and these too were worked out, until Plateros became a ghost town that still had a few residents who hung on because they could commute to the mines around Fresnillo to work. Today the big source of direct income is the Image in the church which attracts thousands of pilgrims each year.

If you're a seeker-out of quaint places, then I suggest you catch a bus over there. You will find a sign reading 'Plateros' in the corner of the bus terminal on the highway side.

ZACATECAS, Zacatecas

Because Zacatecas is among the highest cities in Mexico, plus being so far north,

A Guanajuato, seen from Pipila's statue. The building with the many-windowed facade is the university.

B View from the bridge over the subterranean roadway in front of the bus station in Guanajuato.

A

B

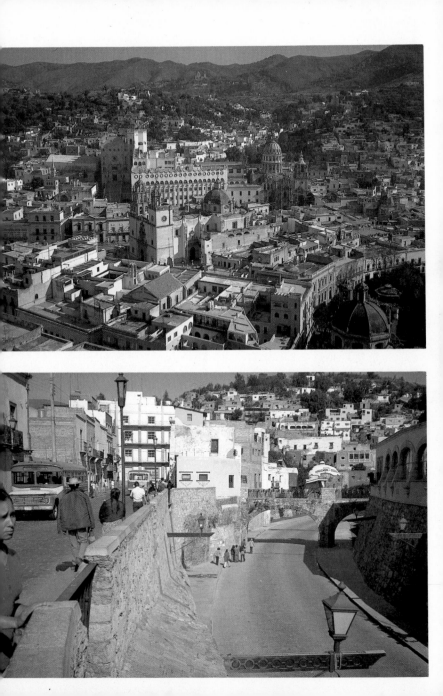

it can get bitingly cold during winter nights and mornings, but the summer climate can hardly be improved on. Even mosquitos, the scourge of Mexico, are not too severe in Zacatecas because the city is surrounded by desert.

A large billboard on the northern outskirts of town proclaims Zacatecas as 'the most colonial city in Mexico'. This statement is open to argument, but all in all Zacatecas does have an awful lot of old buildings dating from the days of Spanish domination, plus narrow, crooked streets designed by their builders for pack animals and carts with a few diligencias as makeweight.

For a city of around 150,000 people, Zacatecas is remarkably compact, even by Mexican standards, and a sturdy-legged sightseer can pretty well cover the whole shootin' match in a couple hours or so. From the bus terminal (located in the bottom of a barranca) nothing much can be seen of the town except a few modern-looking buildings. But amble out of the waiting room and turn right, then right again into the narrow street (almost an alley) that goes up alongside the bus arrival area, then uphill for about five minutes and you will come out on a plazuela. Bear right and continue straight ahead for another two or three minutes and you will enter the Plaza Independencia, too small for the present size of the city. The walk from the bus station to Independencia will take about 10-12 minutes at most.

The cathedral in Zacatecas has an interesting exterior and at one time apparently contained a very great deal of silver and gold ornamentation, as befits a wealthy mining city. Over the years, with revolutions, reforms and miscellaneous civil disturbances, it has been pretty well gutted and the interior is relatively drab now, but most people are impressed by the front, which is elaborately carved and decorated in sundry styles. There is also a notable side entrance, in a totally different motif.

To get to the cathedral, market and various government buildings, go up Juárez (which is the unmarked street at the end of the Plaza Independencia that runs in front of the police station) and turn right on Hidalgo — about the second street above the Condesa/Condes. Keep an eye out for the market if you're a market fancier, although this one isn't much when you consider the size of the city. If you turn left on Hidalgo, you will wind up in a little park and amid the arches of the famous Zacetecas aquaduct.

Places to Stay & Eat
You pass the *Hotel Zamora* just before you reach the plaza. It is a far cry from any Hilton you care to mention, but it's inexpensive.

Next comes the *Reforma* on the same side of the street, right on the corner of Plaza Independencia. (No relation at all to the hotel of the same name in Mexico City.) The current prices probably won't last, but for the nonce it is inexpensive.

Turn left on Juárez at the end of the Plaza Indepencia and head up the hill. In the next block is the *Posada del Condes*, somewhat less expensive than it

A The San Francisco church at Real de Catorce has a splendid collection of *retablos,* pictures giving thanks for, and illustrating, a life-saving miracle.

B The entrance to La Valenciana, at one time one of the world's richest mines. The bus passes here on the way from Guanajuato to Dolores Hidalgo.

C The church at Dolores Hidalgo where the local parish priest, Fr Hidalgo, once raised the cry for independence from Spain.

looks, and an old reliable that's still (but probably not for long) moderate. Across the street from the Condes is the *Condesa* with slightly higher prices — expensive.

The restaurant in the *Condesa* is very popular with the local business types. I often have breakfast there; other meals are OK, but too dear for my peso. Moderate.

Look back down Juárez to where it dead-ends by the plaza and you will see *El Burlador*, an upstairs restaurant decorated with a taurine motif — lots of Mexican bullfight posters, horns and so on. Snow-white table-cloths with blood-red overcloths make it very attractive. Good food. Once in a while a wayfarer needs a place like this for the good of his immortal soul. Very expensive, but worth it.

The best of the economy-model restaurants I know of in Zacatecas is located on the narrow street leading up the hill toward the Plaza Independencia. It is called the *Pavidon* and you can see it from the bus stalls. Not too good for breakfast, but a bargain for the rest of the day's meals with good local cooking — menudo, for instance, is served with no less than five garnishes! Inexpensive.

Getting There
Zacatecas is the intersection for a number of bus routes, and there are direct buses to and from Mexico City, San Luis Potosí, Monterrey, Guadalajara, Juárez and Torreón, to name but a few.

GUADALUPE
Three km from Zacatecas, the 'ex-Convento de Guadalupe' is being converted into a 'tourist centre' by the Government. The old convent was operated as a seminary for much of its functional life. Somehow the gold ornamentation in the Capilla de Napoles has managed to survive over the centuries and is as stunning today as it was centuries ago

when its beauty could only be enjoyed by the professional religious. Guadalupe can be reached by bus from the Central Camionera, by walking or by taxi. It is the big new-looking project on the north side of the road leading to San Luis Potosi or Aguascalientes.

LA QUEMADA, Zacatecas
Unlike the better-publicized ruins in the south-eastern part of the country such as Palenque and Chichén Itzá, La Quemada was not damaged by plant growth, and the original structures have been well preserved by the dry air. The ruins spread over several hundred hectares and are made up of well-constructed buildings of stone and lime-based morter. The ruins were abandoned for some mysterious reason long before the arrival of the Spanish. I feel that if you are only going to see one lot of ruins in Mexico it should be La Quemada, which can be seen largely as the first Spanish explorers saw them, whereas the 'tourist' ruins are mostly restorations, and not necessarily accurate.

La Quemada is on the Zacetecas-Guadalajara road about 50 km from Zacatecas. There is a regular and frequent bus service, although the ticket clerk may not be willing to sell tickets for La Quemada. In that case buy a ticket for Villanueva, about 12 km south, and get off at the ruins. The same thing applies coming from Guadalajara end, except you may have to purchase a ticket all the way to Zacatecas. In this case make sure you get on a bus that goes via Juchipila and Jalpa.

AGUASCALIENTES, Aguascalienties
Aguascalienties is 128 km south of Zacatecas, and has one of the most salubrious climates in all of Mexico.' Its only noteworthy feature is one that the average tourist can't see — the maze of tunnels excavated by some long-forgotten tribe for as yet unknown reasons. The city fathers have long

since sealed off the tunnels to keep small boys from killing themselves in them, and to the casual traveller there is no evidence of their existence, so you'll just have to take my word that they're down there.

Considering its size, Aguas is rather an indolent town. It has an enviable reputation for fine embroidery and knitware, but the finest example of this industry seems to be in the store in the bus station at San Luis Potosí!

Places to Stay
There are lots of economical hotels in Aguas because there aren't enough tourists or business travellers to warrant building new ones, and in Mexico the older hotels are generally cheaper than new.

Hard by the left end of the bus station as you leave by the front door is the *Hotel Continental*. It is convenient and clean, but noisy because of the proximity of the bus station across the street. Moderate.

Right downtown on the Plaza Principal is the *Hotel Imperial*, which was in slow decline 25 years ago. Little has been done to upgrade it since, except to convert the lobby into a pool hall and raise the room rate, but still and all it is right downtown and barely expensive.

Juárez is a peculiar street. It runs past the deluxe *Hotel Francia* on one side of the plaza, goes past the market and winds up at the Calle 5 de Mayo which in turns runs along the opposite side of the plaza and the Hotel Imperial! The *Hotel Don Jesús* is on Juárez between Obregon and Larreategui. Don't be discouraged by the violent green patio — the Don Jesús is good value and moderate in price.

The little *Casa de Huespedes* almost next door to the Don Jesus is typical of its kind. In other words, far from luxurious, but it's inexpensive.

The *Hotel Colonial* is misnamed for it's not colonial at all. It's on 5 de Mayo between San Ignacio and Zaragoza, across from the park. Expensive, but just barely so.

The *Hotel Zaragoza*, on 5 de Mayo and La Mora, is another house that just slips over the expensive classifications, while the *Hotel Roble*, on 5 de Mayo at the end of Juárez, is moderate.

Places to Eat
I must confess that I haven't eaten too much in downtown Aguas, but I have eaten at the *Paris*, by the Hotel Imperial, and my only objection concerned the price: expensive. As elsewhere I've dined well and reasonably with the hardworking ladies in the market on Juárez, very inexpensive.

Across the street from the left end of the bus station as you leave is the restaurant *Hnos Gomez* (Gomez Brothers). This is probably the busiest restaurant in Aguas and one of my favourites, and the reason I haven't eaten in many other places. It serves strictly Mexican items, everything from tortas to flan, and even does a good job with the hackneyed chilis rellenos. Inexpensive.

Getting Around
The bus station is too far from the plaza for practical walking, but city bus service is frequent and cheap. To get downtown, catch a 'C. Macias Arellano', or 'Jesús Maria' bus going from left to right in front of the terminal. To get back, catch the same buses on 5 de Mayo or at the plaza.

LEÓN, Guanajuato
León is the industrial city of Guanajuato with shoes and leather goods its principal products and on the outskirts in any direction you pass shoe factory after shoe factory. It is essentially an uninteresting city, with not enough colonial buildings to say grace over, due to a flood in 1888 that flush-

ed over 2000 buildings down the valley. It is a handy place to branch off the north-south route and catch a bus for Guanajuato and San Miguel Allende.

León has had a central bus terminal for long enough that a number of hotels have sprung up in the vicinity. I've stayed several times at the *Hotel León*, one of several hotels across the street and to the left from in front of the terminal. All are expensive, but extremely convenient.

A good place to eat is at the restaurant on the corner directly across the street from the station. It has a sideline in musical instruments, and does standard Mexican items very well. Moderate.

The restaurant in the bus station isn't bad, either. Moderate.

ENCARNACIÓN DE DIOS, Guanajuato Halfway between Lagos de Moreno and Aguascalientes, Encarnación de Dios is one of hundreds of nice little towns that never receive a second glance from the average traveller. The only reason anyone ever visits Encarnación is because it just happens to be on the way to somewhere else.

The plaza looks almost the same as the one in Lagos down the road, but the town itself is much smaller. However, it does have one thing for it that Lagos doesn't — the trees adorning the plaza are carved into one of the most spectacular topiary displays imaginable. Everything from crows (or are they eagles?) to lions have been carved from the living trees with the utmost patience.

If you have to overnight, as I once did, in Encarnación, there isn't much choice in hotels, but I was very comfortable in the *Hotel Casa Blanca*, next door to the Estrella Blanca bus station. The hotel has an acceptable restaurant. The hotel and restaurant are both operated by an English-speaking family formerly resident in California, and both are moderate.

The Eastern Route via Monterrey

This route has the advantage over the east coast route in that the weather is more bearable due to the greater altitude and there are more interesting things to do and see than the route along the coast which is long on sugar-cane fields and short on anything interesting.

MONTERREY, Nuevo León

Although Monterrey was founded over 400 years ago, it wasn't until 1596 that it became La Cuidad Metropolitano de Nuestra Señora de Monterey. (Somehow over the years the spelling has been changed, nobody today knows why!) Although the city is well over 400 years old it really did not amount to much until the arrival of the railroads and modern highways, whereupon it really got busy and soon became the country's centre of industry. Steel mills, a gigantic brewery, a huge bottle works to supply the brewery, electric motor factories, bicycles — you name it and if it is made in any quantity in Mexico it is made in Monterrey!

The city was always prosperous, but became even more so with the arrival of industrialization, and today it is one of the wealthiest cities in the country. A few years back Monterrey, then with less than 1% of the population, contributed 10% of the taxes to the federal government.

With this background information you could reasonably expect Monterrey to be a beautiful city, with wide and handsome boulevards and gushing fountains at every intersection. And you would be sorely disappointed upon viewing it for the first time. Monterrey is a grimy, hustling, bustling factory town, about equally divided between light and heavy industry, with no environmental laws worthy of mention, and is a grimy, hustling, bustling factory town, about equally divided between light and heavy industry, with no environmental laws worthy of mention, and with a street system essentially planned over a hundred years ago.

There are a few things worth seeing, and quite a bit of historical interest. The new Palacio Municipal, a stunning example of the best of current Mexican architectural thinking takes up the southern end of the Plaza Zaragoza, thereby eliminating much of the city's badly needed open space. The effect of the building isn't helped by the usual man-on-horseback statue of Gra Zaragoza left in the middle of the plaza.

The new building is perched on stilts above the ground floor, with a couple of escalators to reach the second floor from ground level. I have yet to see both of the escalators working at the same time.

Monterrey was the scene of one of the bloodiest battles of the Mexican-American war. The Mexicans fortified the town well, including using the walls that extended above the flat roofs on the traditional buildings as ramparts. When the battle began these roof-top sharpshooters held the city until the Americans began tunneling through the walls with sledge hammers, then throwing grenades through the hole, after which it was considered safe to go ahead and enlarge the hole and begin the process all over again.

Most of the city that Zachary Taylor took is no more, but the historically-oriented travellers will be interested in visiting the Bishop's Palace, then a fort but now a museum in somewhat better shape than when the Americans took it by assault. To reach it go out Matamoros until it crosses Benitez. The Palace is on a hill overlooking the city, and on clear days affords a fine view of Monterrey.

Places to Stay

The hotels in downtown Monterrey are vastly overpriced and no more convenient than staying out near the bus station. After all, one can see everything in central Monterrey, including the Bishop's Palace, in about three hours, so running back and forth sightseeing will not present a problem and it is unlikely any free spirit in good health will spend more than a single day in Monterrey before moving on! I prefer to get a room in Saltillo, 90 km away, and visit on a day-trip basis, but if you want to stay in Monterrey, the hotels reasonably near the bus station are:

Hotel Regis, Jiminez at Reforma. Don't be put off by the cave-like lobby or the garish modesty panels on the balconies. Moderate.

Hotel Norte, Democratia at Mendez. A block from the market, but quiet withal. Expensive, and should really be moderate.

Hotel Habana, Cuauhtemoc between Madero and Reforma. No extra charge for the art deco façade! Moderate.

Hotel Pino Suarez, on Pino Suarez between Colón and Reforma. Moderate.

Hotel Lozano, Pino Suarez at Reforma. Expensive and should be moderate at the most optimistic,but the extra money probably goes for the highly visible sign topping this scratch house.

Hotel America, Cuauhtemoc between Reforma and Colon. Don't let the rock-group posters plastered in the windows discourage you. All rooms equipped with fans. Very convenient to the bus station and often full. Moderate.

Hotel Reforma, next door to the America is usually full, which speaks well for its low rates, if not for the lobby, .which is downright ugly. Moderate.

Places to Eat

Economical eating is a problem in Monterrey, but if you go out the front of the bus station and turn right and then make another right on the first street you will see ahead of you a number of small and inexpensive restaurants, the very worst of which will beat bus station food hands down on both price and quality.

If you're heading downtown these are somewhat out of your way, so turn left on leaving the station, then right on the next street which is Pino Suarez. On your way downtown watch for the little *Cafe Galis* on the right side of the street. The Galis serves typical country food, the kind intended to fuel a man so he can swing a machete or drive a truck hour in, hour out, and does it inexpensively.

There is a *VIP's* close to the bus station. Turn left as you leave the station, then left at the first street. VIP's is at the end of the long block. This chain is expensive, but well worth it for the sparkling sanitary facilities, especially after taking a look and a sniff at the filthy bus station johns. Air-conditioned too.

Sanborn's on Morelos between Escobedo and Zaragoza, serves up the usual expensive North American foods and is the prime source of supply for US magazines and English-language books, but though they sell maps, they don't have one of Monterrey or Nuevo León!

The *City Market*, which really doesn't amount to much when you consider the size of the city; is two blocks along Colón to the left as you leave the bus station. *Madero*, near Juárez, is a market in itself, with sidewalk stands purveying everything from wedding rings to switchblade knives.

Getting Around

The bus station at Monterrey is huge. In addition to the usual post and telegraph offices, it contains a movie theatre, fruit stands, bath house, maker of spare keys, liquor store, copy centre and even a vendor of herb medicines, but

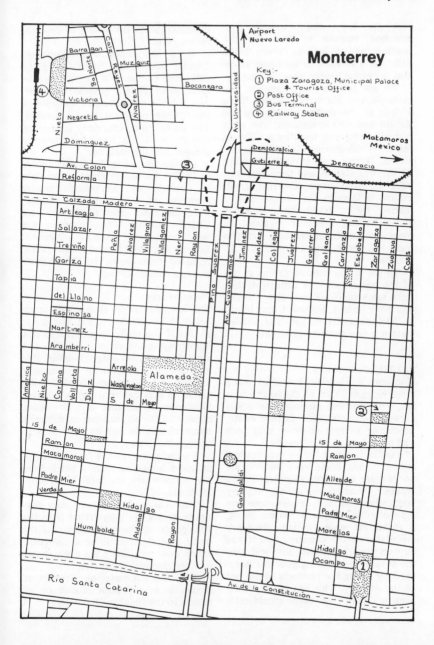

Monterrey

Key:-
① Plaza Zaragoza, Municipal Palace & Tourist Office
② Post Office
③ Bus Terminal
④ Railway Station

with its low, dingy ceilings and complete absence of fans for the comfort of its patrons, I can truthfully say I've been in hard-rock mines that presented a more pleasing aspect.

To get to the Plaza Zaragoza, the main plaza of Monterrey, catch a 'Ruta 1' bus at the shelter outside the bus station and ride towntown. The same bus will bring you back by a different route — Monterrey is all one-way streets. If you want to walk it, go out of the bus station and turn left, then right at Pino Suarez, the first street. Follow it through the famous arch — marred by a cockaminie angle-iron frame hanging across it — about 19 blocks to Humboldt and turn left. The plaza is 7 more blocks. I walk it in 45 minutes.

To get to the railroad station, go out of the bus station and turn right, then right again onto the next street, which will be Villagran. Follow it four blocks to Victoria and turn left. The railroad station is now three more blocks.

SALTILLO, Coahuila

Monterrey's choking industrial smog often extends 90 km all the way to Saltillo. For practical purposes the whole distance is one gigantic factory estate, producing everything from auto parts and phosphoric acid to brandy.

Saltillo is noted for its ponchos and serapes of cotton and wool, but they are no cheaper here than elsewhere in the republic, so unless you are on your way north when you stop, or have come here especially to purchase woven goods, it makes no sense to carry the heavy material over the country. And if you buy on your trip north, you will have the advantage of having your eye sharpened by seeing the products of the rest of the country. This can be important because there has been considerable deterioration in the quality of goods in recent years.

If you're a student of Mexican architecture you will be interested in the cathedral on what is technically the main plaza by the government buildings. It is the northernmost example of the Churrigueresque style of decoration. The inside isn't particularly interesting, though, as it has been systematically pillaged over the centuries.

Saltillo figured in the financial news in 1981 when the governor of the State of Coahuila and his cohorts, mostly members of his immediate family, were dismissed after they stole over US$80 million. The governor was not prosecuted because President Lopez Portillo figured that being removed from access to the treasury was punishment enough!

Places to Stay

The low-price hotel situation is much better in Saltillo than it is in Monterrey, so that if you really have reason to visit Monterrey, get a room in Saltillo and visit Monterrey on a daytrip basis. This is especially convenient in summer because with its greater altitude Saltillo almost always has cool nights, whereas Monterrey in summer is a sweltering mess. And the air, summer or winter, is much cleaner in Saltillo than it is in smoggy Monterrey.

I usually stay in the *Hotel Hidalgo*, an older house less than a block from the plaza where the local buses stop. Moderate.

The *Nuevo Hotel San Luis*, diagonally across the intersection from the Hidalgo is not new, regardless of the name, but it is acquiring an elevator, which does not justify the extra charge over the Hidalgo! Expensive.

The *Hotel Conde* on Trevino at Acuna is a very poor second on all counts to the Hidalgo. Moderate.

Hotel Saade, on Aldama near the Bus plaza is not quite up to the promise of the lobby with its wood panelling, marble floors and trim, and experienced genuine leather-covered overstuffed furniture. Expensive.

The hotel situation should improve with the completion of two small hotels being built across the road from the bus station.

Places to Eat

The *San Luis Inn* is a restaurant, not an inn, and is the second-best restaurant in town, after the Victoria. It is on the ground-floor corner of the building that also houses the Hotel San Luis. The food is passable, but the service is remarkably inattentive, even for Mexico.

The best economical eating in Saltillo is at the *Victoria*, next door to the Hotel Hidalgo. The first time I entered its doors was to use the long-distance telephone and I ate while waiting for the call to go through. After that I went for the eating itself. Inexpensive.

The market is just off the Bus Plaza on the opposite side from the Hotels San Luis and Hidalgo and is the place to get a really cheap, no-frills meal. It is also the place to shop for a poncho or serape or blanket.

Getting Around

The new bus terminal is way out at the edge of town, and Saltillo is a large town. There is excellent bus service to anywhere in the northern part of the Republic, and a pretty fair restaurant on the premises. The station is too new to have attracted any food-stall operators, but I expect that will change within a year or two, and the two new hotels going in opposite the station will logically have a restaurant or two.

The green and yellow micro-buses (vans) marked 'Central-Centro' will take you to downtown Saltillo for M$4 if you don't mind some crowding. I've seen 24 adults, plus God knows how many little kids, in one of the Ford or Chevvy vans!

There is an airport and scheduled air services, but I can't imagine anyone flying to Saltillo except on business.

MATEHUALA, San Luis Potosí

Matehuala is easy to identify from afar — a huge concrete church, shaped like a 200 litre drum split lengthwise and laid on its side, looms over the town. This has to be one of the ugliest churches in Mexico. And as if the church itself weren't horrid enough, some amateur ironworker built the bell-supporting structure out of bits and pieces of scrap iron that looks as if it was left over from a bridge job somewhere.

But the town, while not especially interesting, is a pleasant little place to break the journey for a day or two. Or a month. It is quiet and peaceful, as befits one of the rare cities in Mexico with about the same number of people today that it had in 1960.

Most foreign travellers who stop over in Matehuala do it not because of the ambience but for the trip up the hill to Real de Catorce, an old mining town that looks pretty much as Taxco must have looked a half-century ago, before Bill Spratling showed it the way to prosperity.

The hotel situation is Matehuala is good because of the *Matehuala Hotel*, one of the best values for the peso in Mexico. It is a big old buff-painted two-storey stone barn of a building constructed around a red-tiled patio studded with old-fashioned bridge tables and upholstered chairs with unique holes forming designs in their backs.

For a good restaurant try the *Domi* at the small plaza behind the Matehuala Hotel. A large assortment of typical Mexican dishes and open from early in the morning until late at night. Inexpensive.

If you don't want Matahuala Hotel

and the Domi, there are at least a dozen other restaurants and several hotels.

For a place to eat handier to the bus station for those who are just passing through rather than staying awhile, try the *Market*. This is reached by going out the front and turning left, then left again at the corner and walking alongside the station. The market is right ahead of you with the usual assortment of food stalls.

REAL DE CATORCE, San Luis Potosí

There is a persistent, and probably apocryphal, story that Real de Catorce, which means 'camp of the 14', refers to the 14 bandits who supposedly made their headquarters in the canyon. I have also heard it said that the town got its name from the 14 coins — Spanish reales — that someone discovered in the remains of an abandoned building several centuries ago. Take your choice!

Today Real de Catorce is a sort of Mexicanized ghost town, and its population has gone from an estimated 30,000 or so down to somewhere around 600 or 700. The present residents mostly cluster around the plaza and church and their homes are surrounded by hundreds of skeleton houses lacking roofs and rejas, most of them with front doors securely locked and awaiting the reopening of the mines and the return of their owners. Spooky.

In all likelihood the mines will open again some day because they didn't close down from lack of values but because the town had the bad luck to be located in a canyon. When the revolution came along all it took was one man with a 7mm Mauser and a couple of clips of cartridges on the side hill and he could stop all activity by an occasional shot at anything that moved on the streets below. This happened now and then and it eventually stopped the mining operations. During the years the mines were closed, the drawings of the diggings were lost, the machinery was

carted off, the rails through the tunnel were pulled up, and the once-thriving community of Real de Catorce became a mere shell of the vigorous former self. Nevertheless, it is always possible for a few hungry and determined men to make a few pesos now and then by livestock raising or small-scale mining. Recently the mining has been for antimony, although the original mines were primarily silver propositions.

There is some interest in reopening the mines, and a Swiss firm has been retained to make a survey of the old workings, which extend deep into the mountain that surrounds Real de Catorce on three sides. There is also an attempt to turn it into a craft centre, à la Taxco. Fernando Hernandez is acting as Catorce's Bill Spratling, and already a few of the older buildings have been repaired and restored.

There is a small museum under the church with a few items on display that date from the heyday of the town, among them papers signed by the original Lopez Portillo, a young Spanish mining engineer and the ancestor of the man who eventually became Mexico's President.

There are hundreds of retablos in the church, little pictures, some sophisticated, some naive, celebrating and giving thanks for the miraculous intercession of a saint who saved the donor's life from fire, flood, locomotive, dynamite blast, irritated bull or what have you.

The caretaker of the church will allow you to climb the tower, the best place to view the street after street of roofless houses. In the tower take a good look at the 'chicken ladders', made of logs with notches chopped along one side. These were used for climbing up and down the mine shafts, often while packing murderously heavy baskets of ore. Imagine the result of the slightest misstep in the pitch darkness.

The Casa de Moneda is across the

street from the church and at one time contained minting machinery for the manufacture of silver coins. The equipment has long since been scrapped out, and part of the big old building is currently being used for a private residence.

The rails have been taken out of the railroad tunnel and it has been turned into a one-way vehicular road. If two vehicles happened to meet in the hole one of them would have to back out, so there is a telephone at each end connected to a 'dispatcher' who lives in a shack at the Catorce end.

Deep within the mountain there is a mining tunnel that bisects the vehicle tunnel, and in the drift the miners have built an altar, a common practice in Latin mines, but the only one I know of that can be seen from a bus. Watch for it on the right side — you'll see the candles.

There are two hotels in Real de Catorce, one hard by the place where the bus awaits the return trip and the other 50 metres or so up the hill on the side street, operated by the ubiquitous Hernando Fernandez. Hernando speaks English and has a charming American wife. The two of them are very knowledgeable about Real and its history.

Getting There

There are two ways of getting to Real de Catorce. The less common is by railroad, which is even more inconvenient than it is for the rest of Mexico, and involves catching the train in Saltillo or San Luis Potosí, getting off at Estacion Catorce, and hiking over the hills some 14 km to the Real. Occasionally someone with a jeep meets the train, but this act of mercy is not to be relied on.

The other way is by the bus that runs from Matehuala at about 1½-hour intervals. It leaves from the little bus station by the Las Vegas bar, almost next door to the Matehuala Hotel on

the right as you face the entrance. The first trip up is around 7 or 8 am and the last about 4.30 pm. Although it is possible to go to Catorce during the afternoon, take a quick look around and return to Matehuala that same day, most people either make the up trip in the early morning or stay overnight.

SAN LUIS POTOSÍ, San Luis Potosí

Most of Mexico's old mining towns owe their existence to a silver strike, but San Luis Potosí got its start when gold was discovered in the San Pedro hills, about 20 km from the present city. Prior to this the region was the site of several missions. The early miners, being natural optimists, decided to name their town after the fabulously wealthy mining camp of Potosí, Bolivia, in the hope that some of the luck would spread. It didn't, much.

Although the Mexican operations turned out well, they never achieved the wealth of their South American namesake, but in a few years the growth of the community, coupled with the shortage of drinking water, caused the officials to move the town to its present location. In addition to the gold of the original discovery, silver, lead and some copper were later found at San Pedro, and the future of the fledgling city was assured.

Today San Luis Potosí makes its living from mining, transport and commerce. Although it is not a national monument city, San Luis cherishes quite a number of colonial buildings, mostly clustered near the heart of the city.

The life of most Mexican cities is concentrated on the plaza, and this is even more true of Potosi than most. Four plazas are worthy of mention.

The Plaza de San Francisco, at Universidad and Aldama. The Franciscan order built the monastery on the south side of the plaza and gave it the present name. Next to the church on

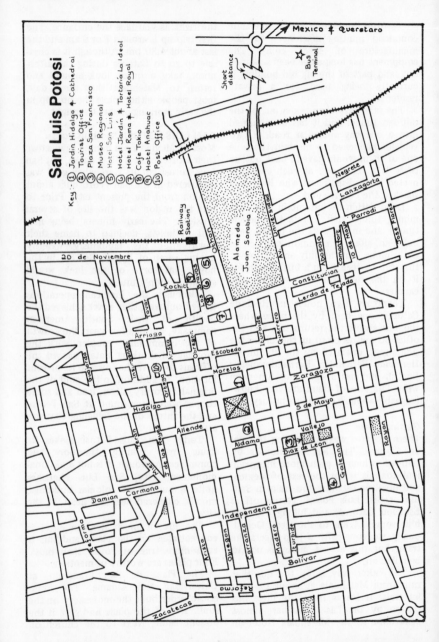

San Luis Potosi

Key:-
① Jardin Hidalgo ✦ Cathedral
② Tourist Office
③ Plaza San Francisco
④ Museo Regional
⑤ Hotel San Luis
⑥ Hotel Jardín ✦ Tortaría la Ideal
⑦ Hotel Roma ✦ Hotel Royal
⑧ Cafe Tokio
⑨ Hotel Anahuac
⑩ Post Office

the west side is the Museo Regional de Arte Popular, specialising in the handicrafts of the State of San Luis Potosí. Incorporated in the museum operation is the Fonda Tipica Potosina. The last time I stopped by the Fonda a local rock group was making the plaza unliveable for anyone lacking ear plugs, but most of the time it is quiet and peaceable and the ideal place for a picnic.

The Plazuela del Carmen at Escobedo and Othón contains the Templo del Nuestra Senora del Carmen, the most interesting of the city's churches and probably the best surviving example of Baroque sculpture in Mexico. Among the interior decorations is a reredo attributed to that Mexican renaissance man, Tresguerras.

The Jardin Hidalgo, at Othón and Zaragoza, isn't a garden, it's really the Plaza Principal. At one time it was called the Plaza de Armas, or parade ground. This is where you will find the Palacio del Gobierno, originally erected in 1770 but reconstructed and extensively repaired time and time again. It was here that Juárez, ignoring petitions for clemency from most of the countries and important personages in Europe, signed Maximilian's writ of execution. The Palacio Municipal was built as a private residence and has been the city hall for only about 50 years. The Cathedral, formerly Parroquia, on the east side of the square was begun in 1670 and took 240 years to bring to its present condition. Perhaps because of the long gestation, the interior is decorated in Byzantine, Doric, Gothic, baroque and so on, while the exterior is (mostly) baroque.

The Alameda at Universidad and Constitucion, is the city's largest and most restful park. It is so big that a person lolling on a bench near the fountain in the middle isn't unduly bothered by the traffic honking its way along the two busy streets on either side.

The Teatro de la Paz, at Othón and Zaragoza, is a pink stone jewel of an old-world type playhouse that is still doing duty as a legitimate theatre. On the right, in the same building, is an art gallery.

Places to Stay

The *Hotel del Rio* is across the street to the right of the railroad station as you face it. Fairly new, but the hideous buff front is discouraging to the stranger. It's the closest moderate hotel to the bus station.

Hotel San Luis is old, but a long, long way from being picturesque. Its best points are its location next door to the railroad station and being the closest inexpensive hotel to the bus station.

The *Hotel Jardín*, on Bravos at Xochitl, is about the nicest reasonably priced hotel in town and only about 30 minutes from the bus station. Best value for the pesos. Moderate and recommended.

The *Hotel Roma*, on Constitución at Bravos, is an old, thick-walled house. Run down, but inexpensive.

The *Hotel Royal*, on Constitución between Bravos and Othón, is another antique building with high ceilings and windows to match. It needs restoration badly, but when and if it is ever restored you can bet your boots it won't be inexpensive any longer!

The *Hotel Anahuac* on Xochitl near Bravos, has Mexican Miracle Modern decor and secured parking. Best bargain in SLP after the Hotel Jardin. Moderate.

Places to Eat

Potosí has oodles of restaurants. These are some of the places I've patronized over the years:

Tortaria la Ideal, on Bravos near Xochitl and the Hotel Jardín, has a sign saying 'service day and night', and I have yet to find them closed. Clean, quick, with a wide assortment of tortas, and inexpensive.

The *Cafe Tokio* is on Bravos between Xochitl and Constitución. Regardless of the name it serves good-quality ordinary Mexican workman's food and does it in a hurry. Also a good place for an American-style breakfast such as 'hot kakes'. The busiest joint in town. Moderate.

The restaurant in the *Hotel San Luis*, 20 de Noviembre at Othón, is about the cheapest place to eat, but the quality pretty well matches the price. Inexpensive.

I once tried the restaurant under the new and ridiculously expensive *Hotel Arizona* across the street from the bus station. Weary of the local corn-based cuisine, I wanted a meal of bread, cheese and wine and a white tablecloth to match. This is a difficult combination in Mexico because places that serve wine are usually aghast at the very idea of a light meal like this. But here I received just exactly what I ordered, served with dispatch and courtesy and nary a raised eyebrow or comment. The price was (need I add?) very expensive, but worth it at the time.

Getting Around

To get downtown from the bus terminal, you can catch a city bus in front of the second-class section that will take you past the Alameda to the Jardín Hidalgo for a couple of pesos or so. If you feel like walking there, go out of the front door of the first-class section and turn left. At the traffic circle swing around to your left and get off on the street directly behind the statue of Juárez. This is Universidad, and the Alameda is now about 20 minutes steady walking.

The bus station at San Luis Potosi is divided into separate 1st and 2nd class sections, in the form of an 'L' with a restaurant at the junction serving both. The terminal is also unusual for the variety of merchandise and services offered. In addition to the usual telegraph and post office it also has a local and long distance phone store, a pharmacy, sweets stands, a book store, two restaurants, a watch and clock shop, a leather-goods store that sells everything from martingales to reatas, and a store that stocks a fine selection of Aguascalientes needlework, which is rather hard to find in its home town.

The railroad station is opposite the middle of the Alameda on the Othón side. Sometimes shown at the end of the Alameda by the overpass but that station has been largely abandoned for many years.

Getting uptown from the railroad station is dead easy. Just walk out the front door and keep going until you hit the Alameda — about 100 metres or less.

There is an airport, but only business people and locals use it.

DOLORES HIDALGO, Guanajuato.

Dolores Hidalgo is the perfect example of a small, peaceful country town, a place where a dog chases a cat — and they both walk! But as a historical site it combines for Mexico the attributes of Concord, Boston, Philadelphia and Mount Vernon rolled into one, for it was here, in 1810, that the parish priest, Miguel Hidalgo, issued his ringing cry for freedom, the 'giro' repeated by politicians great and small all over the Republic each 16 September.

Today Dolores derives most of its income from the fabrication of hand-painted ceramic tableware which is shipped all over Mexico, and from the streams of patriotic Mexicans who arrive by chartered bus, automobile and bus from all parts of the Republic. Unfortunately for the patriots, the church is often locked tighter than a drum; it is still in use as a parish church in spite of its status as an unofficial national monument.

Hidalgo's residence has been turned into a museum containing many of his personal possessions, including, I am told, a peculiar chair with a concealed chamber pot. It is hearsay to me because although I've tried to visit the museum on several occasions I have yet to find the door unlocked. There is a sign on the door saying that the admission is M$15 and also giving the hours of operation, but the latter is to be taken with a kilo of salt.

If you leave the Flecha Amarilla bus station and turn left you will be on Hidalgo, and in a couple of blocks you will come to the Museo Hidalgo complete with identification plaque installed under the direction of the luckless Maximilian.

Across the street is the Artesanias en Piel shop which has a good selection of personal leather goods, such as belts, purses, billfolds and the like. On the same corner is the Mercado de Artesanias, an old house converted into a sales room for the local cermicists' work, mostly tableware. This is far and away the best assortment under one roof in Dolores, and is worth a visit even if you're perfectly content with the Belleek you use at home.

Continuing on Hidalgo will bring you to the tree-shaded plaza with the statue of the great man himself forming a centrepiece.

If the Mercado de Artesanias doesn't have enough pottery, turn right as you leave the Flecha Amarilla station and cross the Rio Laja and you will see wholesaler after jobber, most of whom sell retail, too.

In the same neighbourhood are several huacherias that still hand-make the old-style countryman's footwear, comfortable, long-lasting and cheap — far superior to the stuff sold in tourist meccas such as Taxco and Cancun.

The street names, incidentally, have all been changed a number of times and the only street names that haven't been changed over the past century or so are Hidalgo and Morelos.

Places to Stay and Eat

The hotel situation in Dolores is good in that I have never had any trouble walking in off the street, and bad in that there isn't an awful lot of choice.

The best hotel in town is the *Posada Cocomacán*, on the right corner of the plaza facing the Parroquia. Good restaurant when it's open and quite popular during the fall duck season with nimrods up from Mexico City. Both the hotel and restaurant are moderate.

Along the same street as the Cocomacán and up the hill beside the church is the *Hotel el Caudillo*. Inexpensive. There is also an inexpensive restaurant in the El Caudillo, where I've had both good and lousy meals, depending on who is stirring the cazuelas back in the kitchen.

The *Restaurant Plaza* is on the plaza opposite Hidalgo's old church. Very popular with local business people from the shops around the square. It also has long-distances phone service. Moderate.

Or may may prefer to take your chances at the market. Go along Hidalgo from the Flecha Amarilla bus station and turn left at the plaza. The market is then a block or two. Walking time is five minutes.

Getting There

As Dolores is about halfway between Guanajuato and San Miguel Allende it is a good place to base yourself when you visit either of those popular destinations — it is much more likely to have economical hotel rooms available when everything in either San Miguel or Guanajuato is full to overflowing.

Bus service is excellent, with buses from Mexico City, Guadalajara, San Luis Potosí, San Miguel, Guanajuato and such out-of-the-way places as San Filipe and San Luis de la Paz. Flecha Amarilla has the best service and its own terminal with baggage checking and so on.

The Omnibus de Mexico and Estrella Blanca buses stop along the plaza.

POZOS, Guanajuato

Pozos is another ghost town similar to Real de Catorce or an unrestored Taxco. It is unusual that some of the buildings around the tiny plaza have been refurbished, but the treatment is only facade deep — there is nothing but air behind some of the imposing fronts.

The old mines were mainly strung out along a ridge — go uphill from the little zócolo and keep working your way up and to your left. There are hundreds of roofless houses: at one time Pozos was a city with 40-50,000 people, fine homes, cobbled streets, piped water and its own generating plant, but the revolution put an end to prosperity, and today Pozos is slowly turning into rubble with that charming decrepitude that only Mexico can muster.

To get to Pozos, first go to San Luis de la Paz, which is located 116 km south of San Luis Potosí on the Querétaro road, 86 km north of Queretaro and about 40 km from Dolores Hidalgo. There is frequent bus service to and from all these points.

Pozos itself is about 15 km from San Luis de la Paz and there are several buses a day from the little central terminal in San Luis. The return trip is even easier, because an enterprising taxi driver runs a shuttle service, parking at the little plaza in Pozos until he gets a full load for the return trip. Costs M$15 or M$20.

GUANAJUATO, Guanajuato

Guanajuato is one of the most popular tourist destinations in Mexico, and deservedly so. It has a superb site, a great deal of colonial charm and a rich and entertaining history. Plus it has the facilities to handle a large number of visitors.

Guanajuato is an old silver-mining town, the first strike having been made back in 1548, followed by location after location. These were not nickle-and-dime prospect holes, either — the Conde de Rul, owner of the Valenciana mine, was supposed to have spent a thousand pesos a month on incidentals, yet he had enough left over to pay for churches and monuments.

Because the town is high among rugged mountains where flat ground is at a premium, the city has very little room for streets, and one of them is so narrow it is called 'The Little Street of the Kiss', and there are post cards showing how people can lean out of their balconies and kiss across the street. The narrow, crooked streets contribute a good deal to the attraction of Guanajuato, but also make it extremely vexing to get around on wheels, and Guanajuato is probably the only city in the world where Americans habitually walk!

The incredible traffic problems persist, even though most through traffic now goes underground along the old river bed. This practical state of affairs actually happened almost by accident. The community had always been plagued by flash floods, then finally after an especially severe flusher in 1905 the Government built the 'Tunel Porfirio Díaz' to bypass the river, whereupon all that remained was to construct a few entrances and exits and the city had a ready-made underground roadway.

No city in Mexico has as many points of interest in as small an area as Guanajuato, and there are guidebooks in both English and Spanish wholly devoted to the city, although I have never seen any mention of the Tunel Díaz which makes it all practical!

Sightseeing in Guanajuato proper is dead simple because it is located at the bottom of a narrow canyon with essentially just one street, Juárez which becomes Sopena which becomes Paseo de la Prensa. In this case 'Prensa' refers to the two dams, built in the late 1700s, from which the city draws its water. Guanajuato had piped water before the United States was incorporated.

To get to Juárez from the colonial-styled central bus terminal is simple — just go out the front and over the bridge and you're there!

The iron-framed Mercado Hidalgo is a couple of blocks up the street, a remarkably well-stocked market for a town of its size. The main floor is the food section selling fruit, vegetables, meat, fish, bread and anything else a family is likely to eat, but the interesting feature for the traveller is the balcony encircling the main floor where clothing, copper cookware, cazuelas, toys, shoes, purses and seemingly everything available in Mexico is sold. Some people spend hours on the balcony and leave insisting they hadn't had time to see everything!

When the Mercado was built in 1911, they left the marble floor and entrance columns of the original market and turned it into a tiny, paved plaza, the Jardín Morelos, a totally delightful place where oldsters nod the afternoon away and children play.

Next on Sopena (nee Juarez) is the Plaza de la Paz, surrounded by handsome, imposing buildings. The one with the plaque stating that Humboldt stayed here is the former residence of the Conde de Rul and is another of the excellent designs of that Mexican of many parts, Tresguerras.

Almost next door to the Plaza de la Paz is the lovely Jardín de la Unión, which could be considered the Plaza

Principal of Guanajuato. On the left of the Jardin is the new El Agora de Baratillo, a wonderful place to read away a lazy afternoon at one of the white-painted, cast-iron tables.

Walk through the Agora and you will be on yet another of the secluded plazuelas the Latins do so well, the plaza del Baratillo. It is also called Plaza Gra. Manual Gonzales, and several other names. It has a beautiful fountain, which would be improved no end if the water were turned on. 'Baratillo' means second-hand goods in Spanish, but I have never been able to find anyone in Guanajuato who could explain how it became attached to a quiet little plaza.

Across Sopena from the Jardín Unión is the celebrated Teatro Juárez, another of the efforts of President Díaz. A typical colonnaded classical design, the Teatro is no longer much used, although for the usual small admission fee one can wander around and gawk at the elegant interior. The foyer alone is worth the price of admission. Adorning the front roofline of the Teatro are statues depicting the Muses, the work of W. H. Mullen, of Salem, Ohio. There are nine Muses, of course, but the Juárez only has eight. Question: Who was left out?

Keep going uphill on Sopena and eventually in turns into Paseo de la Prensa. Keep on and you will reach the dams. There are several parks up here, and it is a wonderful place for a picnic. It is about a 45-minute walk from the bus station and takes you through Guanajuato's better residential district, past the Palacio de Gobierno, itself a former private home.

If this much walking doesn't appeal, then go through the Jardin de la Union and turn left on Cantarramas. This leads you back toward the lower end of town, past the imposing University of Guanajuato with its steps that, from the bottom, seem to reach to the sky.

Next Cantarramas changes its name

to Positos after a slight jog. The former residence of the Diego Rivera at No. 47 has been turned into the usual museum. Sketches for some of his famous murals are on display, as are a number of easel paintings. Guanajuato is one of the most reactionary cities of Mexico, an even match for San Miguel Allende and Guadalajara, and during his life-time Rivera was a non-person in his old home town.

Stay on Positos and you will come to the Alhóndiga, the old granary with a bloody history. During the early stages of Mexico's revolt against Spain the Spaniards forted up in the Alhóndiga which was then a new building built to store grain against years of poor harvests. The walls were thick and the doors were sturdy and the rebels and their seige were having no luck at all until a young miner named José Barajas volunteered to set fire to the massive portals. Barajas's nickname was 'Pipila' which means 'hen-turkey', but nobody remembers today whether he got it because of a high-pitched voice or the way he walked.

So Pipila had a slab of sandstone tied to his back as a sort of early-day flack vest and he braved the hail of bullets and destroyed the doors, opening the way for the insurgents to take the warehouse, a deed commemorated by the huge statue on the hill overlooking the town from the south-west. The rebels had to fight every inch of the way when they took the Alhóndiga after Pípila breached the door, and the last Spaniards died on the roof with sword in hand. Later a number of Royalists were taken prisoner and incarcerated in the Alhóndiga. The incensed people of Guanajuato broke into the place and murdered nearly 250 helpless men.

But the fortunes of war always favour first one side and then the other, and it was soon the Spaniards' turn to capture Guanajuato, and they set out

to inflict the usual draconian justice. Royalist General Calleja made it his first order of business to order everyone in Guanajuato be executed, including men, women and children. A number of men had been killed when a priest, José María de Jesús Belaunzaran, interposed himself between the executioners and their victims and stopped the slaughter by force of personality and the cross he held on high.

Later the Spanish captured and executed Hidalgo, Allende, Aldama and Jimenez and their heads were returned to Guanajuato and hung from hooks at the four corners of the Alhóndiga, hooks which are there to this day for you and all the world to see.

Now the bloody old Alhóndiga is a peaceful museum showing paintings and odds and ends pertaining to the history of Guanajuato.

The best known tourist attraction in Guanajuato is the Pantéon, a collection of mummies that are exhibited in a gruesome museum of their own. When the corpses are put into niches in the graveyeard they shrivel and dry up, rather than disintegrating. At the end of five years the bodies are evicted from their niches unless their relatives come up with additional rent. Most of the bodies are put in a common grave, but the more interesting are put in cases in the museum. Among the 'interesting' mummies are a miner still in boots and overalls, and a woman who died in childbirth, complete with half-delivered foetus.

To get to the Pantéon, turn right on leaving the bus station and follow the street uphill past the railroad station. There are signs and it would take considerable effort to get lost. The walk takes about an hour, the return somewhat less. Non-walkers can get a cab from the rank in front of the Central de Autobuses. Expect to pay M$50-75 for the ride, depending on how well you haggle.

Another don't-miss are the Entremesses Cervantinos put on during the spring by the University students. They are mostly in mime, so a lack of Spanish is no bar to their enjoyment, and are performed outdoors, as they were meant to be.

A recent development is the annual two-week International Cervantes Festival, sponsored by the State of Guanajuato. This is a major cultural event with internationally-known dance companies, singers and other performing artists. Held in April or May, months when the weather is especially fine.

The Iglesia de Can Cayetano, on the road to Dolores and about the same distance from town as the Pantéon, is better known as La Valenciana, to the best of my knowledge the only instance of a church named after a mine!

The Valenciana was built by the Conde de Rul and the cost was divided between the Count and the miners working at the La Valenciana mine across the road. The name of the architect is long forgotten, but the church is one of the best, and best-preserved, examples of Churrigueresque decoration. In my opinion it is one of the most beautiful exercises in colonial church-building in the country. And the interior matches and justifies the exterior. There are three Churrigueresque altars, in marked contrast to the usual Mexican church which is a medley of periods, styles and techniques. Pay close attention to the pulpit, one of the best demonstrations of the wood-worker's art I ever laid eyes on.

Even allowing for the fact that the church is slightly lopsided and out of balance because the planned second tower was never built — apparently local politics prevented — this is *the* church to inspect in Mexico.

The Valenciana mines that paid for it all, one way or another, is directly across the road from the church. It was shut down about 50 years ago after sev-

eral hundred years of continuous operation. The machinery was removed but within a few years new hoisting gear was installed and operations resumed, albeit on a smaller scale. It is a fascinating place with the huge patio formerly used in the milling process, many old stone buildings, most of them roofless, and some old, old air compressors and bit sharpeners. I wandered around at will, with nary a word from anyone, probably because the miners couldn't conceive of anybody except another miner being interested in their activities, but I don't guarantee you will have the same good fortune.

If you are interested in the rehabilitation of old buildings, then visit Marfil, about 3 km from town toward Silao. Marfil was originally the suburb where the better-off mine people lived, and was severely damaged by the same flood that led to the construction of the Tunel Díaz in Guanajuato. By the end of WW II it was practically a deserted ghost town and in horrible condition. In common with Alamos, Taxco and San Miguel, Marfil has been largely re-built through the efforts of well-to-do Americans who have retired in the area. And as with Taxco, the restoration of Marfil is largely the result of the effort of a single individual, an American named Belloli. He is to be commended.

Places to Stay

Guanajuato has lots of hotels to take care of its burgeoning tourist business, but even so it occasionally fills up with not a room to be had. If that happens I suggest you try Dolores Hidalgo. If you don't have any luck in Dolores, then double back and try León, which is a large, main-road city with a number of moderate or expensive hotels very near the bus station. And if you have no success in either of these places I suggest simply giving up on the whole idea and plan on coming back the next year with

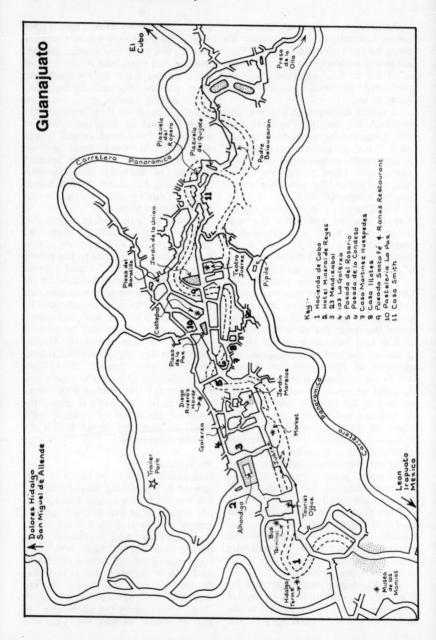

Guanajuato

El Cubo

Presa de la Olla

Carretera Panoramica

Plazuela del Ropero

Plazuela del Quijote

Padre Belauzaron

Jardin de la Union

11

Teatro Juarez

Pipila

Plaza del Baratillo

Cathedral

10

Plaza de la Paz

8

9

Diego Rivera's House

5

Jardin Morelos

Galerza

Market

3

Alhondiga

Tourist Office

Bus Terminal

2

1

Hidalgo Thermal

Carretera Panoramica

Trailer Park

Dolores Hidalgo
San Miguel de Allende

Leon
Irapuato
Mexico

Museo de las Momias

Key:-
1 Hacienda de Cobo
2 Hotel Mineral de Reyes
3 23 Mendizabal
4 103 La Galerza
5 Posada del Rosario
6 Posada de la Condesa
7 Casa Martinez Huespedes
8 Casa Illotes
9 Posada Santa Fé ✦ Ranas Restaurant
10 Pasteleria La Paz
11 Casa Smith

advance, money-down reservations.

Paid reservations are always advisable during week-ends in April and May when the Entremeses are on.

The *Posada la Condesa*, a block down the street from the Plaza de la Paz, has a sort of impressive lobby, what with suits of plate armour and all, but don't be fooled, it's not nearly as expensive as it looks. Moderate, and usually full.

The *Hotel Mineral de Reyes* is on 5 de Mayo past the Alhondiga to the five-storey cream building with balconies, on the left side of the street. Red flower pots on the individual balconies are a thoughtful touch. I've enjoyed several sojourns here once I learned to duck the concrete beam above the last steps as I came down the narrow front stairs. Best value in Guanajuato. Moderate.

The *Hotel Murillo*, on the second street behind the bus terminal off 5 de Mayo, looks like a nice hotel for a wayfarer but it really caters to the large-family trade. But if there are two or three couples in your group this is a good choice and dead cheap when the tab is split four or more ways.

The *Hotel Alhóndiga*, across the street from the Murillo, seems to function at about the same level as the Reyes, but I have never been able to catch it with the front desk manned, and I have been told by other travellers that this is by no means an unusual state of affairs.

Another good bet, although a bit more expensive, is the easy-to-overlook *Hacienda de Cobo*. As you cross the bridge in front of the Central de Autobuses look down the old creek to your right and you will see a white, igloo-like structure with 'Hacienda de Cobo' painted thereon. To reach it, turn right on Juárez and go until the sidewalk jogs to the left around a store. Just before this you should find an inconspicuous iron gate opening on a sloping driveway. This is the pedestrian entrance to the Hacienda. It is more

motel than hotel, and the automobile entrance is on the other side on the road coming in from Silao. Lots of thoughtful little touches, such as a couple of bottles of Electropuro bottled water, crown-sealed, in each room. Expensive, but worth it.

There are a number of hotels practically side by side on Juárez after it crosses 5 de Mayo. They used to be inexpensive, but recently they have all jacked their prices up all the way to expensive. They are far from worth their prices but they are among the first in town to rent all their rooms.

In the Jardin de la Unión, on the left, is the *Posada Santa Fe*, a ridiculously expensive hotel with a sidewalk cafe. The Santa Fe people have extended themselves with the Lady's Bar El Truco.

Guanajuato is such a popular destination that nearly all the hotels have not only raised their rates but have been able to keep pretty well filled in spite of it. The only inexpensive place to stay that I know of is the *Casa Martinez Huespedes* on Alonso, a short street that branches to the right from Juárez near the Jardín Morelos and returns to Sopena a few blocks farther up. I've never stayed there because it always seems to be full when I try to register, but it looks like a rather nice huespedes. If you can get in it is inexpensive.

Places to Eat

For a quick comida, washed down with a bottle of Negra Modelo, it's hard to beat the little *El Cedro* restaurant near the tourist information booth on Juárez and only a short block from the bus station. Heavily patronised by country families in for a day in the big city, but they somehow have always managed to fit me in at one of their six tables. Inexpensive.

A little further up the street, there is a three-storey, open-sided building next to the Mercado Hidalgo. This is actually a sort of restaurant department store where the girls who used to operate on the sidewalk on the opposite side of the market now have their permanent stalls. No two of them serve exactly the same thing, and I've had everything from a pozole to blood sausage sandwiches there at one time or another. Best value in town for a wide assortment of basic dishes. Very inexpensive.

Do-it-yourselfers will enjoy the *Pasteleria Santa Fe* on the Plaza de la Paz across the caca-coloured Basilica de Nuestra Senora de Guanajuato. It's both a bakery and a pastry-shop and a good place to pick up some of the ingredients for a picnic. Very inexpensive.

If price is no object, absolutely the best place in town to eat is the *4 Ranas* restaurant, overlooking the Jardín de la Unión and the Teatro Juárez. It is actually the dining room of the Hotel San Diego and is located on the second floor thereof. It has good food and an extensive wine list, and is another place where I've never been served a bad bottle of the red. The 4 Ranas wins Guanajuato's best restaurant award going away, but it's a place to be saved for those special occasions because it is ridiculously expensive.

The restaurants in Guanajuato's little bus station are a good choice for breakfast, especially the one that costs a peso to visit.

There is a simpatico sit-down bar on the Jardín Unión opposite the Agora. Lots of atmosphere and heavy, dark-polished wood, more like a better private club than the average Mexican saloon. Brick-red paint job out front, but no sign.

Getting There

Considering that Guanajuato is not on the main road to anywhere it has extremely good bus service, and you can catch a bus to Guanajuato from the Central del Norte in Mexico City, or San Luis Potosí or Guadalajara or even Matamoros, but don't waste time waiting for a direct connection which may run only a time or two each day. Get a bus to Querétaro or León and then get another bus from there; Querétaro, especially, is a good shot, and one bus company or another has a bus every half hour or so.

Forget the railroad; and there is no air service.

SAN MIGUEL DE ALLENDE,
Guanajuato

San Miguel de Allende is one of the four most photogenic and picturesque cities in Mexico. Its only peers are Guanajuato, Pátzcuaro and Taxco, and San Miguel is the one with the largest and most visible American colony.

As a retirement community San Miguel has a number of advantages. First-off, until a very few years ago run-down buildings were dirt cheap and could be fixed up very economically. The weather is superb, unlike Alamos where somewhat the same situation prevails but where the weather is hot as blue blazes in summer. Miguel is rather more intellectual than the other three, due largely to the Instituto, and perhaps most important of all, there are so many English-speaking people around town all the same that a retiree can get along just dandy without learning three words of the national language.

The town was founded by a Spanish priest, Juan de San Miguel. For several centuries it was called San Miguel el Grande to distinguish it from the numerous smaller San Migueles that clutter the map of Mexico to this vey day.

One of the original conspirators in the revolution against Spain was a young man from San Miguel el Grande named Ignacio Allende. For his efforts he was executed by the Crown and his head wound up on a hook at one corner of the Alhóndiga in neighbouring Guanajuato. Immediately upon throwing off

Spanish rule the town of San Miguel decided to honour their favourite son by adding his name to the town's existing name, a very common Mexican practice. The locals call it 'San Miguel' and let it go at that.

San Miguel owes its present-day beauty to the practice of the wealthy people of Guanajuato of building their homes away from Guanajuato, which has always been rather a difficult place to live, although a nice place to visit. And although San Miguel was eclipsed by its neighbors up the road at Pozos and Guanajuato, it was once the centre of a prosperous mining district in its own right.

San Miguel is one of the handsomest towns in Mexico, with fairly wide streets and quite moderate grades for a mountain community. Many of the streets are cobblestones, which makes it unwise to wear high heels. Many of the old buildings were occupied throughout their existence by families with the resources to keep them in good repair, and the town is full of beautiful, unrestored structures. San Miguel is another 'monument town' where plastic-fronted movie theatres and dirty Pemex stations are verboten in the central city. For years it was a popular movie set for Hollywood and Churubusco film makers, and the 'The Brave Bulls', 'Serenade' and other major pictures were shot here.

The oustanding building in town, and its most distinctive landmark, is the Parroquia. It started out in life as a rather nondescript Franciscan church, but the town wanted something unique to grace their plaza, and during the late 1800s it was rebuilt under the direction of an illiterate Indian stonecutter named Ceferino Gutierrez who in turn apparently received his inspiration from a postcard view of Europe's great cathedrals — stories disagree as to which one. The end result has to be seen to be appreciated. 'Plastic Gothic' is one description that would be difficult to be better. Admire it from the outside — the inside is living proof that not all Mexicans have good taste.

Almost directly across the street from the bus stations is the Instituto Allende, the institution that can fairly take the credit for the renaissance of San Miguel. The Instituto is housed in a former convent and when it was started San Miguel was just another semi-ghost town sitting on the side of a hill and listening to its roofs cave in. The Instituto attracted well-off Americans who fell in love with the place and later returned to rehabilitate the then-cheap old houses and make San Miguel their home. Even without the history it is entertaining to wander around the extensive grounds of the Instituto. To give some idea of the size of the place, there is a hotel located on the premises that has a parking lot and is still fairly well separated from the enclosing structures.

The Instituto has some competition nowadays, from the Academia Hispano Americana, located at Reloj and Insurgenties in an old mansion complete with the usual beguiling patio. The Academia emphasizes its Spanish language classes and is one of the best schools of its type in the Republic. Students can take board and room with a local Mexican family and thereby entirely avoid hearing and using English. This 'immersion system' of language instruction is probably the most efficient technique going and the Academia has excellent results overall.

But essentially San Miguel is a Mexican town that has been around for hundreds of years, with its own traditonal enterprises that have nothing whatsoever to do with battening on the foreign visitors. For instance, San Miguel is the principal supplier of the 'colonial' lamps seen all over Mexico.

On the way uptown from the bus station on Zacateros there are several factories and shops selling lamps and

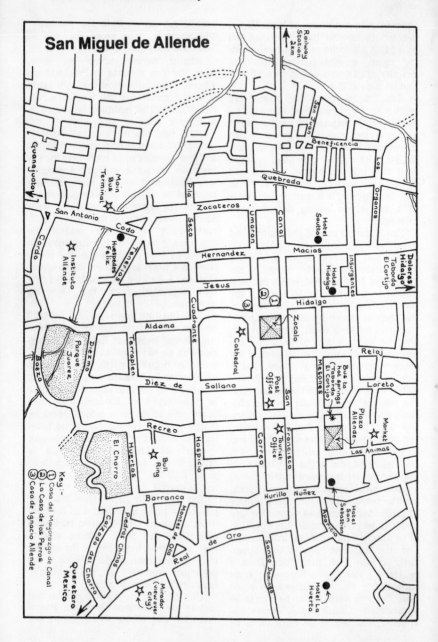

San Miguel de Allende

Key:-
1 Casa del Mayorazgo de Canal
2 La Casa de los Perros
3 Casa de Ignacio Allende

kindred items, such as candle-holders, vases, table lamps, ash trays, salvers and so on. The goods in the shop of H Llamas, mostly of brass, are of a particularly high order of craftmanship.

Other stores along here sell items made of sheet iron, tinplate, brass, silver, aluminum and even gold. Unlike the shops in Taxco, these largely provided items of a utilitarian, rather than decorative nature.

On the plaza, to the right as you face the Parroquia, is the Colibri, a book and art supplies store that stocks Mexico's most extensive selection of English-language paperbacks and also selected magazines from the US. The two amiable ladies who run the Colibrí have been around San Miguel for donkey's years and are a priceless source of information about the place.

The grocery store with the best stock in town is located under the same set of portales as the Colibrí. It has a large stock of things Americans are likely to buy, such as pancake mix and white granulated sugar, and is also a good place to pick up the makings for an al fresco meal, which can be devoured in the Bosque, three blocks out one of the streets running alongside the Parroquia.

Calle Reloj is the street that leaves the Jardín across from the church and on the right. On Reloj is one of the most unusual old buildings in Mexico, the Casa Cohen, with six entrances, five of which wear Stars of David carved above their doors. The Casa Cohen nowadays sells everything from spray paint cans to solid brass tables.

Places to Stay

The *Quinta Loreto*, on Calle Loreto at the new Paseo, is a long, low motel that used to have very spacious grounds until a good part was taken up by the new paseo. Swimming pool. This is the most popular place for long-term guests in San Miguel and reservations

are usually essential. Moderate and best value in town.

The hotel *Casa Colonial*, on Canal between Macias and Hidalgo, is a pleasing establishment in an old private home with an open-top patio. Another place where you'd best have reservations. Moderate.

The *Posada de las Monjas* is on Canal between Quebrada and Beneficencia, or to put it another way, below the arch on Calle Canal. It is in a former convent — witness the name — that has been the victim of a new addition. The older part, which I prefer, is expensive (and getting ready to edge into the very expensive category). The rooms in the new section are more costly and also more like rooms in an elderly Hilton.

San Miguel is a town that doesn't take much interest in the plight of the impecunious, and there are far more ridiculously expensive hotels than there are moderate. I'd about given up entirely on finding a cheap hotel when I was told about the *Casa de Huespedes Felix*. I didn't get to inspect the rooms because they were all occupied whenever I tried, but it seems neat, well-kept, well-run and a cut or three above the average Latin-American rooming house. It is actually in sight of the bus stations, to the left as you leave them. Inexpensive, but probably not for long.

Places to Eat

One of the better low-budget eateries is right next to the Flecha Amarilla bus station. The sign says 'Restaurante'; the place serves standard country fare, mostly to countrymen in town on business. Inexpensive.

The restaurant at the *Quinta Loreto* is justly popular with foreigners and serves Americanized food. It gets very little play from locals as a result — the indigenes feel the cooking is too bland! It is a best bet for breakfast, although you would be well advised to omit the ham, which like most Mexican 'ham' is a ham-based luncheon meat. There are set serving hours, like a boarding house, rather than continuous as with a bonafide restaurant, and the place serves all comers. Moderate.

After the Loreto, the next-best breakfast spot is the *Carrusel* on Canal between Macias and Hidalgo, less than a block from the Jardin. The Carrusel serves American, Mexican and 'Continental' style breakfasts until high noon. It is an odd place, a padded-seat saloon by night, which uses the bar entrance as a short-order joint during the day, dispensing hamburgers, hot cakes, bacon and eggs and so on. Expensive.

On the corner of the plaza by the Parroquia is the all-new *Terraza* restaurant. The Terraza was one of the oldest restaurants in San Miguel, but it was forced to close a few years back to make way for a religious equipment store. Now it has moved a few doors up Calle Correo from its previous location and the tables are now out in the open on the terrace. It is the best place in town for people-watching and sidewalk cafe-ing, and is popular with foreigners, rather than residents, probably because of the prices — quality is OK, but it's expensive.

La Hoja Seca, back down on the corner of Umaran (Correo under another name) and Macias is just the opposite of the Terraza — it's popular with Mexicans but practically unknown to the foreign colony. The Hoja Seca is owned by a retired musician named Roque Carabajo, a native of San Miguel, who achieved the dream of most performers and retired and went back to his old home town and opened a restaurant. The name comes from his greatest hit. Señor Carabajo is well-known among Mexican music lovers and occasionally people will drive up from Mexico City in their Mercedes and Chryslers just to spend an evening listening to him play and sing. I've eaten there a dozen times or so over the years and I don't recall seeing anyone but locals in the place. Expensive.

Popular with the younger set is the *Posada la Fuente — Mama Mia's* on Umaran up the hill from La Hoja Seca. The food is designed to appeal to Americanized tastes and runs heavy to hamburgers, pizza, fruit salads and beer. Moderate.

If cost is no object, then the best place in town is on Zacateros on the way in from the bus station. It's called *Genios* and is located in a dowdy storefront on the left side of the street. A plain rustic sign doesn't shout its message and is easy to overlook. Unpretentious or not, Genios can come up with such things as tripe à la mode de Caen, sweetbreads in wine and oysters Rockefeller. Ridiculously expensive and worth it.

Getting There

Getting to San Miguel is easy. Several buses a day give direct service from the Central del Norte in Mexico City, and there is hourly service to Queretaro, Celaya and Dolores Hidalgo/Guanajuato.

There has been no railroad service for years, unless you are willing to go via San Luis Potosí!

Mexico City

The Mexicans simply say Mexico when referring to their capital, and on some maps it is called La Ciudad de Mexico. The English-speaking call it Mexico City, but by any name it must rank as one of the great cities of the world.

It was laid out by the Spanish to their standard pattern in the early 16th century and has been the subject of improvements and alterations on an almost annual basis, the most notable of which was Maximilian's Paseo de la Reforma. A cosmopolitan, cultured individual, he wanted his capital to have a wide boulevard suitable for strolling ladies and gentlemen, the equal of Paris's Champs Elysées, and in this undertaking, at least, he succeeded admirably. Today his Reforma is one of the centrepieces of the city and one of the world's great boulevards. When first built it ran only to Hidalgo, but during the past few years it has been extended all the way to Gonzalez.

The Spanish founders, however, intended that the Zócolo would be the heart of their city as it is in most of Mexico, and they took advantage of the city's flat terrain to lay out a huge plaza, one of the largest in the country and about equal in size to the plaza in Mérida. Around the Zócolo are the National Cathedral, the City Hall, Capital and the president's office. The National Pawnshop is an afterthought.

The Spanish are also responsible for the Alameda, the expansive park a few blocks away, but in their day it was used for burning those unlucky enough to fall afoul of the Inquisition, and it was not until the reign of President Díaz that it began to take on the pleasing aspect it has today.

Mexico City has been the capital of Mexico since the days of the Aztecs. Cortés and his allies took it from the Aztecs by force of arms and made it their own capital in part, I suspect, because it provided a large selection of ready-cut building stones in the form of the pyramids dotting the region.

From time immemorial Mexico City offered financial opportunity. First to the old Conquistadores, who became enormously wealthy men if they survived, and lately to millions of the wretched and impoverished poor who automatically turned their faces to the capital as they were starved out of their home villages. Currently it is estimated that about 300,000 people a year move to the capital and this, coupled with the natural increase in a population that translates 'the pill' as 'la aspirina' has strained the finite resources of the city to the breaking point. To the foreigner the best evidence of this is the eye-watering, throat-searing, all-pervasive smog that hangs over the city for weeks on end. On days when this smog is about average it can put Los Angeles to shame and it poses a real problem for travellers with respiratory difficulties.

The population explosion has caused public transport to be all but unusable during certain hours of the day, made the downtown sidewalks almost unwalkable, and caused theatre lines that routinely stretch for blocks. Foreign travellers would be well advised to do as the more affluent natives do — to stay in Cuernavaca or one of the other outlying towns and commute to the city on the excellent bus lines.

The above remarks notwithstanding, Mexico City is one of the most fantastic communities in the world, and one I've enjoyed for years, although I will admit that it becomes much less fun with each passing year.

Street names

Mexico City has the most confusing street naming 'system' in the world.

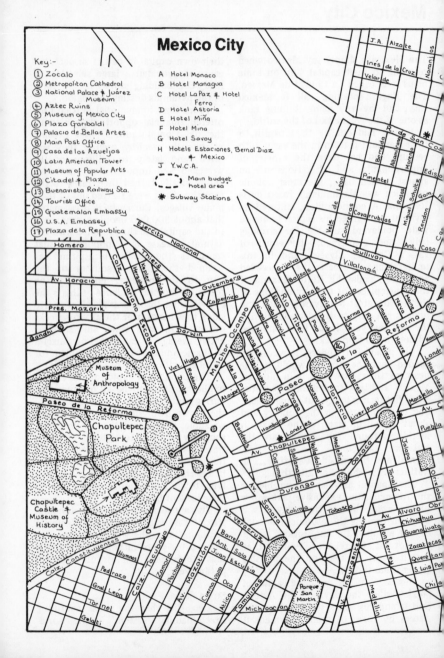

Mexico City

Key:-
1. Zócalo
2. Metropolitan Cathedral
3. National Palace & Juárez Museum
4. Aztec Ruins
5. Museum of Mexico City
6. Plaza Garibaldi
7. Palacio de Bellas Artes
8. Main Post Office
9. Casa de los Azulejos
10. Latin American Tower
11. Museum of Popular Arts
12. Citadel & Plaza
13. Buenavista Railway Sta.
14. Tourist Office
15. Guatemalan Embassy
16. U.S.A. Embassy
17. Plaza de la República

A. Hotel Monaco
B. Hotel Managua
C. Hotel La Paz & Hotel Ferro
D. Hotel Astoria
E. Hotel Miña
F. Hotel Mina
G. Hotel Savoy
H. Hotels Estaciones, Bernal Diaz & Mexico
J. Y.W.C.A.

Main budget hotel area

Subway Stations

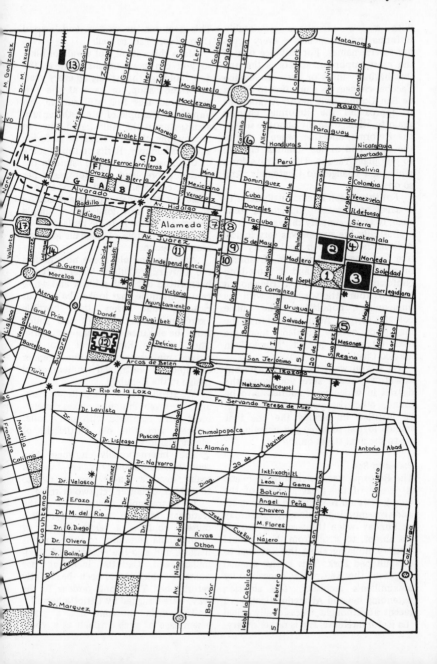

With a few exceptions — notably Reforma and Insurgentes — every street has several names. For instance one of the most important streets is the one that begins — more or less — as Mexico Tacuba, changes its name first to Rivera de San Cosme, switches to Alvarado as it approaches the Reforma, changes again to Hidalgo on the opposite side of the Reforma, and then when it gets to the other end of the Alameda changes to just plain Tacuba. Then it runs for a while and changes to Guatemala. And so on.

For this reason I occasionally refer to a street as 'Alvarado/Hidalgo' or some such, to try to simplify things.

Basically the system was very logical back in the days when Mexico City was, like Los Angeles, a number of suburbs in search of a city, and it caused no confusion at all to have a 'Hidalgo' in three or four little towns, but with the burgeoning population the little colonias merged. As an indication of the magnitude of the problem, there are over 60 streets named 'Morelos' in Mexico City!

So if you want to go anywhere but downtown, make sure you know the district in which your address is to be found, otherwise your cab driver will be justified in picking the one that sounds logical to him, and charging to get to the next street on the list.

Places to See
The **Reforma** was designed to be — and is — one of the great avenues of the world. I would recommend that you set aside one morning, preferably a Saturday or Sunday when the week-day crowds are absent, to stroll from the National Lottery Building along the Reforma to Chapultepec Park. This is the original length of the Reforma as conceived by Maximilian's architect. The addition extending beyond Alvarado/Hidalgo is a recent afterthought, occasionally called 'La Reforma Nueva' and is rather dreary.

This goes for the western end beyond Chapultepec Park as well.

Make this a stroll, not a walk or hike, so you can gawk unashamedly at the new buildings that spring up every year, or window-shop, or gaze at the few great residences that still survive. An impressive example of late 19th-century architecture is the multi-tiered, towered brownstone at the corner of Reforma and Guadalquivir. It sits on top of some of the most expensive real estate in the world, where land sells for pesos per square *centimetre*, and each time I make my stroll there I pause and admire and wonder how long before simple economics cause it to be replaced by a 22-storey example of Bauhaus Mexican Modern design.

Another fine old home now houses the University Club at Lucerna. It has been fitted out with a black and white canvas marquee that looks like a circus cast-off, but even this horrible excrescence can't detract too much from the elegance of the basic structure. The Japanese Embassy at Rio Nilo strikes me as probably the premier example of restrained contemporary design in the Republic.

My stroll ends at Chapultepec Park, and its seven museums, lakes, amusement park complete with scary roller coaster, and the old battlefield of Molino del Rey.

The internationally-renowned **Museum of Anthropology** is here, but you really need a whole day to devote to its tour, or better yet, two or three.

In Chapultepec Castle itself is the **National Museum of History**. This musem contains a large amount of memorabilia pertaining to the country's history, and also the residence of Maximilian and Carlotta including her quarters which have been beautifully refurbished. The formal gardens, by the way, were designed by Carlotta herself.

The main museum has a grand assemblage of such artifacts as a whole room full of pianos, the largest collection of horological instruments this side of the British Museum, and a carriage collection that rates a building of its own. It is worth spending several hours wandering around in the History Museum. More time is needed to see the other museums.

When you stroll back along the Reforma, this time on the opposite side of the street, the Molino del Rey is on the far side of the park, at Chivatito. This was the scene of a major battle in the Mexican-American war. The Americans were under the impression that the Molino was a munitions plant, and they took it at considerable cost, only to find it was of practically no military importance. The Americans then stormed the fortress of Chapultepec from the rear, an engagement which gave rise to two persistent myths: in Mexico the 'Niños Heroes' street signs and monuments refer to that losing engagement, and in the USA it is the basis for the 'Halls of Montezuma' line in the Marine Hymn. (In fact no marines were involved in that particular engagement.)

The Molino del Rey is the red building by the President's official residence and it is now a barracks and closed to the public, as is the local version of the White House, Los Pinos.

If you have a spare hour or two on the return leg, swing over to the corner of Rio Lerma and Rio Amazonas and go through the home of the late President Venustiano Carranza, now the least-visited museum in the city.

Carranza was a former senator who made a tidy fortune during the Díaz regime, and his home reflects his wealth. It is seldom visited, and a pity, too, because it gives an opportunity to see what lies behind the oft-forbidding exteriors of the mansions. And it is proof positive that the President of a mud-hut country is not expected to live in squalor with his constituents.

I admire the design and workmanship in the parquetry floors, the beauty of the tastefully-done stained-glass windows and the rich furnishings, all of which are meticulously maintained and in perfect condition. Even the antique Oliver typewriter which Carranza used in writing his many proclamations still rests on his desk, and his office looks as if the great man had merely stepped out for a quick word with his cook.

But of course this is Mexico and there has to be a jarring note. In this case it is the new building next door housing many photographs pertaining to the Carranza regime — but none of Villa! This is 'modern' in style and clashes horribly with the graceful stone house beside it.

The Alameda and its environs are worth an afternoon.

The Palacio de Belles Artes occupies one end of the Alameda and is the home of the fantastically popular Ballet Folklorico de Mexico, the country's sole claim to international fame in the theatrical line. The Folklorico program constantly changes, and there are actually three companies, but it is still difficult to get tickets at times. The best seats in the house go for M$200, and it may be necessary to buy a ticket a day or three in advance. Make sure you don't arrive late — the Tiffany glass curtain and the beautiful lighting display are worth the price of admission.

The Belles Artes building also houses one of the best art museums around, with major works by the big five: O'Gorman, Orozco, Rivera, Siquerios and Tamayo, plus other indigenous artists and travelling shows. If you're an art buff, this is a must.

Half-way down the Alameda and across the street on Avenida Hidalgo is the Plaza Santa Anita, one of the smallest in the city, and the Mercado de Artesanias, the least-known arts and crafts centre. Here you can watch the ladies deftly manipulate their primitive back looms just as their ancestors did centuries ago, weaving tipico cloth for jackets, serapes, skirts and wall hangings. Or you can browse shops selling silver and leather goods.

The old church of red stone on the right as you face the little plaza from the street is Santa Anita. Spanish-built, it leans about five degrees to the left due to subsidence, but there's nary a major crack in the facade.

The **Casa de los Azueljos** — or House of Tiles — could well be the best-known building in the Republic, and one of the best examples of Mudejar decoration. It was built in 1596 without tiles. These were added by one of the descendants of the Count of the Valley of Orizaba who had married a wealthy woman. It has a varied history, often bloody. One of the former owners was murdered on the grand staircase, and at one time it was the home of the Jockey Club. It is now owned by the Sanborn chain, with the usual shops on the ground floor. The restaurant is located in the original patio, and the general offices are on the second floor. The feature that contributes so much to the attraction of the House of Tiles is that it began as a private home and Messrs Sanborn did not make any stupid and degrading structural changes, and essentially the house remains as it was back in the days when grand balls were held in the patio. A definite must. It is reached by passing the Alameda on Juárez which changes its name to Madero.

While in the neighbourhood step into the **Main Post Office**, at the corner of Cárdenes and Tacuba/Hidalgo. It is one of the best instances of spare-no-expense 'colonial' designs in Mexico City, although it was completed under Diaz in 1907. The inside lives up to the promise of the exterior, with beautiful bronze and woodwork much like a profitable private bank of the day. For philatelists the second floor stamp collection is a pleasure and a delight.

Another point of interest in the same neighbourhood is the 44-storey **Torre Latinoamericana,** at Juárez and Cárdenes near the end of the Alameda. Its construction was a major engineering accomplishment because of the softness of the ground and the continuing subsidence. The very best view of the city is from the observation deck or, better yet, from the tower on top of the building. Buy a ticket in the lobby — the elevator from the lobby only goes part way. At the top end of the elevator trip you can either admire the view or climb some stairs to the flat roof. And if you're still game — I'm not! — it is possible to climb still higher, into the tower proper, some 150 metres or so above the street. The gigantic city is fantastic at any time of day, but absolutely breath-taking after dark when it seems as if the whole valley lights up. The view is best immediately after a rain, when the ever-present smog is at a minimum.

Proceed along Juárez/Madero five blocks and you come to the **Zócolo,** rather drab and uninspiring of itself. Its official title is the Plaza de Constitución. Originally the Zócolo had a fine collection of greenery, but it interfered with the aim of some cannoneers who were bombarding the Palacio Nacional during some revolution or other, and the trees fell victim to the gods of war. Naturally, the Government never quite got around to replacing them.

Later most of the street car lines converged on the Zócolo, and when the trams were phased out — a great mistake as later events proved — the square was concreted. The Metro is beneath it, and there is an underground walkway running diagonally under the Zócolo to the Pino Suarez Metro station, built so that pedestrians could avoid the intolerable congestion of the weekday downtown sidewalks.

The time to see the Zócolo is at night,

and not during the day when the jostling multitudes interfere with contemplation. At night, too, the well-planned lighting system enhances the buildings surrounding the plaza, something that the hazy sunlight does not.

The **National Cathedral** that occupies most of one side of the Zócolo is worth an hour or two. The cathedral is built on the site of an earlier church which was razed in 1573 and it in turn was constructed on another building. The cathedral was pretty well finished in 1667, but it took another 130 years to add the towers, and the building still wasn't quite complete. As it now stands, the cathedral is a mismatch of different styles and designs and technically speaking the whole thing doesn't work very well. The lantern and dome are by Tolsa, for instance, and are not really appropriate for the ediface. The end result of all this combining of ill-assorted bits and pieces is simply a huge building that manages to dominate the Zócolo by sheer size.

The cathedral was seriously damaged by a fire in 1967, supposedly started by faulty wiring, and the repair work is still under way. (Mexican wiring today is still the same invitation to disaster as the installation that nearly destroyed the interior of the cathedral.)

The small church to the right of the cathedral as you face it looks like a part of the cathedral, but it isn't. It's the Sagario Metropolitano, a separate church, both physically and politically, in its own right. It is in a different parish and serves as the local church for the large number of people who live nearby.

The **Palacio Nacional** is another building that was accumulated rather than built, a process that took 235 years. It is a veritable treasure trove of salons, ballrooms and beautiful halls, and much of it is open to the public. Over the centre entrance hangs the bell that Fray Hidalgo rang when he called for Mexican Independence. It is rung each year on 15 September at 11 am by the President who then recites the original grito. This brings an immense throng to the Zócolo. On any other day tourists by the thousands enter to view the vast murals by Diego Rivera, a task that pretty well occupied the last quarter century of his life. The murals are unfinished because the Master died on his project and although his sketches exist and it would be a simple matter to complete the work it was decided to leave them as they are as a monument to the Republic's greatest painter.

Entrance is by the centre door. The right-hand entrance as you face the building is reserved for El Presidente, and the left leads to the Juárez Museum, mostly of interest to Mexicans and the few history buffs among the foreigners.

A pre-Cortés site is being excavated to the side of the Sagario and on the opposite side of the street. First discovered in 1913, work has been under way most of the time since, and new and interesting discoveries are still being made. Most of the objects taken from the hole have wound up in the Museum of Anthropology in Chapultepec Park, but there is still enough left to warrant a look-see.

Some bargain-hunters are more interested in the **Monte de Piedad** than all the rest of the buildings in the Zócolo put together. The Monte de Piedad is the national pawnshop, with branches all over Mexico. It was started by the Conde de Regla, a miner who made a huge fortune around Pachuca, in 1775. The building itself was built by Cortés as a vice-regal palace. The pawnshop is operated by the Government in the public benefit and makes loans on almost anything, except livestock, that can be brought through the door. There really aren't all that many bargains, but now and then there is a sleeper.

Another old home, now converted into a museum, is at the corner of

Pino Suarez and El Salvador. Originally called La Casa del Conde de Santiago de Calimaya, it was built in 1528 and until 1964 occupied by descendants of the builder. It has now become the **Museum of the City of Mexico** and should be on the must-see list of any visitor who desires an overview of the history of the area, from the pre-Aztecs to Pancho Villa. Even for those with a total and complete lack of interest in things historical it should be included in any reconnaisance of the area for the building alone.

On the other side of the Reforma from the Zócolo is the **Monumento de la Revolución**, which has to be the ugliest monument under the sun, anywhere. Located at the end of Juárez, it started out to be a new capital building, the last major effort of the Díaz era, but it was no more than well underway when Díaz was deposed, whereupon all work stopped. When things quietened down there wasn't enough money left to complete the structure, so someone had the happy idea of converting it into a monument to the revolution just concluded. The two wings that had been partially built were demolished, the bodies of Villa, Zapata, Carranza, Calles, Madero and Cárdenes were interred there and it became a monument. Mexicans don't think much more of it than I do, and they often refer to it as 'El Elefante'! About all that can be said for it is that it is huge, 62 metres high, with other dimensions to match.

The **Museo de San Carlos** is on Alvarado opposite Aldama, but for some reason a few guidebooks and maps show it on the opposite side of the Zócolo. Locally it is sometimes known as La Casa de Buena Vista because for years it was the home of the family of that name. The building itself is superb. Designed by the same Tolsa who did the dome of the Cathedral, it is a much better job. The San Carlos Museum houses the best collection of European paintings in Latin America, and continually presents travelling shows. On the second floor of the semi-circular mezzanine is an interesting collection of sculpture by Mexican artists.

Markets. Mexico City is so large that it has a number of good-size markets. They are fairly well arranged as a general rule, with different types of merchandise segregated into specific areas. My favourite is the Lagunilla, on Allende at Rayon. Not as big as some of the others, it has two fairly large buildings and is really more of a bazaar than a market. A fine place for shopping for such practical items as comals, huaraches, belts, lamps and so on. The easiest way to get there is by Metro. Go to the Allende station and walk north on Allende.

Near here is the Sunday Market, an incredible open-air market specializing in the wildest assortment of new, slightly used, and used-up merchandise under the sun, displayed on stands, on the pavement, on the sidewalks, on trays and pinned to suit jackets. The Sunday Market is only for experienced hagglers for here you are dealing with people more concerned with the worth of the customer than the value of the merchandise. Nevertheless I was told of one valuable antique porcelain tray purchased here for a pittance that was later sold for enough to underwrite the lucky purchaser's trip to Mexico!

The **Virgin of Guadalupe** is the most venerated saint in the Republic. The story has it that an Indian named Juan Diego was told by the Virgin that a church should be built at the place where they met. The bishop didn't believe Diego's story, and requested additional proof. The Virgin appeared to Diego a second time and instructed him to pick some flowers on a hill where no flowers had ever grown. He did so, transporting them in his serape. When he gave the flowers to the bishop the image of the Virgin was imprinted on the cloth, and today the cloth hangs over the altar in the Basilica in a gold frame.

The annual pilgrimages grew to involve so many people that there was not enough room to come anywhere near accommodating the multitude at the original church, and at present there is a gigantic basilica being built, designed by the same architect who did the Museum of Anthropology.

Near the Basilica is a well, El Posito, rumoured to have miraculous curative powers, and the ill and infirm come here from all over the country to partake of the amazing fluid.

Many of the pilgrims to Guadalupe still follow the ancient practice of approaching the Basilica on their hands and knees, sometimes crawling for several km. This is an ongoing spectacle, but on 3-12 December it reaches a degree of frenzy that astonishes foreigners. So many people come to visit the Virgin that they wind up sleeping on the streets in the area around the church because the city's hotels are full. There is another, somewhat less well-attended, pilgrimage during Easter Holy Week.

25 years ago Guadalupe was out in the countryside, and it was fashionable to walk out to Sunday Mass from the town centre, but now the city has engulfed the little village and the walk is no longer very popular. Most people take the Metro out and get off at the Basilica station.

In the opposite direction are the **Floating Gardens of Xochimilco** which were once just that. In the beginning twigs were woven into rafts capable of supporting a thin layer of earth. Flowers and vegetables were planted, and eventually their roots grew through the floats and anchored the rafts. Eventually the rafts became small islands. Today the term 'floating gardens' usually refers to the boat-loads of flowers picked for the Mexico City markets.

Xochimilco is extremely popular with the locals as a picnic site, and hun-dreds of families spend Saturday and Sunday here, eating, drinking beer, and enjoying the domestic scene. (You can load up with picnic supplies at the supermarket at Taxqueña.)

To hire a boat and a poler to propel it costs around M$200 an hour, a lot more than it's worth for one or two people. I'd say skip it unless a fairly large group can split the cost.

Xochimilco is a city in its own right, with about 125,000 inhabitants, and the easiest way to get there is to take the Metro to the end of the line at Taxqueña and change to one of the red PCC tram cars that stop outside the door of the Metro station.

Places to Stay

The hotel situation in Mexico City has been getting worse year by year. Part of it is due to the rampant inflation that has the Republic by the pursestrings, and the rest is caused by the merciless application of the law of demand and supply. There have been no low-price hotels built in the capital for years, and every year a few are torn down to make way for new office buildings. This has created a sellers' market in economical housing unequaled short of London.

This is not to say that there are no reasonably-priced hotels left, but those that survive are in less desirable neigh-bourhoods and very definitely aren't in the 'Zona Rosa', where the imitation Gucci shop is located, where the super-expensive spas have their town offices, and where the majority of the fancy restaurants and some of the very best hotels do business. But surprisingly, there are inexpensive hotels within three or four blocks of the Alameda, and one or two not too far from the Zona Rosa itself, which is generally around the Sheraton Hotel on the Reforma.

The vicinity of the Plaza San Fernando, at Guerrero and Alvarado, used to be laced with inexpensive hostels but these days they are nearly all very expensive. For years I used to stay at the *Hotel Monaco*. I liked the house, the location, and the comfortable little tree-shaded plaza across the street, but during the past few years the rates have skyrocketed to very expensive.

Similarly, the *Hotel Managua*, across the plaza from the Monaco, the *Hotel La Paz* and the *Hotel Ferro* on Mina, the *Hotel Astoria* on Zarco off Mina, have all elevated themselves into the very expensive classification, or are planning on doing so very shortly. The *Hotel Mina* at Salgado and Mina is a quiet, well-run older family hotel with a mosaic facade and was happy to get M$150 a night a few years back; now it is very expensive, too.

Things get better as you go along Alvarado away from the Reforma. The last street before reaching Insurgentes Norte is Bernal Díaz and in the first block on Díaz there are the *Hotel Estaciones*, the *Hotel Díaz*, and the *Hotel Mexico*. This is a dreary industrial neighbourhood, mostly devoted to the express package departments of the various bus companies and very congested during week-days. All these hotels are moderate, but have been known to drop into inexpensive because of expressions of dismay on the face of the prospective guest.

Hotel Savoy, on Zaragoza right off Alvarado, is a newish hotel conveniently located, but without a centavo wasted on ambience. Expensive.

A bit farther along Zaragoza is the green-fronted *Hotel Miña* (not Mina), even less attractive from the street than its neighbours. A glance through the entrance tends to dishearten those with too much luggage — there are no less than 34 steps up to the second-floor lobby. But once the heights are scaled the Mina turns out to be quite comfortable, with large rooms and firm, lump-free mattresses. Expensive.

The aged *Hotel Cortez*, on Hidalgo a few steps off the Reforma looks from the outside like a genuine inexpensive find, but it is now a part of the Best Western chain of motels and hotels and is ridiculously expensive.

The *Asociación Cristiana Femenina* (YWCA) is (I am told) an excellent selection for women travelling alone. It is on Humboldt, just off the Alameda, and about as conveniently located as can be. Moderate.

A good hotel for walkers is the *Hotel Marin* at the corner of Caso and León. (León intersects the Reforma near the Colón monument and the Sanborn outlet.) Don't be misled by the three styles and types of brickwork in the front. Over the years a couple of additions have been grafted on the peculiar half-hexagonal building. The Marin gets almost no tourist play and so is little affected by the vagaries of that volatile trade. It often has rooms available when everything else in town is full. Moderate.

A practical alternative to actually staying overnight in Mexico City is to get a hotel in Cuernavaca. This can be a necessity at times, especially in summer, when it is practically impossible to rent a hotel in the capital. Also it avoids the smog, which can be extremely irritating. But if you decide this is the way to go it is best to get a room ahead of time and not to wait until the very last minute — Cuernevaca can fill up too!

Places to Eat

One of the best *VIP's* restaurants is just one block off the Reforma on Ramirez. Chain operations make every effort to standardize their branches, but the fact remains that they aren't equal. VIP's is a business-like outfit and although it is definitely US-oriented the majority of the customers are from the local community, and in the case of the VIP's on Ramirez many of them are from the editorial sides of the several newspapers in the area. There is another VIP's not too far away, on the corner of Insurgentes and Reforma, but I definitely prefer the one on Ramirez. Expensive.

The *Parillada Zurich*, on the Reforma down the street from Sanborn's Lafragua and Reforma branch, is a restaurant specializing in quesos al carbón — charcoal-grilled cheese. The Reforma today is about evenly divided between Burger Boys and super-expensive hotel dining rooms, and the Zurich falls somewhere in between; although primarily a place to grab a quick snack, it does pretty well in the meal department. Ideal for Saturday afternoon, when it is uncrowded. Inexpensive.

About as close as you can get to a genuine American hamburger will set you back around M$60, or as much as the average comida corrida. And even for M$60 you can't seriously expect to receive a Big Mac. The Mexican version resembles a British wimpy more than it does its US counterpart.

The largest assortment of low to medium price restaurants in Mexico City is located at *Insurgentes Plaza*, the Metro station three blocks off the Reforma on Génova. The Plaza is about 200 metres across and lined with everything from a Burger King to a restaurant accepting every credit card known to man. Plus bookshops, natural food store, record outlet and even a Conasupo Supermarket. It has the widest choice imaginable and is not too far from Chapultepec Park.

The *Centro Centural Liberias Reforma*, on the Reforma between Lafragaua and Juárez, is a combination coffee house and bookstore. This is not too unusual in Europe, but is a rare combination on this side of the ocean, north or south. Only Spanish-language books are sold, but I've seen customers reading English, German, French and Dutch publications with their café con leche or Cerveza Corona. This is a hangout for writers, readers, scholars and print-media professionals, and I have yet to see anyone reading one of the ubiquitous comic books. Moderate.

When Guerreo crosses Alvarado it becomes Rosales and on this short street are located two of the handiest and most economical restaurants to the Alameda. First is the *Restaurant Leo*. The Leo makes a sort of folded-over, deep-fat-fried taco they call a 'quesedilla'. It is a near cousin of the gordita of Guadalajara, and filling. In addition to this specialty, which keeps one girl busy on the fryer, the Leo has a fairly complete list of such basics as refrescos, cervesas, milanesas, enchelades, etc. Inexpensive.

Or you can go some 50 metres toward the Reforma from the Leo to the *Cafe Rosales* and have a go at that internationally-famous Canadian delicacy, chop suey. If your taste buds don't lust for ersatz Chinese, try their pastry with a cup of coffee. In any event the tab will be inexpensive.

Sanborn's *House of Tiles* serves American-oriented food with a Mexican overtone. The soda fountain is the place for a quick snack or a chocolate sundae. For a main meal I definitely recommend eating in the old patio, two storeys high and glassed over. The soda fountain is expensive, and the restaurant ridiculously expensive but worth it just once.

The little arts and crafts market off the Plaza Santa Anita, halfway along the Alameda on Hidalgo, contains a couple of 'tipico' restaurants, and I make a point to eat in one of them, the *Restaurante Fonda Santa Anita Alameda*, at least one afternoon each time I visit Mexico City. Inexpensive.

GETTING THERE
By Air

The vast majority of travellers arrive in Mexico City by air, and Mexico City International is, and always has been, the crossroads of Latin-American air travel. There are so many airlines flying to Mexico City that it almost seems as if there is always an excursion or special promotional fare. See the 'Getting There' chapter for more details.

There is a M$100 departure tax, and Mexican airlines charge 15% for late cancellations and 50% of the fare for no-shows unless the seat happens to be sold to someone on standby.

Expect the airport to be undergoing repairs and/or alterations. It has been worked on for 20 years that I know of and no sooner do they finish one project then they commence somewhere else.

The airport is not too far from the centre of things and the most popular way to get downtown is via one of the VW vans called colectivos. They take off as soon as they are loaded, and if you let the driver know you aren't in any hurry you will probably wind up on a grand tour of the central part of the city. Price: about M$50.

There are also special city buses that stop in front of the terminal and run to the Alameda. They have luggage space, charge around M$15, and show a sign that says Centro or Alameda or the like.

The all-out cheapest way to get downtown if you travel very light is to catch a trackless trolley from in front of the terminal to the Aeropuerto Metro station; the fare is only a couple of pesos. At the Metro station catch a train going in the Observatorio direction and get off at either Pino Suarez or the Zócolo and change to another train going in the Tacuba direction. Get off at Hidalgo, which is at the corner of Hidalgo and the Reforma, only a couple of blocks from the Alameda; or at Revolución, on Alvarado not far from the Monument to the Revolution.

Don't try the Metro during the rush hours in the morning and afternoon, and note that hand-carried luggage is definitely not permitted.

By Bus

Things are a little more complicated for those arriving by bus as there are no less than four intercity bus stations.

The largest and most popular is the huge Terminal del Norte, which handles almost all of the buses going to the northern part of the country, including some services to and from Veracruz and Mazanillo. As you enter the concourse you will see ticket booths selling taxi tickets. If you want a taxi, tell the young lady where you are going, buy your ticket, and find a taxi going in your direction. This is another colectivo arrangement.

If you don't want a taxi, keep right on going past the ticket booth and look for a city bus marked 'Terminal Norte — Plaza Insurgentes' which will take you to the heart of town, turning around at the Insurgentes Metro station. The Metro is in the process of being extended to the Central del Norte.

If you don't intend to stop over in Mexico City and plan on continuing immediately to Cuernavaca and Acapulco, you will need to change bus stations to the Central del Sur. There is a shuttle bus running between these two popular stations marked 'Centro Medico — Hospital la Raza', or perhaps 'Central del Norte'. To go downtown, catch a No. 7D.

The Central del Sur is hard by the Taxquena Metro station. Go out the front door of the bus station, turn right and follow the crowd. The Metro will take you direct to Hidalgo and the Reforma.

The Terminal de Autobuses de Pasajeros de Oriente handles most of the passengers to Veracruz, Puebla, Yucatan, Oaxaca and Guatemala. It is located at the Lazaro Metro station for the benefit of those without hand baggage. You can also take a Ruta 100 bus to the Alameda and the Reforma. Most of the Ruta 100 buses continue on to the western terminal, the Terminal Poniente de Autobuses, near the Observatoria Metro station. It's the smallest and handles traffic to and from Toluca.

GETTING AROUND

Public transport in Mexico City is a disaster during the rush hours, cabs are unavailable except perhaps at the terminals, buses are jammed and pass customers at every stop. And these remarks go triple for the Metro which has gotten so bad — five million passengers a day — that there are separate lanes at many stations for women and children to save them from being crushed.

I have found it best to skip travel altogether during the rush hours, which is not so bad as it sounds because downtown Mexico City's points of interest are within walking distance of each other.

There are guards stationed at the Metro stations around the rush hours to turn back people with bulky backages, suitcases and what not. I've even seen a few well-dressed gentlemen refused admittance because they carried

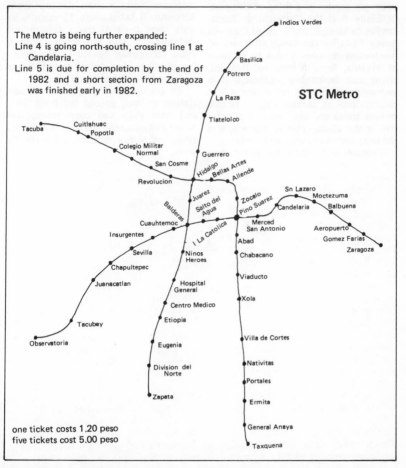

The Metro is being further expanded:
Line 4 is going north-south, crossing line 1 at Candelaria.
Line 5 is due for completion by the end of 1982 and a short section from Zaragoza was finished early in 1982.

STC Metro

one ticket costs 1.20 peso
five tickets cost 5.00 peso

ordinary briefcases. Outside of the rush hours I have never had any problems riding the Metro with my small shoulder tote bag.

For some obscure reason, some Europeans like to travel with huge framed packsacks and I've seen them turned back even during the late evening hours when the cars were running with about a dozen passengers apiece.

There is only one railroad station in Mexico City now that the narrow-gauge passenger service is a thing of the past. Officially it is the Terminal de Ferrocarriles de Mexico, but is called Estación Buena Vista by the locals after one of the leading families. Trains to all parts of Mexico, from Mérida to Mexicali, arrive and depart here, although it is impossible to buy a ticket for a trip passing through Mexico City — in this respect trains are like buses. A popular trip is the all-day ride to Oaxaca, and the long, long trip down to Mérida.

Because train fares are lower than bus fares, except sleepers, the trains tend to be crowded with people to whom a couple of pesos is important money. The second-class cars become travelling garbage dumps practically as soon as a train leaves the station, and the first-class is only slightly better. If for some reason you elect to take a train, by all means go pullman, even if it is a day trip and you will be unable to use the berth.

The Buena Vista Station is on Insurgentes Norte a short distance from Alvarado. It takes about 15 minutes to walk there from Alvarado/Hidalgo and Reforma. Or you can catch a bus at Plaza Insurgentes headed for the Terminal del Norte bus station and unload as you pass the railroad depot.

To get downtown from the railroad station by bus, go out the front door and turn right and cross Insurgentes Norte and catch the first bus that comes along. All things considered, I prefer to walk.

South & East of Mexico City

Places east of Mexico City, including Veracruz, Oaxaca, San Cristobal las Casas and the Yucatán, can all be reached by bus from the Terminal de Autobuses de Pasajeros de Oriente. The terminal is hard by the San Lazaro Metro station, and is also accessible by the Ruta 100 bus that you can pick up on the Reforma downtown. The leading lines, first-class, are the ADO (Autobuses de Oriente) and the Cristobál Colón which runs all the way to the Guatemalan border by Comitán. Service is frequent and good and only slightly more than second-class.

Trains for Veracruz, Mérida and Oaxaca leave from the Estacion Buena Vista on Insurgentes Norte.

The region also has excellent air service provided by Aeromexico and Mexicana, plus a host of local air lines.

PUEBLA, Puebla

Many cities in Mexico can, with justification, lay claim to a rich and lusty history, but Puebla has been involved in almost everything that has happened in and to the country since Cortés first tramped through on his way to take on the Aztecs.

It is also involved in the USA's history. Back in 1847 the city was captured quite easily by General Winfield Scott who was on his way to take Mexico City and win the war. He had fought several pitched battles on his way up the hill from Veracruz, most notably battle of Cerro Gordo, and he decided to leave Colonel Thomas Childs behind with around 400 sick and wounded men who were unfit for service. Scott anticipated no particular difficulties, believing that General Santa Ana would busy himself with readying for the eventual defence of Mexico City. Things didn't work out precisely as anticipated, and Santa Ana, who badly needed a fresh victory after a series of defeats brought on mostly by his own ineptness, elected to recapture Puebla instead of concentrating on the main issue at the capital.

Childs got wind of the impending attack and collected a number of cattle, a few hundred sheep and some military equipment and forted up in the zócolo. As Santa Ana had around 2500 men in his effort he naturally expected a repeat of the Alamo episode and a great propaganda victory. Things didn't go as Santa Ana planned — they all too seldom did! — and the Americans refused to surrender. They held out for about a month, at which time Santa Ana was forced to withdraw when Colonel James Lane arrived with reinforcements from Veracruz.

A few years later, during what the Mexicans call the French Intervention, the troops of Napoleon III were soundly beaten by a Mexican force under the command of General Ignacio Zaragoza. The date of the battle, 5 May 1862, accounts for the celebrations every year and all the streets named 5 de Mayo. In 1863 the French besieged Puebla and took it in two months, a date that is not commemorated. And then, on 2 April 1867, General Porfirio Diaz retook Puebla.

Since those bloody days Puebla has been fairly peaceful, not to mention prosperous. Today Puebla derives the bulk of its income from manufacturing, and the original city is surrounded by factories manufacturing cement, glass, cloth, bricks and the colourful 'Puebla tiles' which are shipped all over North America.

This tile is made by same process as the famous Talavera polychrome tile in Spain and was one of the first manufacturing operations in the New World. It resists weathering remarkably well,

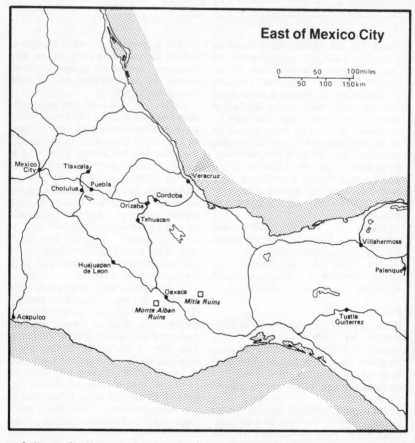

East of Mexico City

0   50   100 miles
  50   100   150km

Mexico City
Tlaxcala
Cholula
Puebla
Cordoba
Orizaba
Veracruz
Tehuacan
Villahermosa
Huajuapan de Leon
Palenque
Oaxaca
Mitla Ruins
Monte Alban Ruins
Acapulco
Tustla Guiterrez

and its application to the domes of countless Mexican churches and building facades contributes greatly to Mexico's unique appearance.

The best example in Puebla of the use of the native tile is in the building called La Casa de Alfeñique (or the Wedding Cake House by English-speakers). Located at Avenida 4 Oriente and Calle 6 Norte, it now houses the Regional Museum. Alfeñique means almond cake and it got its name because of the ornamentation, plus the generous use of white Puebla tile, that make it

look like an outsize frosted cake. Even if museums generally leave you as cold as a margarita, the place is worthy of visiting.

Another museum is now located in the ex-Convento de Santa Rosa, at Avenida 4 Oriente at Calle 3 Norte. This was at one time a huge operation of the Dominican order, and today it is mainly interesting for the kitchen. Known locally as La Cocina de Santa Rosa it is a fantastically well preserved tiled kitchen that was used for hundreds of years. In conjunction with the kitchen is a crafts museum and sales-room, but it is the kitchen itself that is interesting, both to tourists and locals, and it's worth a visit by anyone interested in eating and/or cooking.

The Capilla de Rosario, also known as the Templo de Santo Domingo is on 5 de Mayo at Avenida 4 Poniente and is noted for its beautiful and decorative tile work. The Templo gets its informal name from the Rosary Chapel, the most thoroughly-decorated ecclesiastical building in the city. The walls, ceilings, supporting columns and even the portales are covered with gold, figures and carvings. The image of the Virgin on the altar is jewelled, and a visit to the chapel will give the visitor some idea of what most of the great churches were like before the Reform Laws and assorted revolutions and martial disturbances stripped most of them of their riches. And I don't know why the chapel was spared.

Another place that shouldn't be overlooked is the Convento de Santa Monica, often called the Secret Convent. On Avenida 18 Poniente at 5 de Mayo, it is another place with a long and fascinating history. It was originally built in 1606 as a sort of half-way house for respectable women whose husbands were out of town, an idea that failed because the respectable ladies of Puebla refused to cooperate, or because their husbands took them along. The next step was for it to be operated by the church as a convent and reformatory for prostitutes. There is no record of whether this scheme worked any better than the previous effort, but it had a longer run. When the Reform Laws abolished convents in 1857 the establishment went underground and in 1862 the visible part became a women's college and was called Santa Monica.

The secret convent lasted until 1934 until it was closed by the government. Today the convent is a museum, and anyone with the paltry price of an admission ticket can enter through an apartment by way of a door disguised as a china cabinet. Quite fascinating.

Those interested in military artifacts can go out to Forts Guadalupe and Loreto. This is were Zaragoza put himself on street signs all over the Republic by soundly defeating the French. In addition to being rather interesting in their own right, the forts are on a hill and offer a commanding view of the city and the surrounding countryside. To get there, catch a bus marked 'Fuertes' by the zocolo, or walk there in about 40 minutes from the zona centro. Go out 5 de Mayo to Avenida 38 Oriente and turn right and go to 2 Norte. Turn left, then right, on Calzada de los Fuertes.

Places to Stay

The economical hotel situation is fairly good, but bear in mind that the first hotels to fill during the summer are the cheaper places, and Puebla is popular with history-minded Mexicans as well as tourists from far-away parts. Most of Puebla's hotels are designated by a large white plastic sign bearing a big H in red with the hotel's name beneath it in black as a sort of afterthought.

The *Hotel Ritz*, on Calle 2 Norte between Avenida 4 Oriente and Avenida 2 Oriente is warranted to be no relation whatsoever to the caravanassary of the same name in Paris. The institutional buff lobby has seen about two decades since a touch-up on the paint job, and the kitchen exhaust fan from the restaurant next door discharges into the foyer, but don't let's knock too hard because Puebla doesn't have much leeway when it comes to hotels in the inexpensive classification.

There are two *Palacio* hotels in town, both on Avenida 2 Oriente near Calle 2 Norte, and both too pretentious and costly to give value received. Ridiculously expensive.

Hotel Embajadores, 5 de Mayo be-

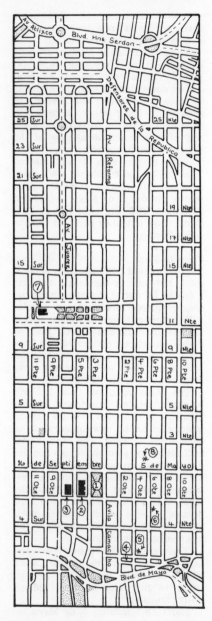

Puebla Central

1 Plaza de Armas
2 Cathedral
3 Post Office, Tourist Office & Casa de la Cultura
4 Mercado El Parian & ADO Bus Terminal
5 Museo del Estado 'Casa del Alfeñique'
6 Museo de la Revolución 'Casa de los Serdán'
7 Museo de Historia Natural (Acuario Municipal)
8 Capilla de Rosario (Templo de Santo Domingo)

tween Avenida 4 Oriente and Avenida 6 Oriente, probably never roomed any ambassadors in its life. It could use a new coat of paint — that pinkish hue is cloying on either a hotel or a concrete truck. Patio shows marked Moorish influence, and the rooms are larger than one has a right to expect. All rooms have two or more beds, and the rent split among four would make it inexpensive.

The *Hotel España* is on Avenida 6 Poniente between Calle 3 Norte and 5 de Mayo. A small working-man's hotel, it is at least as interested in peddling lottery tickets as renting rooms. Inexpensive.

Posada Los Angeles is on Calle 4 Norte near Avenida 2 Oriente. In the beginning this posada was a casa de huespedes, but a few years back they promoted themselves to posada when they got enough money ahead to buy a neon sign. Close to the bus station and good value. Moderate.

The *Hotel Latino* on Calle 6 Norte at Avenida 2 Oriente is in the same block as the ADO bus station. It offers a brown and white tiled lobby and fairly large rooms. It is usually full, but worth a try. Expensive, but good value.

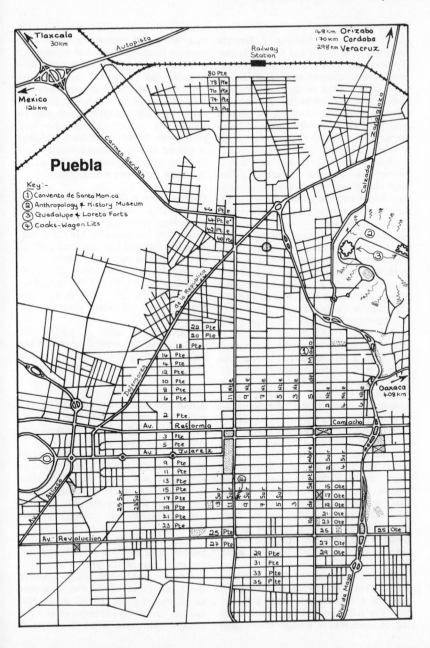

Puebla

Key:-
① Convento de Santa Monica
② Anthropology & History Museum
③ Guadalupe & Loreto Forts
④ Cooks-Wagon Lits

Places to Eat

Sanborn's is on Avenida 2 Oriente between 5 de Mayo and Calle 2 Norte. Typical Sanborn's with books in English, magazines, American and Americanized food, and a good photographic department. This one keeps its cigars humidified. A good place to shop for maps if you need seven or eight maps of Zacatecas, but for Puebla city and state maps you're out of luck! Expensive.

Restaurant la Princesa, on Calle 3 Norte just off the Reforma, offers tablecloths and such domestic wines as Los Reyes and has all the other characterstics of a very expensive restaurante. It ain't. Moderate.

The *Hotel Restaurant Suba Vd* has no other identification. It is on 16 de Septiembre across the street from the cathedral. Enter through a knitware shop, turn right at the back through a black-painted iron door, and go upstairs. Inexpensive, as should be.

Super Tortas Angel, on Calle 2 Sur at Avenida 5 Oriente, is another of Mexico's many misnamed businesses. Although it sells quite good tortas the Angel is the place where everybody buys raised Bismarks, called jelly doughnuts in parts of the USA. A couple of these, a litre of pasteurized milk and a seat on a bench in the zócolo will make a very inexpensive lunch.

Vittorios, a bar-cum-pizza joint, is on the plaza opposite the Princesa, and serves real pizza, too, with more filling than crust. Vittorio's uses Machego cheese from Chiapas (instead of the Mafia-made mozarella employed in the US) and with outstanding results. They also serve wine. There are two 'happy hours' a day when two drinks go for the price of one. Expensive, but well worth it.

There are several *El Grecos* around Puebla, but the one on the corner of Avenida 4 Oriente and Calle 4 Norte, near the ADO bus station, is outstanding. It specialises in a huge 'taco Arabe' which I thought would be made with pita bread but instead is made with oversize flour tortillas — real whoppers.

There are sidewalk cafes under the portales on Camanco and 16 de Septiembre and they are very popular with the locals as a relaxing place to solve the day's problems, or just to watch the throng weaving its way among the tables. It has been said that if you sit at one of these tables it won't be long until everyone in Puebla passes in parade, and I can well believe it.

Getting There & Getting Around

Puebla is a transportation hub, and buses leave from San Lazario in Mexico City every few minutes. ADO is a first-class bus line and the preferred method of travel in this part of the world.

To get downtown from the ADO first-class station, go out the front door and turn right. The plaza is now two blocks away. Walking time is five minutes.

ADO has a habit of putting the sanitarios on the second floor, and the stairway leading to the toilets is hidden behind the snack-and-postcard counter.

CHOLULA, Puebla

About 15 km from Puebla, Cholula makes a convenient side trip. It is the current location of the University of Americas, usually listed as being in Mexico City. This is an institution of higher learning that has a large American enrolment. Not only is this a great place to acquire a working knowledge of Spanish as she is spoke, but it is the only US-accredited college in the Republic.

The average tourist visits Cholula because it is said that there is a church for each day of the year, a story I've heard all my life and which I doubt, never having met anyone who conducted an inventory. But I will agree that Cholula is a perfect example of conspicuous consumption when it comes to churches and there are enough of them to stock another Mexico City. The most noteworthy of all the churches is the little Sanctuario de los Remidios built on top of the Tepanapa Pyramid a few blocks east of the plaza. It was the largest of the Mexican pyramids, so large that over 8 km of tunnels have been explored within the structure. The pyramid itself is now a museum, and some of the tunnels have been illuminated for the benefit of the visitor.

Cholula's history has been bloody. Cortés was invited to Cholula by the Indians and while there got word of a conspiracy on the part of Moctezuma to murder him and his men. The Spanish were never ones to turn the other cheek and Cortés nipped the plot in the bud by slaughtering some 6000 or so Aztecs during the course of a single night.

TLAXCALA, Tlaxcala

Another enjoyable side trip. About 30 km from Puebla, with frequent bus service, Tlaxcala is the capital of the tiny state of the same name — Mexico's Rhode Island. The town has a population of about 40,000. And with its elevation of 2285 metres it has one of the most enjoyable and smog-free climates in all Mexico.

Tlaxcala gives an overall impression of cleanliness, and the ample plaza is well maintained. Like Puebla there is a sidewalk cafe under the portales, but otherwise the two places have nothing at all in common. The Iglesia de San Francisco, about one km along the road to Puebla, is claimed to be the oldest church in the New World. On the pulpit of the adjacent chapel is the hard-to-decipher inscription, 'Aquí tubo principio al Santo Evangelio en este nuevo mundo' (Here the Holy Gospel had its beginning in the new world).

For building buffs, I recommend the Sanctuario de Octlán. Unusual for Mexico, the facade is white plaster,

elaborately carved. The towers have bases covered with red tiles and the elevated parts covered with more white plaster. Also a rarity in Mexico, the interior is as spectacular as the outside, with lots of carved wood and polychromed and gold-leafed figures. The Sanctuario is about 750 metres from the plaza — ask any local for exact directions.

Tlaxcala is a good place to buy handwoven cloth, although very little of the actual weaving is done there. Much of it is done in Santa Ana nearby, and the Sunday Market in Santa Ana is probably the best shot in the Republic for blankets, serapes and so on — far, far superior to Saltillo in the north.

TEHUACÁN, Puebla

Tehuacán is the supreme example of the quiet, peaceful, utterly charming Mexican town where nothing much ever happens and never has. It has an almost-perfect climate, too. The area abounds in mineralized springs, and for centuries before the arrival of Cortés and his hardbitten crew the Indians had come great distances to bathe in the healing waters.

During the 19th century the springs were operated as spas, and Tehuacan occupied the same place in Mexico as Baden-baden, Bad Gasswasser and Bath in Europe. The businessmen of Tehuacan felt deeply that the benefits of the waters should not be confined to the wealthy of the Republic, and began bottling it and shipping all over North America. Then it was discovered that a lot of people denied themselves the benefits of the mineral springs because they disliked the stuff, and so the astute entrepreneurs began to add flavourings to conceal the 'mineral' taste, a practice that continues to this day.

Although 'Tehuacán' is a brand name and there are a number of water bottlers in the area, it is better to ask for 'Agua Tehuacán' in most of Mexico, rather than 'agua mineral'. Anywhere in the Republic, ordering 'Agua Tehuacán' will get you a bottle of mineral water, even if the actual brand stocked is Garci Crespi or one of the several other competing brands.

Tehuacán has one of the most captivating plazas in Mexico, with wide sidewalks, handsome shade trees and cool concrete benches. The plaza is partially surrounded with portales, and under the arches are sidewalk cafes.

There really isn't much to do in Tehuacán. As with any country town there is nothing at all in the way of night life, no old forts as reminders of long-lost battles — apparently the old-timers never figured a few mineral-water outcroppings were worth fighting over! The only industry worth mentioning is mineral water bottling, and the plants look like any Coke or Pepsi plant in the US, or anywhere — same machinery, same smell.

You could spend a half hour inspecting the Templo del Carmen, easily visible from the plaza. It has some unusual tile work on the dome and is more interesting on the outside than the inside.

Next to the church is the Museo del Valle de Tehuacán, not much as regional museums go in Mexico, but then Tehuacan is not a big and aggressive city, either, and the Museo is in perfect step with the peaceful tenor of the community.

The little Palacio Municipal is a multi-tiled jewel of a building on the plaza that looks as if it has been standing there since Juárez was a cigar roller, but it was only completed in 1959, the local authorities having had the rare good taste to construct it along ultra-traditional lines.

Places to Stay

The *Hotel Spa Peñafiel* was one of the old deluxe hotels where the filthy rich come to take the waters during the 1800s, but it has fallen on evil times because the wealthy don't go to spas in droves anymore. It still costs an arm and a leg to stay here, and they can be awfully insistent about the clients taking their meals on the so-called American plan, but it is definitely worth strolling out and visiting the place, and maybe having a cold bottle of brew if you can't stand the thought of drinking any of the mineral water that runs out of the 'cave' next door. The Spa Penafiel is located on the way in from the Puebla-Orizaba highway.

On your way downtown from the ADO bus station you will pass the *Hotel Mexico*, a time-honoured establishment and a rarity in Mexico — it boasts that it accepts American Express cards! Wander in through the lobby as if you were a guest, or thinking of becoming one, and take a look at the patio with its Spanish-styled fountain. All is colonial style — bar, restaurant and so on. But ridiculously expensive.

Continue on Independencia — the street you're on — past the plaza and in the next block you will find the *Hotel Hibernia*, reconstructed from one of the early great houses. Only two storeys surround the unusual patio, but the ground floor is a good seven metres high. Expensive.

Turn right off Independencia onto the next street after the plaza and you will be on Calle 3 Sur, although there probably won't be a street sign in sight. In about 35 metres you will come to the *Casa de Huespedes Veracruz*. The sign says 'hot water all day'. Inexpensive.

If you continue along Calle 3 Sur to the corner of Avenida 1 Oriente — the next street — you will see the weather-beaten sign and peeling paint of the *Hotel Madrid*. The Madrid has a pleasing patio with concrete benches surrounding a sunken fountain, caged birds a-singing and leaded glass windows separating the lobby and the patio, quite large rooms, lots and lots of ambience, and all this for about half what you would expect. Inexpensive.

Places to Eat

The place in Tehuacán is the *Restaurant Peñafiel* on the plaza. Take your choice and eat indoors or out on the sidewalk beneath the portales. Widely varied menu, mostly of 'international' food, although a few Mexican dishes are included for the more traditionally-minded customers. Good selection of wine, mostly domestic, some imported, but only one brand of beer. The Peñafiel is an excellent choice for those who can afford to fork over $250 for a lunch with wine — ridiculously expensive.

The little *Café Lupita*, across the zócolo from the fancy Peñafiel is both good and reasonably priced, a welcome and unlikely combination. Big Humphrey Bogart fans churn the air on the occasional hot day and chase the insects away. Red table-cloths and that rarest of all amenities in the Republic: attentive service, prompt and caring. And wonder of wonders, an espresso machine that works and is used. Try the queso fundido which loosely translates as cheese fondue, but this is not quite the stuff the ski lodges serves as an après-ski snack. This is Mexicanized and instead of toast you get lovely, fresh, little flour tortillas. It works out better than it sounds. Inexpensive.

Getting There & Getting Around

Getting to Tehuacán is dead easy. It is on the Puebla-Oaxaca route, and also on one of the Mexico City-Veracruz routes. Lots and lots of buses. Masochists may take the train from Mexico City or Puebla. To get downtown from ADO bus station, go out on the street in front and turn right and the plaza is only about a five-minute walk.

ORIZABA, Veracruz

This is an unattractive industrial centre, specializing in the industries that delight in erecting tall smokestacks and belching evil smells high into the air. But not quite high enough — the pollution laws in Mexico are more a joke than a deterrent. The most interesting feature of Orizaba that I could discover is the retired juice jack, No. 1002, on display in the street divider on the way from the highway to the ADO station.

The trip down the hill from Tehuacán should be made at night for those with a dislike for heights. There are a few places where it is an awful long way down.

CÓRDOBA, Veracruz

This is another of the many Mexican towns in which nothing very much has happened in a very long time. The high point of its existence, historically speaking, was when General Augustín Iturbide, soon to be emperor, and Viceroy Don Juan de O'Donoju, soon to be unemployed, signed the Pact of Córdoba which made Mexico free of Spanish domination and an independent nation.

The building on the plaza in which the treaty was signed eventually became the Hotel Zevallo and by means of systematic lack of care gradually became a wreck. Recently the rear part of it collapsed under the accumulation of dry rot and years and the Hotel Zevallo is no longer in business as a hotel, although a few old-timers still pass their time playing chess and dominoes in the relatively safe front part of the patio.

As Mexican cities go, Córdoba isn't very old, having been founded under the direction of the Viceroy Fernandez de Cordoba in 1618. The Church of the Immaculate Conception on the plaza reflects this relatively newness, being considerably more modern in appearance than most plaza churches in Mexico. The building is painted a peculiar light green with white trim and seems to change colour with changes in the weather. It is the only Catholic church I have ever seen with medallions of palm trees mounted on the facade.

Córdoba is close enough to the Atlantic coast to attract strolling marimba bands, and you can enjoy spending a few evening hours at one of the cafes under the portales on the north side of the plaza, drinking some of the famous local coffee and encouraging the musicians now and then with a few pesos.

To get to the plaza leave the ADO station by the door opposite the restaurant and turn right — the plaza is only a four-minute walk.

Places to Stay

As you enter the plaza from the direction of the bus station you will see a huge, dark, unlovely, new-looking building diagonally across the square. This is the *Hotel Mansur*, not nearly as new as it appears. Not a bad hotel at all, but ridiculously expensive; every imaginable credit card gladly accepted.

A little farther along to the right of the Mansur, and facing the far side of the church, is the *Hotel Virreynal*, an older house with a clean tiled lobby containing comfortable old-fashioned chairs where both guests and strangers feel free to take a few minutes ease when the mood strikes them. The rooms are large and well-equipped for a hotel of today — there is a spittoon in every room. Expensive.

If you leave the plaza just before the Mansur on the street that used to continue across the plaza in front of the church before it was turned into a paseo, you will see the *Hotel Los Reyes*, Córdoba's answer to the old problem of lodgings for the moderately unrich. To get to the desk you climb a wainscoted stairway. The rooms are not overly small, unless you plan on giving ballet lessons, or swinging a cat. Moderate.

To find really cheap places, continue past the Virreynal and at the corner turn left. About three squares away you will see an ancient church that

apparently blocks the street. If you go to the church and turn right onto the cross street you will find several low-priced casas de huespedes. Inexpensive.

Places to Eat

One of the best places to eat, if not the best, is the restaurant off the lobby of the *Hotel Virreynal*. Enter either from the lobby or from the street. Aged wood, tables with clean white tablecloths, and highly professional waiters are in its favor. Espresso coffee, excellent cafe con leche and quite an extensive menu of both Mexican and international items. Naturally a place like this is very expensive, but worth it.

The *Restaurante Parroquia* is on the plaza beneath the portales on the north side. Mainly because of the similarity of names, Córdoba regards the late Manuel Benitz, El Córdobes, as one of its own, and there must be 20 fine Spanish bullfight posters on the walls. Another place with competent waiters, and the ideal place to meet the local gentry. Expensive.

Between the Hotel Mansur and the Virreynal is a passage leading through the centre of the block to the *Restaurante El Brujo*. The passage is only a block long, but that short distance is enough to remove the Brujo from the high rent district, and far enough from the plaza to eliminate overcrowding. Nobody seems to know how the Brujo got its name, and there is certainly nothing supernatural about the place. The food is about average for small towns, and the prices are inexpensive.

For really economical eating, turn left on the street just past the Virreynal. This is a sort of open-air food market, with about a dozen restaurant carts peddling everything from tacos both ways. Very inexpensive.

For a treat, go along this street to the church and in front there is usually a cart selling deep-fried churros and plantains. The latter are delicious, and the former require the digestive tract of a billy goat. Very inexpensive.

If all this walking, eating and drinking is catching up with you, on the side of the church on the plaza, facing the Hotel Virreynal, there are five public toilets behind the candle shop. Cost M$1 and well worth it.

VERACRUZ, Veracruz

Veracruz's excuse for existence is that it is the principal seaport for the central part of Mexico, and the Atlantic-side port for Mexico City. It is rich in history, and its modern history really starts with Grijalva in 1518, followed a year later by Cortés. It was here that Cortés burned his ships and formally launched the conquest of Mexico.

Since those days every invader attempting to take Mexico has found it necessary to first take Veracruz, which although well fortified has never presented any vexing problems. The French took Veracruz in 1838, and it was here that the infamous Santa Ana lost his leg in repelling the bill-collecting mission.

The French were back, in company with the British and Spanish, in 1862, and once again took Veracruz and its shielding fortress, Ulúa. For political reasons England and Spain withdrew, and France went at Mexico alone, and today this operation is known in the Republic as the 'French intervention'.

The Americans also took their whacks at Veracruz, and captured the city in 1847 en passant on their way up to Mexico City, and in 1914 the Americans once again overcame the town, an action that was roundly denounced in both Mexico and the US, although it did not lead to a formal declaration of war. The action still rankles patriotic Mexicans.

The Veracruz battle under General Winfield Scott in 1847 is still of interest to military historians as it was a first in so many spheres of war. It was the first genuine combined operation in which soldiers, sailors and marines operated together on land. Heretofore the soldiers had fought on land and sailors on sea, but in this battle Scott had the cooperation of the naval commander who supplied both the heavy naval guns for use ashore and the trained gunners to fire them. And Scott engineered an amphibious landing that is a textbook operation to this day. He built hundreds of light-weight compact lighters and ferried several thousand men and their equipment ashore from the massed troop transports.

The Spanish in their day spent a fortune fortifying Ulúa on Gallega Island, about one km from Veracruz, between 1746 and 1771, and they regarded it as impregnable. Among other things it had over 250 cannon of various calibres, metres-thick stone walls, and a built-in moat.

The Americans elected to take the city first and turn their attentions to Ulúa later. They landed their naval guns on the dunes a few km south of the city and manhandled them overland with a surprising lack of resistance on the part of the defenders who just had to know what was going on. This was the first of a long string of blunders by the Mexican commander.

The Americans began the seige of the city by spending a little over a week consolidating their position, then they surrounded the city on the dry side, set up their heavy naval guns and called on the authorities to surrender, and informed the Mexicans that once the shooting started no one would be allowed in or out. Naturally the Mexicans refused to lay down their arms, and the Yanks began to systematically demolish Veracruz building by building, block by block, using both ordinary land field pieces and the much heavier naval cannon.

After two days of merciless around-the-clock shelling the Mexicans pleaded with Scott to allow the women and children to leave, but he pointed out that he had offered them their chance and it had been refused, and he continued the bombardment. Scott also stated that there would be no truce, only surrender.

The shooting had commenced on 22 March, and the city capitulated on 27 March, whereupon Scott began preparations to attack the 'impregnable' Ulúa. But it turned out to be unnecessary. Ulúa's commander had closely observed the American technique in taking the fortified city and had seen the terrible havoc wreaked by heavy naval ordnance on stone-built structures and wanted no part of it for himself, his men, and his rock fort. He surrendered without firing a shot and abandoned Ulúa without even destroying the huge stock of military stores. The munitions came in very handy in the Americans' advance on Mexico City because they were at the end of a supply line thousands of km long.

Santa Ana seriously considered shooting the commander who surrendered the country's most prestigious fort and thus opened the road to Mexico City, but I don't believe this was ever done.

San Juan Ulúa was more successful as a prison than a fort, and it served as a prison under both the Spaniards and Mexicans. Latins have never been high on prisons as reformatories, and a prisoner in Ulúa was there to be punished and punished he was. A popular tourist attraction are the oubliettes where the extreme high tides actually came up into the cells. It was said that anything over six months was a life sentence.

The old fort is one of the best-preserved examples of Spanish military construction extant and is well worth visiting aside from the macabre aspects. The walls are so thick that guardrooms and stairs were built within. Their tops were wide and smooth to facilitate supplying the guns that were mounted along their outer edge. There were semi-circular iron tracks set in the stone to facilitate traversing the heavy artillery, high observation towers for spotting, and several drawbridges that could isolate the firing points. No wonder the Spanish, and later the Mexicans, regarded Ulúa as an invulnerable bastion guaranteeing the safety of the country's most vital city. Unfortunately this Latin faith in fixed positions was never justified.

Ulúa is Veracruz's most interesting feature. Allow at least three hours to absorb the finer points of the magnificently useless old pile. To get there, catch a S J Ulúa bus going from right to left in the second street seaward from the plaza. Or you can walk there in 40 interesting minutes. Go straight through the plaza to Zaragoza and turn left. Cross the overpass over the railroad yard and turn right by the old stone substation. Continue on through the container yards (the largest in the Republic) and pass beneath the Conasupo grain conveyors and follow the signs. The S J Ulua bus back to the plaza parks by the ticket office.

The tourist office doesn't spend any of the 10-peso admissions on lighting, and it is definitely advisable to take a flashlight along.

Ulúa has a number of guides, mostly mono-linguals who cope with the tours of Mexican adults and school children. Be suspicious of these people — I heard one telling an awe-struck group of the 'heroic resistance' put up by the fort during the Mexican-American war!

Other than the fine old fort, Veracruz doesn't have much to offer a traveller, and unfortunate weather conditions. During the summer it is hot and sultry and downright uncomfortable, with millions of mosquitoes and hungry little flies. During the winter the weather is about like Miami's, but now and then with no warning whatsoever a 'norther' will strike.

The infamous norther is a cold wind that starts up around the North Pole and picks up speed passing through Moose Jaw. It gets colder and more powerful crossing the Great Plains with nothing but a few barbed-wire fences to impede its progress. When it finally hits Veracruz it will cause the temperature to drop 20 degrees in a matter of minutes, and with an astronomical chill factor. So if you're going to be away from your hotel for any length of time take a coat.

On your way out the Paseo de Malacón and the waterfront from the plaza you will pass a considerable number of stands selling such goodies as turtle-shell combs, miniature lighthouses and other items specifically intended for the tourist trade. If any of this dreck happens to tempt you remember that dickering is the name of the game.

Stand in front of the Hotel Vigo at the corner of Molina and Coss to view what has to be one of the ugliest buildings in the country. Apparently the designer set out to plan a conventional pyramid, thought better of it, and made two parallel cuts from top to bottom, ending with a sort of semi-pyramid with two up-and-down sides and two sloping sides.

The newstand under the portico on Independencia at Zamora, kitty-corner from the plaza, stocks a few US magazines and also the English-language *Mexico City News*.

Just past the Hotel Avenida, at Díaz Miron and Aragón is the gigantic supermarket Chedraui, part of a chain operation. It sells everything from baked goods such as the morning pan dulces, to the latest Beatle reissues. Fresh fruit, though, is handled by the barrows lining the curb out front. About a 15 minute walk from the ADO station.

Places to Stay

Considering that Veracruz has some grand hostelries intended for wealthy customers awaiting the arrival or departure of steamships, the town has a remarkably large assortment of economical hotels.

Right next door to the ADO bus station is the *Hotel Central*, badly misnamed because there is nothing central about it, but quite convenient for travellers by bus who feel a need for a night's rest after the long run down the hill from Mexico City. Expensive.

The bus station is on Díaz Miron at Orizaba, and if you pass the Hotel Central on your way downtown, at about the third intersection you come to the *Hotel Tabasco*, two storeys with a cream topside and a light blue lunch stand on the ground floor. Moderate.

In the next block after the Tabasco is the tile-fronted *Hotel La Paz*, actually more of a motel than a hotel, with off-street parking, which always tends to raise the rate. Expensive.

Farther in on Díaz Miron, about a dozen blocks from the bus station, is the *Hotel Avenida*, four storeys with the *Café Noche y Dia* ('Coffee Night and Day') restaurant on the ground floor. The hotel is fairly new and so large that it takes longer to fill than most. Moderate.

Things are generally more expensive downtown, and hotels are no exception.

The *Hotel Rias*, on Zaragoza near Lerdo across from the Aduana Maritima, has a couple of great advantages. It is just far enough from the plaza to avoid the strolling orchestras that tend to play all night in the plaza, usually several at the same time sawing different songs. And it is somewhat cheaper than it would be if it were directly on the plaza. But still it's expensive.

Another place far enough from the plaza to avoid the worst of the noise is the *Hotel Vigo* on the corner of Molina and Coss, a couple blocks cheaper than

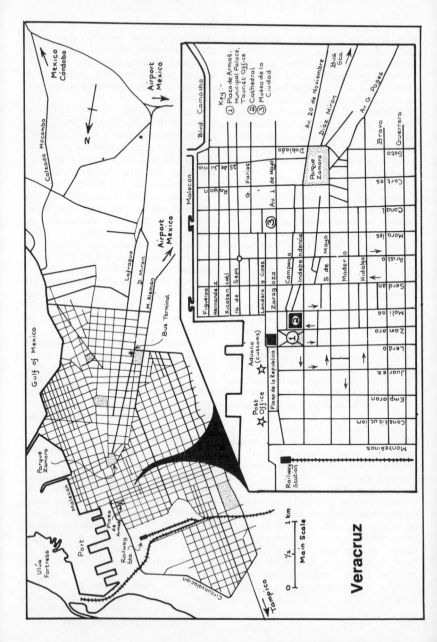

Veracruz

Key:-
① Plaza de Armas, Municipal Palace, Tourist Office
② Cathedral
③ Museo de la Ciudad

Main Scale

0   ½   1 km

the plaza proper. An older house, but not as run-down as many of the older hotels in Veracruz that gave up trying when people switched to planes from ships. Expensive.

The *Hotel Amparo* is on Serdán and Zaragoza and is the cheapest place near the plaza, but make sure the fan works during the summer — if only to drive the mosquitoes away. Moderate.

Places to Eat

The restaurants around the Plaza de Armas are intended for drinking beer, listening to marimba bands, spitting shrimp hulls on the tiles, and conversation, not for serious eating.

A popular way to spend a languid Saturday afternoon in Veracruz is to gather a few friends, book a table in front of the Bar Santiago, order a few bottles of Agua Tehuacán mineral water, a fresh bottle of Viejo Virgil or San Marcos brandy, a bucket of ice, and tell stories and watch the level in the bottle sink with the sun.

Come right down to it, Veracruz is not really a very good eating town, probably due to the hot muggy climate. Even pescado Veracruzana, the fish stew that can give bouillabaisse a fair run for its money and takes its name from this town, was far, far better cooked up north at Guaymas than I've ever had it in its hometown.

The above remarks notwithstanding, there are a few places I've been patronizing for years.

At Serdán and Zaragoza is the *Cochinito de Oro*, probably the best economy restaurant in town — but don't order the baby pig. As with so many Mexican business names, the Cochinito is not to be taken seriously. Moderate.

By the fish market, a block to the seaward from Coss, is a solid string of little restaurants, most specialising in seafood. The tables are on the opposite side from the plaza, and it gets almost no play at all from tourists, but I'm of the opinion that the *Dia de la Marina* is better in almost all respects (except seeing and being seen) than anything except the La Paella on the zócolo. Popular with dining-out local families. Inexpensive.

One of the best places to eat in Veracruz, and the best on the plaza, is the *Restaurante la Paella* behind the church. This is the only restaurant on the plaza itself that concentrates on feeding the public, rather than serving drinks. The name, again, is not to be taken too seriously, although I've had an excellent Paella Velenciana a time or two. It isn't a spartan establishment and neither is it too Spanish. Expensive, but usually well worth the price.

Getting There & Getting Around

Veracruz is a transportation centre, and there are buses north and south along the east coast, and to Mexico City, leaving constantly. (This makes it dead easy to catch a bus up to Córdoba which, with its altitude, is a much better place to stay than Veracruz.)

ADO stations almost never have baggage checking service, but the station at Veracruz is an exception, sorta. There are a number of lockers against the wall toward the restaurant. Anywhere else they would be coin-operated, but in Veracruz a 'ficha' (not to be confused with a flecha or fecha) is required; there is no sign indicating where to purchase a ficha, but you get it from the bookstore.

To get downtown from the Central Camionera, you can catch a bus running along Díaz Miron from left to right in front of the bus station and stay with it until you reach the plaza. If you want to walk, go out the front door and turn right on Díaz Miron. There is a confusing set of intersections at the Parque Zamora, but continue straight ahead past the park, and then angle slightly to your left at Rayón and you will wind up on Independencia. The Plaza de

Armas, also known as the Plaza de la Constitución, is seven blocks more. Walking time: 40 minutes.

To get back to the bus station, retrace your steps or walk over on 5 de Mayo and catch the same bus back. 5 de Mayo is one block over from Independencia on the landward side.

HUAJUAPÁN DE LEON, Oaxaca

During the winter of 1980-81 a severe earthquake struck the State of Oaxaca. The epicenter was near the cross-roads city of Huajuapán and it caused considerable damage and a large number of fatalities. Only a few months later there was little evidence remaining of the disaster. Approximately half-way between Puebla and Oaxaca, Huajuapán is by no means a garden spot, but if you absolutely have to lay over, there is an economy-model hotel not too far from where the buses stop. It is right on the main stem, dressed in a coat of dark green paint and somewhat better than the town deserves. Moderate.

OAXACA, Oaxaca

Oaxaca is, with justification, one of the most popular tourist destinations in Mexico. In addition to wonderful year-round weather, travellers come for the ancient Zapotec and Mixtec ruins, the museum in the former convent, the band concerts in the plaza, and just for the relaxed atmosphere.

Each year more and more tourists arrive, until at times it seems there are more foreigners in the plazas than there are locals, and there are quantities of tourist-oriented shops, but part of the charm of Oaxaca comes from the local people who pursue their lawful occasions with little or no contact with outsiders. It is one of the few large communities where numbers of people still converse in their pre-conquest languages, and Zapotec and Zapotec-accented Spanish are everywhere in evidence.

The State of Oaxaca has well over a million non-Spanish speaking citizens, a severe problem to a government that is attempting to impart a knowledge of rudimentary birth control techniques, and families with half a dozen little kids led by a pregnant nursing mother are not at all uncommon.

One of the most popular stops on the tourist round of inspection is the Church of Santo Domingo at Gurrion/Constitucion and 5 de Mayo/Armentia y Lopez, the most impressively-decorated church in the country to my way of thinking. To step inside the front doors when the sun is at just the right angle is to be dazzled by the gold leaf which seems to cover the whole altar end of the interior. It is a big place, with walls as thick as six metres in places. When construction started in 1575 churches were expected to be able to double as fortresses. There is a popular story to the effect that it was started with a bankroll of M$2.50, but this I doubt. When the construction was finished it had cost in excess of M$2 million, and this I don't doubt.

The exterior is Baroque, with niches occupied by statues. The splendid chapel on the right as you enter is the Capella de la Virgen del Rosario, in itself as large as some churches and more elaborately decorated than most.

As you enter, look up toward the choir loft. The odd tree with all the figures growing on the branches is actually the family tree of the Guzmán family, Sr Guzmán being the instigator of the church.

For many years the convent attached to the church was a military post, but recently it has been converted into a regional museum, with heavy emphasis on the artifacts recovered from the nearby ruins of Mitla and Monte Alban, including gold jewellery recovered from one of the tombs at Monte Albán. Pretty it is, but I am somewhat more impressed by the superb design and construction to match of the old

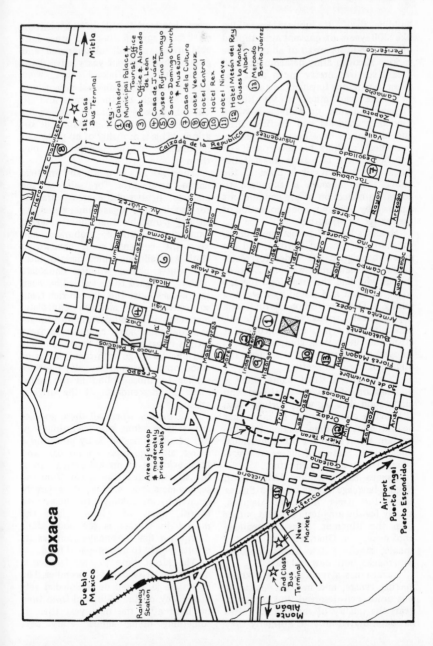

Oaxaca

Key :-
1. Cathedral
2. Municipal Palace #
3. Tourist Office
4. Post Office & Alameda de León
5. Casa de Juárez
6. Museo Rufino Tamayo
7. Santo Domingo Church & Museum
8. Casa de la Cultura
9. Hotel Veracruz
10. Hotel Central
11. Hotel Rex
12. Hotel Nineve
13. Hotel Mesón del Rey (Buses to Monte Albán)
14. Mercado Benito Juárez

building itself. It survived something like 300 years of convent use, topped off by a century or so of abuse by the various Mexican army detachments, and it still survives pretty much as it was when the masons finished their work.

I have read much of the Rufino Tamayo Museum, on Morelos between Tinoco y Palacios and Porfirio Díaz, and all reports have been enthusiastic, but when I'm there it is never open, and I've been there at least a dozen times when the sign says it is open to the public. The museum is supposed to contain a collection of pre-conquest art amassed by Tamayo, not a collection of the master's own output.

Mexico's beloved Juárez, the promulgator of the Laws of Reform, and the man who signed the order for Maximilian's execution, was a Zapotec Indian who had the great food fortune to be adopted and raised by a wealthy family in Oaxaca. His home is on Garcia Vigil between Carranza and Quetzalcoatl. Maintained as a museum, of course, it affords an interesting glimpse of life as enjoyed by the upper classes during the middle of the 19th century.

Except for a street name there is no mention of another local boy who made good in a big way, Porfirio Díaz, although a good case can be made that he did more to drag Mexico into the modern world than any other individual since Cortés. Statues of Juárez are everywhere; Díaz is all but forgotten.

Oaxaca has a lending library with English-language books on Piño Suarez across the street from the Alameda, mostly for the long-term resident, rather than the itinerant. The Universitario bookstore, on Guerrero just off the zócolo, stocks a few English-language paperbacks, both new and used.

Oaxaca has a reputation as a knife-making centre, and in past decades it was quite well deserved. But of recent years the quality of the Oaxaca knives has deteriorated no end. Formerly they were hammered out of high-carbon steel from springs, files and other suitable items, shaped, oil-tempered and ground, but in recent years knives have been sold in Oaxaca that were etched with the traditional designs and with the eagle on the handle and all, but which were absolutely useless for any purpose other than mantle decorations. (This is probably of no particular importance to the people who buy them.)

There are lots of useful and practical native handicrafts for sale at the markets: lightweight charcoal braziers for cooking over a gas flame; water jugs slightly permeable that allow water to dampen the surface, evaporate, and keep the contents cool; handwoven cloth with alluring tipico designs, ideal for winter skirts; wooden chocolate beaters, intended to be twirled between the palms to give the layer of rich foam so essential to Mexican chocolate; huaraches of several designs with tough-as-a-hog's-nose soles hand-carved from retired tyres; beautifully decorated belts and buckles to go with them; lamps of wood, onyx, glass and clay; clay figurines similar to those found in the ruins, made by descendants of the original artists.

The market where all these goodies are available, along with everything you can possibly imagine, is by no means a secret, although there are no signs and little evidence of market activity from the street. Across the street from the second-class bus station, it is largely ignored by, or unknown to, the average tourist, many of whom believe the market in Oaxaca is the poor affair downtown that nowadays confines its efforts mostly to non-prepared food.

The nicest time to visit Oaxaca is during the latter part of December. The Fiesta de la Virgen de la Soledad gets under way on the 16th, and from then on until after the new year there is something doing almost every day.

Especially interesting is the Noche de las Rábanos on the 23rd. On that night wonderfully carved radishes — rábanos — are sold in the plazas, as well as little bañuelos, a sort of deep fat fried pan dulce. These latter are served on small clay plates which are smashed with great ceremony after the bañuelos are consumed.

The whole town blossoms with nativity scenes which, since snow is largely an unknown quantity, are constructed with Spanish moss as a base. These are built in windows facing the street, or even in one corner of a front room and the street window left uncovered so the passers-by as well as the family may enjoy. On Christmas Eve elaborately decorated trucks, and even handcarts, parade through the downtown section.

All in all, it is awfully hard to beat Oaxaca in December. Best of all, the weather is the kind of weather one associates with Mexico: cool mornings, warm sunny days, followed by cooling evenings. The air is invigorating and the townspeople seem even happier than usual. Poinsettia plants are to be seen everywhere as little brown Indian women pack them through the streets. The country people bring in huge grey-green bundles of Spanish moss and pile them along the little Alameda de Léon. There is a feeling of happy Christmas-anticipation easily transmitted to even the first-time English-only visitors.

Ruins of Monte Albán & Mitla

Part of Oaxaca's attraction for tourists is due to these two great nearby ruins. Monte Albán is closest to town, and the one most often visited by foreigners. It is a gigantic place, occupying something over 40 square km. The plaza is 200 by 300 metres, which compares very favourably with the larger big-city plazas in modern Mexico.

Monte Albán thrived for over 20 centuries and then, for unknown reasons, was abandoned by the people and turned into a vast necropolis by its neighbours. Shortly thereafter the site was occupied by the Mixtecs. No builders they, the Mixtecs simply moved into the old Zapotec buildings. In those days the area was very densely populated, as indicated by over 260 sites discovered so far.

Archaeological investigations at Monte Albán have been under way for over half a century. A great deal has been learned of the lives and history of the early inhabitants, and a number of excellent guidebooks to the ruins have been written and are available in English, Spanish, French and German both in Oaxaca itself and the little museum at Monte Albán. If you obtain one of these books and spend some time reading up on the subject before you make the trip out there, it will greatly enhance the pleasure of the visit.

Plan to spend a little time. Monte Albán will take several days to tour; anything else won't really do it justice.

Monte Albán is about nine km from Oaxaca. Many visitors take a cab from the plaza which is an expensive way to go unless there is a full load to split the fare. Most arrive by bus. The 'bus station' for the Monte Albán coach changes from time to time, but at present it is at the Hotel Mesón de Angel, on Mina between Mier y Teran and Díaz Ordaz. Buses run throughout the day, so it is possible to go out early and return late. Check the schedules — as with the station they are subject to whimsical change from time to time. And be sure to pack a picnic lunch. Although there are usually food stands neither the stands themselves nor the quality of their food is to be relied on.

Mitla, Oaxaca's other major ruin, is approximately 45 km from the Plaza de la Constitución, and it is not nearly as extensive or as interesting as Monte Albán, so it is the least visited of the two sites. But if you have only a single day to spend, I'd suggest Mitla. It can be pretty well examined in two or three hours, whereas a short visit to Monte Albán doesn't allow much more than a quick glimpse of the ball court or the Danzantes.

Getting to Mitla is simplicity itself. Hike out Trujano to the second-class bus station and board the Mitla bus at gate 15. The buses run every half-hour or so and the trip takes about an hour and a half. Fare is approximately M$15.

Places to Stay

Although Oaxaca has hotels by the dozen, it has visitors by the hundred, with the predictable result that the hotels get filled up quite often, and a few of them make the most of this opportunity to overcharge.

The *Hotel Veracruz*, two blocks to the left as you leave the first-class bus station, is newish and would be extremely convenient for the person who arrives late at night via first-class bus except that it tends to fill up early on. But if you are lucky enough to get a room you will have one of the better buys in largely-overpriced Oaxaca. Moderate.

The *Hotel Santo Tomás*, Abosolo near Juárez, is an older motel-like place displaying the oval logo of the Mexican Hotel Association which has always seemed to me — perhaps unfairly — to be a good indication of an overpriced house. The Santo Tomás makes considerable effort to give value with an accommodating staff and efficient maid service. Expensive.

The *Hotel Modelo* on the zócolo is probably one of the most overpriced in Mexico, with all the less desirable attributes of a poorly-run casa de huespedes in a played-out mining town, including cheap padlocks on the ill-fitting doors, rocky beds, complete lack of warmth in the 'hot' water and a perambulating cockroach population that must number in the thousands. The reason I mention the Modelo here is that Oaxaca oftens fills to the brim and any room at all is difficult to find. After all, the joint is right on the main plaza opposite the Hotel Señorial, and easy to locate in the ultimate emergency. It is a classic example of what happens when too many prospective guests chase too few rooms. Ridiculously expensive.

Most of the economy hotels are between the zócolo and the second-class bus station.

The *Hotel Central*, on 20 de Noviembre between Hidalgo and Independencia, for years was the low-priced standby in Oaxaca, but then it fell on evil ways and grew sloppy and careless. Recently management has got its act together and the Central is again worthy of mention, and a good choice for those who feel they just have to be close to the plaza. Expensive.

If you go to the corner of Trujano and Díaz Ordaz you can see four hotels, moderate or inexpensive. Stroll around, look them over and make your choice. And remember sometimes a bit of polite haggling will help defeat the high cost of living in Mexico.

The *Hotel Jiminéz*, on Mier y Terran between Trujano and Hidalgo is really more of an economy-model motel than a hotel. Parking in the courtyard for a few vehicles. Moderate.

The *Hotel Paris*, a new hotel at Trujano and Galeana, has a beige facade, comfortable beds, hot water, small rooms, and a price about 25% higher than it ought to be. Expensive.

The *Hotel del Pacifico*, at Mier y Terran and Trujano, is also fairly new and offers the same amenities as the Paris but a somewhat more reasonable price. Moderate.

The *Hotel Ninive* is another new hotel at Perifico and Las Casas, which is the next street south of Trujano at the stoplight by the railroad tracks. You can watch for it as you leave the second-class bus station and start toward the centre of town. It is so far from the plaza that the price is moderate.

There is a real, up-front casa de huespedes in the first block of Trujano after you leave the traffic light by the railroad tracks. No name, just a small sign stating the type of enterprise within. Inexpensive.

Back up town, the *Hotel El Presidente* on 5 de Mayo between Abasolo and Murgui is in the tastefully rebuilt former Convento de Santa Catalina. This is a really first-rate job of conversion and well worth a visit for an inspection trip, but I feel their rates border on the outrageous. Ridiculously expensive.

Places to Eat

Oaxaca is a fair eating town, with most of the lower-priced restaurants serving Oaxacan regional items as well as standard Mexican fare. Mexican is better. But first I will mention a couple of places to avoid.

One is the restaurant in the ADO bus station. ADO operates its own restaurants, which are definitely not up to the standards of its buses. Among other objectionable habits they show a distressing tendency to serve reconstituted orange juice, and Bimbo bread, the ultimate insult in a land that makes bolillos! And because of the low standards of ADO food they don't do too much business, which in turn means that food spends too much time in the steam table. These remarks go double in spades when applied to the Oaxaca first-class terminal.

The other one to avoid is a restaurant right on the Plaza Constitucion that calls itself the *Fuente de Sodas el Tule*. It has the best restaurant setting in town and traps a few unwary travellers with its rather elaborate menu. If you go there stick to beer and/or soda fountain items and take a table overlooking the square. In the same block as the Señorial. Ridiculously expensive.

Eating anywhere around the plaza

in sidewalk cafes turns out to be expensive and not very good, but try the *Restaurante Alameda*, on Trujano between 20 de Noviembre and Virgil. The Alameda makes a diligent effort to acquaint its customers with the unique cuisine of Oaxaca, which differs radicaly from the better-known Mexican fare. Here a 'cecina enchelada' has no tortilla involved, for instance. There are a few Mexican items on the menu too. Expensive.

Prices drop as you get farther away from the zócolo, and the *Kosinto* is no exception. Located on Hidalgo between Díaz Ordaz and J P Garcia, it is larger than it looks from the sidewalk. Really a room and a half in size, it features standard Mexican food at moderate prices; recommended.

As you go out Trujano toward the second-class bus station the restaurants gradually get smaller and cheaper, and the Kosinto is situated in the midst of an area thick with inexpensive restaurants.

For the real people's restaurants at people's prices, keep walking out Trujano until you come to the end at the railroad tracks. The long, low brick buildings to the left of the big Central Commercial Popular building are the new market. Skip the first building and try the second and third, entering from the bus station end. There are at least a dozen food stalls serving both Oaxacan and Mexican specialties. Well-prepared and at inexpensive (or lower) prices.

If the yen for snow-white tablecloths overcomes you, then try one of the hotels around the plaza, but especially the *Señorial* and the *Monte Albán*. Their menus are singularly unimaginative, but their wines are dependable. Gourmet they ain't, but they give fairly good value even though the prices average out very expensive.

Getting There & Getting Around

Oaxaca has excellent first and second-class bus service, and there are buses for Puerto Escondido, Puerto Angel, San Cristobál las Casas, Mexico City, Veracruz, Villahermosa, the Guatamalan border, and dozens of little back-woodsly towns that don't even appear on maps.

To get uptown from the second-class bus station, turn left as you come out on the broad divided avenue. Go past the big Centro Comercial Popular store and cross over the railroad tracks and the Perifico at the traffic light. Then take the street that angles off to the left. Eventually this street bends to the right to become Trujano which leads you to the plaza. Walking time: 15 minutes.

To get from the first-class bus station to the centre of town, turn left on leaving the station. Go three blocks and turn left again on the well-travelled Avenida Juárez and follow it 11 or 12 blocks, then turn right on either Independencia or Hidalgo — either one will take you to the Plaza de la Constitución in three blocks. Walking time: 20 minutes.

There is a city bus service, but it is more trouble to get to or from the bus station by a city bus than it is worth. If walking is inconvenient then catch a taxi.

There is railroad service to Oaxaca from Mexico City via Puebla and Tehuacán. It takes about 15 hours when the trains run on time, and running on time is not a universal trait among Mexican trains. There are two trains, a day train and a night train. Both are infernally slow.

Oaxaca has excellent air service, with both Mexicana and Aeromexico having several flights a day to Mérida, Veracruz, Mexico City, Villahermosa and so on.

The Puerto Escondido bus is a popular way to reach the beautiful Pacific coast beaches. The road has been under construction for something like 20 years to my knowledge, and it will soon be finished, I am told, but during rainy weather the bus is sometimes unable to make the trip. The road to the less popular Puerto Angel is paved all the way. Both are about 250 km from Oaxaca.

If you don't contemplate the eight-hour bus ride down to Puerto Escondido with any joy, Aerovias Oaxaqueñas will fly you there in about an hour for M$600. The planes are DC-3s and Convairs and they fly at low altitude, ideal for sightseeing. Often they go by way of Salina Cruz, which more than doubles the distance flown. Most of the passengers are business people who have flown the area time and time again, so nobody thinks it worthwhile to announce the name of the airport when they land, and now and then a person going to Puerto Escondido gets off in Salina Cruz. The flight time is about the same and both are on the coast. Salina Cruz has a railroad, a pipeline, a refinery, a drawbridge (usually open) at the harbour entrance, and a dirt air strip. Puerto Escondido has none of these.

TUXTLA GUITÉRREZ, Chiapas

Twenty-five years ago Tuxtla was a modern small town dedicated to making money by supplying the necessities to a large part of Mexico, and since then nothing has changed at all except its size. The only reason to stop overnight is having to wait for a bus out of town, for Tuxtla is the transport centre of the State of Chiapas, with bus services to Villahermosa, Mexico City, Oaxaca, San Cristobál las Casas and Guatemala.

There is no railroad. The airport offers flights to Mexico City and way points.

The first and second-class bus stations are some distance apart, and the streets are a bit confusing, so if for some reason it is necessary to transfer between them, take a taxi.

Places to Stay

For those with the bad luck to have to lay over there is a hotel near the second-class bus station. Turn right on the dead-end street in front of the station, cross over the pedestrian way at the end, and follow it to the left to its end. To your right, about half a block distant, is the *Hotel Ricamar*, a box-like construction, fairly new. Moderate.

Almost directly across the street from the first-class station are two hotels with little to choose between them except their paint jobs: the *Hotel Santo Domingo* and the *Hotel María Teresa*. Unfortunately they both have the habit of filling up early because both are moderate and highly visible.

If they are filled, keep going right on past them and turn right at the next intersection. In the next block are three more hotels that are unlikely to be filled as all are either expensive or very expensive.

And make sure the fan or air conditioning is operating — Tuxtla is relatively low and can get terribly hot during the summer.

SAN CRISTÓBAL LAS CASAS, Chiapas

It is but a short 43 km from Tuxtla to Cristóbal las Casas, but in that distance there is an increase in elevation of some 1615 metres, and an infinite increase in colonial atmosphere.

Cristóbal is one of the unspoilt jewels among Mexican cities, one of the most determinedly colonial towns in the Republic. Plus it is the only place where large numbers of Indians from the surrounding countryside persist in wearing the traditional costumes, unique to each village, when they visit the market. It is common to see Zinatecans in their beribboned hats, Chamulas in white or black tunics with coloured sleeves indicating their village, and men from Huistan in odd 'diaper' pants, and lots of others.

During the last 50 years or so Cristó-bal has been a magnet for both Americans and Europeans who appreciate the small-town way of life, and scholars studying the numerous tribes. Some are attracted, too, by the excellent climate which is much like Guadalajara's.

Recently the ready availability of low-cost air fares from Europe, plus an increasing awareness of Mexico's unique qualities, has brought ever-increasing numbers of French, Swiss, German, British and other Europeans to las Casas, and today the place is a veritable Babel. Increasingly signs are going up stating that the business people can speak French, German and English, whereas a few years ago one was fortunate to find a shopkeeper who could speak reasonably unaccented Spanish!

The city was founded in 1528 by Diego Mazariegos, a compassionate man who was soon replaced by a heartless individual named Juan Enrique de Guzmán, every bit as cruel as his namesake, Nuño de Guzmán. But the town really dates to 1545 when Bishop Bartolomé de las Casas made his appearance with a group of Dominican priests. Las Casas, like Vasco de Quiroga in Pátzcuaro, soon made himself the protector of the Indians and eventually the town added his name to the existing Cristóbal.

Most of the architectural charm of las Casas is due to the old tile-roofed buildings, many of them dating back to the days of Guzmán and las Casas himself.

Las Casas has always been a progressive community, perhaps stemming from the days when it was the capital of Chiapas. In the plaza is a lacy cast-iron bandstand with a plaque stating 'The First Normal School in America Was Founded Here In 1828'.

Art exhibits are held in the Auditorio de Bellas Artes on Hidalgo by the arch of the Templo y Arco del Carmen. Mostly work by local artists is shown, some of it very good indeed.

The 'Reoveco' bookstore on the

plaza by the Hotel Ciudad Real, stocks English-language books, mostly paperback fiction, but also regional guidebooks.

There are public toilets on the back of the Palacio Municipal on the opposite side from the Turismo office.

And of course any Mexican town with a fine climate, colonial buildings and delightful ambience has to have at least one cultural centre with classes in Spanish, art and, usually English. In las Casas it is the Centro para Intercambio de Estudios Linguisticos Occidental. The usual efficient method of immersion language teaching is used in which the students live on the local, Spanish-speaking economy. If you're intersted, address a letter to: CIELO, San Cristóbal las Casas, Chiapas, Mexico.

The market in las Casas is not very large but it is one of the most interesting in the Republic because of the fantastic variety of costumes of the merchants and customers. Best time to take in the market scene is during the early morning hours.

Places to Stay
An important part of a pleasant stay is an affordable hotel. Many of the visitors are Europeans quite accustomed to staying in low-priced hotels, and San Cristóbal is well supplied with hotels in any price range.

The *Ciudad Real* is as centrally located as it can possibly be, right on the plaza. Easily the best hotel in town and, partially because of the plaza location, ridiculously expensive.

The *Hotel San Martin*, on Guadalupe between Utrilla and Belesario Dominguez, is not quite on the plaza but still only a block away. The rooms are arranged around a three-storey patio and are bright and airy, especially those on the top floor. Because the rates are reasonable and the location desirable the San Martin is often full, especially during the summer vacation season. Moderate.

The *Casa de Huespedes Pola*, on Insurgentes at Pino Suarez, is the bargain find of las Casas. The Pola boasts a rustic decor and an international clientele. When I browsed through the register on one page were listed guests from Finland, Great Britain, West Germany, France and Spain. It is close to both bus stations and only five or six blocks from the plaza. Inexpensive.

The French-speaking traveller will feel right at home at the *Casa de Huespedes Chamula*, whose owner makes quite a point of being French-speaking. The Chamula is on Pantaleon Dominguez between Corzo and Leon.

The *Posada Abueleta*, on Tapachula near Tuxtla, has to be the cheapest place to stay in las Casas, especially for those with their own sleeping gear. It's a sort of cross between a casa de huespedes and a youth hostel where people can save around M$25 a night by dossing down in the dormitory. Inexpensive, with or without sleeping gear.

The *Casa de Huespedes Margarita*, on Guadalupe between Dominguez and Colón, has a brown and white facade, blue and white tiled floor. It is another

ex-private mansion, one storey and built around a conventional patio, and a cut or two above the usual casa de huespedes. Because of its reasonable prices and convenient location the Margarita is usually full. Inexpensive.

Places to Eat

The *Rosticera la Casa Blanca Restaurant*, on Guadalupe between Utrill and Dominguez opposite the Hotel San Martin, is just exactly what it says on the sign, a place that sells roasted chickens, and a restaurant. Bigger than it appears from the sidewalk, it does a booming business with both locals and foreigners in the morning with café con leche and pan dulce. Good service. Moderate.

Los Arcos, a block off off the plaza on Madero. I don't know why, but the Arcos is not greatly frequented by visitors, although popular with local residents. Food is strictly Mexican and OK; they do liver especially well. Another place that is a lot larger than it appears from the outside. Moderate.

The *Olla Podrida* on the corner of Mazariegos and Allende gets a lot of beard-and-sandal customers. It can't seem to decide whether it is a bakery, gimcrack shoppe or a restaurant and winds up not doing any of them too well. Moderate.

La Ideal Pan Regional y de Mexico, on Mazariegos near Allende, across the street from the Olla Podrida, has an assortment of baked goods totally unlike the usual Mexican bakery, particularly a small-town bakery. Their

wide, flattish whole wheat bread together with a chunk of white Chiapas cheese, a bottle of vino tinto and a park bench on the plaza make my afternoon complete. Inexpensive.

The *Hotel Ciudad Real* has a restaurant rather than a parking lot in the patio. Service poor, food fair, which is not what one would expect in a ridiculously expensive establishment.

The ladies up at the market do the cheapest and about the best meals in town. I've been eating with them almost from the time the concrete was poured, and I'm of the opinion that the extra walk out from the centre of town is well worthwhile. Very inexpensive.

There is a restaurant called *El Triangulo* across the Carretera Panamericana from the Cristóbal Colón bus station. You can actually see it through the big plate glass window in the front of the waiting room. It does a good business with truck drivers heading down Guatemala way, inexpensive.

Getting There & Getting Around

Almost everybody arrives in las Casas by bus. There are quite a number of buses every day, and the distance from Tuxtla is too small to warrant bothering with airplanes. To get downtown from the second-class bus station, go out the front door and turn left, then right at the first street. Go two blocks and turn left on Hidalgo — you will be able to see the arch over the street a couple of blocks in front of you. Continue on Hidalgo until you reach the plaza three blocks beyond the arch. Walking time

A   The balcony of the restaurant in the Gran Hotel, Taxco — a good place to sit in the evening and watch the action in the Plazuela San Juan.

B   Campesino in Taxco.

C   Taxco shows more Spanish influence than almost any other Mexican town.

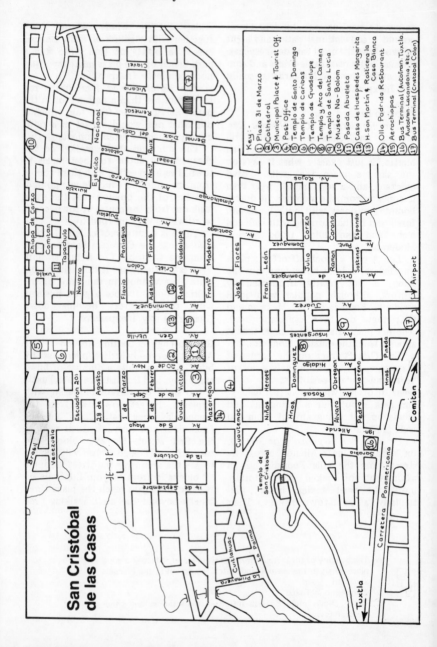

San Cristóbal
de las Casas

Key:-
1. Plaza 31 de Marzo
2. Cathedral
3. Municipal Palace + Tourist Off.
4. Post Office
5. Templo de Santo Domingo
6. Templo de Caribas
7. Templo de Guadalupe
8. Templo y Arco del Carmen
9. Templo de Santa Lucia
10. Museo Na-Bolom
11. Posada Abuelita
12. Casa de Huespedes Margarita
13. H. San Martin + Rosticeria la
    Casa Blanca
14. Olla Podrida Restaurant
15. Aerochiapas
16. Bus Terminal (Autobran Tuxtla,
    Autotran Lacandonia, etc.)
17. Bus Terminal (Cristobal Colon)

is 15 minutes or so.

To get downtown from the Cristóbal Colón first-class bus station leave the waiting room and turn right on Insurgentes, the plaza is just seven blocks. Walking time is 10 minutes.

VILLAHERMOSA, Tabasco

Villahermosa is a transport hub and heavily involved in Mexico's latest oil boom, and there are drilling rigs working almost within the city limits. The town has embarked on an ambitious scheme to rid itself of the cars that were choking it to death, and a number of streets downtown have been closed to vehicular traffic and turned into charming pedestrian malls.

Because of the overwhelming influx of people connected in one way or another with the oil business Villahermosa has become an exceptionally inconvenient place for the casual traveller, and in the summers of 1980 and 1981 scores of people wound up sleeping on the floor of the ADO bus station because every room in town was rented for weeks in advance.

If you have the ill fortune to get stuck in Villahermosa, perhaps waiting for a bus connection, then it is worth it to go second-class, especially toward the Yucatán. It will mean spending more time on the trip because second-class buses stop at towns too small to appear on most maps, but it beats the hell out of waiting two or three days for a bus that may never appear.

The second-class bus service from Villahermosa is extensive, and it is seldom difficult to get a bus to Tuxtla, Veracruz, Mérida, Campeche, Coatzacoalcos or even such out-of-the-way places as Macuspana or Tenosique. Villahermosa is also where you catch the bus for Palenque either first or second-class. The former is faster, the latter oftener.

To get from the first-class bus station, often called the 'ADO station', to the second-class station, go out the front door and turn left and walk to the end of the street. To your right at about 45° and across the divided street is the reddish false front with sign 'Central de Autobuses', almost in line with the microwave tower. It's about a six-minute walk.

To get uptown from the ADO station, go out and turn left, then right at the end of the street. This is about a 30 minute walk. From the second-class station, go out the front and turn left and walk about 25 minutes.

A taxi from either station will cost M$25-50.

Villahermosa has excellent scheduled air service, with flights to Mérida, Oaxaca, Veracruz and Mexico City among other places.

PALENQUE, Chiapas

Palenque is one of the more spectacular Mayan ruins. They are located among thousands of square kilometres of heavy jungle growth and surrounded by hills. The ruins were abandoned some time around the 12th century and unlike Monte Albán, never reoccupied. The ancient buildings are beautifully designed, and there are stelea with elaborate bas-reliefs. Extensive use is made of ornamented stucco and all in all the effect is awe-inspiring.

Palenque has a tree, or cross, on the Temple of the Foliated Cross that is unique in America, but which has a nearly-identical duplicate at Angkor Wat in Cambodia. There are also sculpted figures holding a flower and they, too, have their counterparts in a Buddhist temple in India.

Guidebooks are available in Palenque Village — can you imagine a 'village' of over 30,000 people? — in Spanish, English, and usually French and German, that will go far toward explaining the ruins.

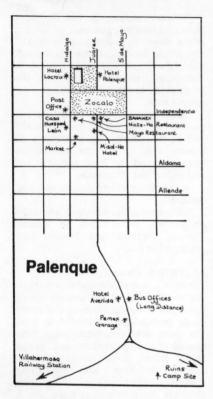

Palenque

Places to Stay & Eat
Since visitors to the ruins constitute a major source of income for the town of Palenque, it logically follows that there are several hotels, most of which are entirely too dear for penny-pinchers like myself. There are a number of hotels, motels and trailer camps on the road between Palenque and the ruins, but I feel it is better to be in town where there are an assortment of restaurants and other facilities.

When I'm in Palenque I tend to stay right on the Parque Central at the *Hotel Palenque*. This is an older house with a double room rate, depending on whether you want to pay M$26 a day extra for air-conditioning. For myself, I'll take a fan over air-conditioner any day, especially if the fan is a Humphrey Bogart. Rates are moderate/expensive.

If the old Palenque is full, I walk up Juárez half a block from the plaza and check in at the *Misol Ha*, smaller than the antique Palenque, and another place with a dual rate. Air-conditioning costs a whopping M$63 over the fan-equipped rooms. Moderate/expensive.

Another reason for staying in town rather than in the midst of the jungle is that it is easy to obtain the makings for a picnic lunch, a practical necessity for those intending to spend a day at the ruins.

It is hard to beat the *Restaurante Nicte-Ha* on the Parque Central. It serves both Mexican and Yucateco specialties: mole poblano, chicken pibil, etc. I was in the Nicte-Ha one evening when a Frenchman mistook the bottle of Salsa Habanero on the table for the milder Tabasco and applied it accordingly. It took him about three bites to discover that not only is the habanero one of the hottest peppers but it also tends to get hotter with the passage of time! Moderate.

One can always beat the relatively high prices in the uptown restaurants by strolling the few blocks to the market. This is extremely practical for breakfast but doesn't work at all for supper because the market girls go home early. They all serve about the same dishes, and I remember with affection the fina sopa de chicharrones I had a few years back and have never been able to locate again in Palenque.

Getting There & Getting Around
Palenque is one of the few places where there are many arrivals by train, usually from Mérida or Campeche on their way back to the US after flying to one of the international airports in Yucatán. But by and large the most practical way of getting there is by ADO bus from Villahermosa. Next is by second-class bus

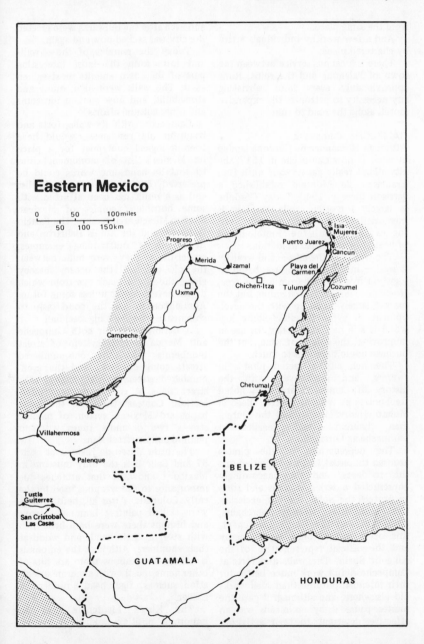

Eastern Mexico

0   50   100 miles

50   100   150km

Progreso

Merida

Izamal

Uxmal

Chichen-Itza

Campeche

Chetumal

Villahermosa

Palenque

BELIZE

Tustla
Guiterrez

San Cristobal
Las Casas

GUATAMALA

HONDURAS

Isla
Mujeres

Puerto Juarez

Cancun

Playa del
Carmen

Tulum

Cozumel

from the same place.

And a few wealthy individuals arrive by chartered plane.

There is local bus service between the town of Palenque and the ruins. Runs approximately every hour, obviating any necessity to patronize the expensive motels along the road to ruin.

CAMPECHE, Campeche

Although Hernández de Córdoba landed at what is now Campeche in 1517, the city didn't really get its start until Don Francisco de Montejo established a garrison there in 1540. Today Córdoba is largely forgotten while Montejo is memorialized in numerous ways, not the least of which is the Montejo brand of beer, down the road in Mérida.

The wealth of the city — and wealthy it was! — in the beginning was based on logwood dye derived from a local tree, *Hoematoxylon campeachianum*, but the market largely dried up with the development of synthetic dies. Some logwood is still harvested today for use in 'improving' the colour of wine, but the business doesn't amount to much.

The rich city attracted pirates in swarms, and interwoven with the history of Campeche are such noted freebooters as William Parker, Diego el Mulato, Henry Morgan and the Dutchman, Laurent Graaf, recalled in Campeche as Lorencillo.

The depredations of the pirates aroused the usual Latin reaction among the residents, and they accordingly constructed a series of walls and forts to protect the noble families, ecclesiastical authorities, wealthy merchants, politicians and the King's Lieutenant, this last a sort of bush-league viceroy and the official representative of the King of Spain. The walls and forts at Campeche didn't work much better for their intended purpose than such works did elsewhere, and although it gave the pirates pause it by no means was an effective deterrant to their activities,

and even after the bulwarks were erected the city was sacked now and again.

Today the remains of those walls and forts form the most interesting part of the town and its most valued asset. The walls were high, bulky and stone-built, and now contain museums and other cultural efforts.

Campeche, with its walls, forts and beautiful old residences, would have been a logical contender for a place on Mexico's list of monument cities so that its handsome works could be preserved, but it never made the list and as a result has been afflicted with some horrible examples of Mexican Modern Miracle architecture. The Palacio Gobierno and the hotels Baluartes and El Presidente outstanding examples, especially as they were built between the old city and the ocean, thereby giving the city a black eye from which it will never recover unless some future Administration has the good taste to commence swinging a big steel ball.

A definite plus for both Campeche and Mérida is their system of street numbering with the odd-numbered streets going one way and the even-numbered streets at right-angles, with street signs at each and every intersection. Contrast this with the usual haphazard Mexican system of naming streets two or more times with no method and no street signs.

The little Museo de Historia at Calle 57 and Calle 8 is the only museum in Mexico I know of that attaches due importance to the weapons used by the early Colonials. After all, before there were skilled painters limning viceroys and bishops there were hard little men with steel in their hands and wood at their shoulders. Although the emphasis is largely on weapons there are lots of other items, mostly with a marine orientation, such as a figurehead, a rudder and a tiller.

The King's Lieutenant had an important position, and lived accord-

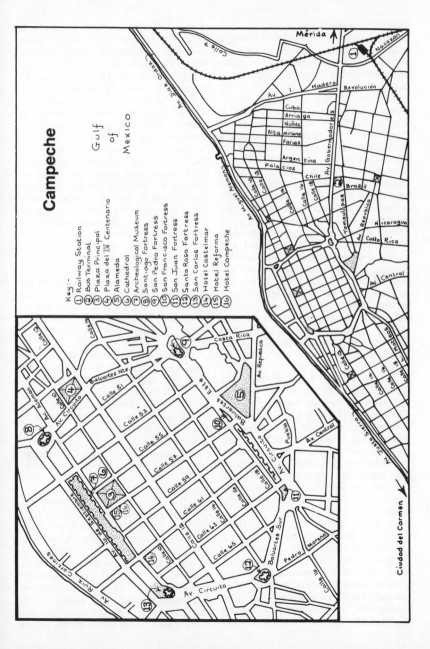

Campeche

Gulf
of
Mexico

Key:-
① Railway Station
② Bus Terminal
③ Plaza Principal
④ Plaza del IV Centenario
⑤ Alameda
⑥ Cathedral
⑦ Archeological Museum
⑧ Santiago Fortress
⑨ San Pedro Fortress
⑩ San Francisco Fortress
⑪ San Juan Fortress
⑫ Santa Rosa Fortress
⑬ San Carlos Fortress
⑭ Hotel Castelmar
⑮ Hotel Reforma
⑯ Hotel Campeche

ingly. If you stroll up Calle 14 you will find La Casa de Tiente del Rey between Calles 59 and 61. Admire the Baroque entrance and the iron-studded door and inspect the interior if you get a chance.

Places to Stay

The arm-and-a-leg-expensive hotel *El Presidente* is a typically over-priced installation on the waterfront below the Water Gate at the foot of Calle 59. Go through the gate and angle through the parking lot on your right. I never have very good luck with Presidente hotels, and the one in Campeche is no exception. My room came with two F ('frio') faucets in the shower, the door to the hall could only be opened part way and cold condensate from the air-conditioning pipes dripped down the back of my neck. All in all not the sort of service one would reasonably expect in any hotel, and most emphatically not in a house where the tab starts at M$850! I stayed there for the best of reasons: arriving rather late in the day in mid-summer I found everything else in town full.

If, when you come through the Water Gate, you head for the big, multi-layered squarish building to your left instead of heading for El Presidente, you will arrive at the *Hotel Baluartes*, which looks brand new, but is around 25 years old. In the same category as the Presidente, it is much better operated and hence fills up much sooner, and although the price is ridiculously expensive it still offers good value for lots of pesos.

It seems as if the elderly *Hotel Castlemar*, on the corner of Calles 8 and 61, has always been a part of the Campeche scene with its large rooms, thick walls and high windows that swing wide to catch the cooling trades of an evening, but nowadays there is a huge, modernistic, tasteless box of a building blocking the view to seaward, but not quite all the breeze. The Castlemar is another hotel built on the bones of an old mansion. Excellent value, moderate price; recommended.

The plaza at Campeche doesn't amount to much as plazas go, which may be the reason the *Hotel Campeche*, on the plaza opposite the church, at Calle 57 and Calle 8, doesn't see fit to jack up its rates. Inexpensive.

The *Hotel Reforma*, on Calle 8 near Calle 57 is an old-fashioned viajero-style house that sometimes hangs its washing in the patio to dry, a homey touch. Usually full of country people, perhaps because the rates are so reasonable. This is the cheapest you can do downtown, which may not be too much of an advantage, considering the size of Campeche. Inexpensive.

The *Hotel Cuauhtémoc*, on Calle 57 at Calle 10, less than a block from the plaza, is another spectacular old mansion fallen into trade. Large rooms, good beds, cane-bottomed chairs in the lobby that are ideal for the tropics. Expensive.

Out on Gobernadores at Calle 45 (also Chile), directly across the street from the bus station, is the *Hotel Central*. A fairly new building with furnishings to match, the Central tends to fill up sooner than other hotels in town. It is popular with bus and truck drivers, for Gobernadores is the road to Mérida once it leaves the Campeche city limits. Expensive.

Places to Eat

The best place to eat in Campeche, by popular agreement, is the *Restaurant Miramar* at Calle 61 and Calle 8. Like the neighbouring Castlemar it seems to have always been a part of Campeche. It has waiters who know their business and offers a good, professionally-prepared meal. The Miramar advertises 'all brands of beer', and I believe it. The wine, however, is grossly overpriced and I have seen fellow diners return bottles that had sat too long upright. (The return was accepted with good grace.) During the afternoon the Miramar fills with affluent locals, often with families in tow. Very expensive, but well worth it for an occasional treat.

The *Cafe Continental*, on Calles 61 and 8, opposite the Miramar, is a small coffee-shop operation that does good business with the bureaucrats working in the upended shoebox across the street. Much cheaper than the Miramar, but with considerably less panache. Moderate.

The restaurant on the ground floor of the *Hotel Campeche*, Calle 57 at Calle 8, facing the plaza, is heavily patronized by working-class local people. Good value for the money. Inexpensive.

Both the *Hotel Baluarte* and the neighbouring *El Presidente* have restaurants. Standard Mexican/international menu and very expensive.

The market is located outside the old city wall on the opposite side of town from the ocean, at the ends of Calles 57 and 59. Because this is a seaside city the food stalls specialize in sea food, and make a good job of it. Cheapest eating in town short of buying the ingredients and dining al fresco. Very inexpensive.

Getting There & Getting Around

Campeche is on the main bus line to and from Yucatán and a large number of buses going to and from Mérida stop here, but many of them are full and the ticket agents don't know how many seats they can sell until the coach arrives.

Campeche also has air service, so if you can't get on a bus you might decide to fly. It is only 176 km by road to Mérida, and I have known several people who failed to get on a bus in reasonable time and pooled their assets and took an air taxi. Contact Viajes Campeche, on Calle 10 between Calles 57 and 59, half a block from the plaza.

Campeche also has railroad service

to Mérida and Mexico City. This is a practical way of getting to Palenque station and quite popular with backpackers as it eliminates going into Villahermosa and doubling back.

To get from the bus station to the Plaza Principal, go out on the heavily-travelled Avenida Gobernadores and turn left. At the first baluarte it changes its name to Calle 18. Stay with it past the market to either Calle 55 or 57. Turn right and the plaza is four blocks away. Walking time is 15 minutes.

MÉRIDA, Yucatán

As with so many of the cities the Spanish built during the early years of the conquest, Mérida is constructed on the remains of a much older Indian city, and the plaza is supposed to have been laid out on the remains of the pyramid that was torn down to provide building material for the homes of the conquerors. Be that as it may, the plaza is extraordinarily attractive and of a size appropriate to the size of the city — about 200 metres square. The story has it that a ship carrying Indian laurels intended to grace the Prado in Habana was wrecked off the Yucatán coast and some of the cargo wound up in Mérida where they still enhance the beauty of the plaza.

For some reason the plaza in Mérida has had more names than any square in Mexico, some of them being Plaza Principal, Plaza de la Constitución, Plaza de Armas and even, on some present-day maps, simply Jardín.

The Cathedral, aside from its size, has little of interest either in the architecture of in the decoration. The only reason to visit it is to see the wooden figure called El Cristo de las Ampollos (the Christ of the Blisters). Apparently it was carved in the village of Ichmul from the wood of a tree that was reported to have burned during the night. A few years later the church which sheltered the Cristo burned, but the image was unharmed except for some blisters. It was brought to its present resting place in 1645. A rip-roaring fiesta is held on 28 September to honour the Christ of the Blisters.

The most imposing of the colonial buildings is the Casa de Montejo, built by the son of the original Montejo. Located on Calle 63 across from the plaza, it was built before anyone thought of such foolishness as equality, and among the decorations on the facade on either side of the entrance are the carved figures of caballeros with a foot on the bowed head of an Indian. The building is now open to the public for the usual few pesos admission fee and should not be overlooked.

Mérida became a very wealthy city through henequén which was used mostly to make cordage. As with any prosperous city the rich men built large and imposing homes for their families, the best collection of these mansions is on and around Paseo de Montejo. To reach the Paseo from the plaza go out Calle 60 to Calle 47 and turn left. The Paseo is between 56 and 58, number 56A under Mérida's street numbering system. About a dozen blocks.

One of the pleasures of Mérida for locals and tourists alike is to load into a calesa drawn by a placid nag and tour the town in dignity and comfort. This is an enjoyable way to see the Paseo de Montejo. The calesas also double as taxis, and it is not at all uncommon to see a countryman and his wife and children and innumerable bundles get out of a calesa in front of the railroad station or one of the bus stations. 'Calesa' is a semi-obsolete Spanish word meaning 'chaise'.

Merida has dozens and dozens of stores, stands and vendors selling craft articles and locally manufactured goods. The 'guayabera' shirts sold all over Mexico are mostly made in tiny backroom factories in the city, although they are just as expensive, or as cheap, in Guadalajara as they are in Yucatán where they are made. In Mérida it seems as if there is a shirt factory or store in every block, and sometimes two or three. One that I like and that marks its prices (many don't) is the Jarana on Calle 62 between Calles 59 and 61.

Mérida does good leather work. One good leathergoods shop with reasonable (and marked) prices is Casa Rubio, on Calle 56A between Calles 63A and 65, across from the post office. This has about everything imaginable in the leather line, including covers for Bic lighters, dozens of wallets and billfolds, passport cases, and belts.

The Casa de las Artesanias del Gobierno del Estado do Yucatán, on Calle 63 between Calles 66 and 64, is entered via the patio of the school. This apparently discourages those few foreigners who have heard of it. A handicraft salesroom that's practically a museum of contemporary Yucatán handmade goods, it has everything a countryman can think of making — hand-made kitchen chairs, mortar and pestle sets, real clay piggy banks, turquoise rings, 'Panamá' hats, and beautiful huipils, just like the girls in the market have been wearing for hundreds of years. All merchandise is price-tagged and is generally of better quality and lower in price than the stuff in the stores and stands around town. The bulk of the customers are local people rather than tourists.

While you're visiting the Casa de las Artesanias spare a few minutes for a stroll around the school buildings housing the shop. It is an art school with interesting displays of students' and instructors' work from time to time. The beautiful old building was originally a monastery and has been tastefully converted.

So-called 'Panamá' hats are woven around Mérida out of henequén fibre. This is the fibre used to make sisal

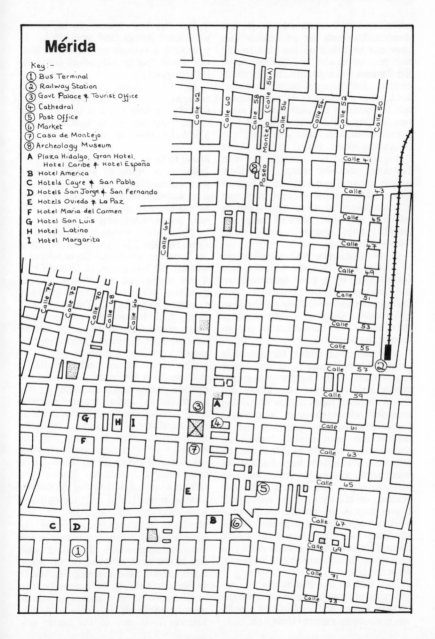

Mérida

Key :-

① Bus Terminal
② Railway Station
③ Govt Palace & Tourist Office
④ Cathedral
⑤ Post Office
⑥ Market
⑦ Casa de Montejo
⑧ Archeology Museum

A Plaza Hidalgo, Gran Hotel,
   Hotel Caribe & Hotel España
B Hotel America
C Hotels Cayre & San Pablo
D Hotels San Jorge & San Fernando
E Hotels Oviedo & La Paz
F Hotel Maria del Carmen
G Hotel San Luis
H Hotel Latino
I Hotel Margarita

ropes, and it is extremely tough and durable. The hats are so flexible that they can be rolled up for packing and still recover nicely. The Spanish word for Panama hat is jipijapa, locally shortened to 'jipi'. The pochismo for 'hippy' is also 'jipi', which can cause confusion and occasionally ill feelings when someone touting for a store walks up to a bearded tourist and says 'Jipi? Jipi?'

Anyone that looks at all like a foreigner will be invited to shirt factories, jewellery shops, jipi warehouses — you name it. It is best to ignore these types because they get a commission on every sale, which is added to the selling price of the goods. Another good reason to avoid shops without price tags.

A popular item with travellers are the hammocks that are actually used for sleeping by a good percentage of the residents of the Peninsula, both Indian and otherwise. They are the ideal hot-weather sleeping arrangement as they allow free circulation of air all around the body.

The hammock, widely thought of as originating in Yucatán, is an import from Haiti, and before hammocks people slept on straw mats. Many still do. In Yucatán today hammock-making occupies whole families. Hammocks come in three sizes, generally: single, double and matrimonial. Inspect all three sizes so you will be able to tell the difference. Although they are sold in many stores and on the street, the best place to buy a hammock is at the big market, or at the Casa de Artesanias. If you shop in the market, compare the workmanship, sizes and prices because all three vary from stand to stand. Remember that in these hammocks you lie diagonally, not fore-and-aft as people do in the US.

The bulk of the hammocks you see are made of henequén and are what the country folk — and a lot of city people, too — use every night of their lives.

But the best hammocks are made with linen strings, and you can bet if you find a flax-strung hammock that the workmanship will be of the very highest quality.

If you need photographic-size batteries, the Foto-Mercado on Calle 67 between Calles 58 and 56 has a good stock. These are rather hard to find in Mérida for some reason.

Places to Stay

Despite the influx of well-off tourists who automatically opt for the expensive hotels, restaurants and so on, Mérida is well supplied with more modestly priced establishments.

The *Hotel España* is on the little Plaza Hidalgo (also known as the Plaza de Jesús and the Parque Cepeda Peraza) on Calle 60 between calles 59 and 61. It is an unrestored grandhouse that is definitely worth viewing on its merits as a prime example of Yucatán's past glory. With its spacious rooms, grand staircase and fine old doors it would be an ideal place to spend a month or two some winter. Very expensive.

The *Hotel Posada Central*, Calle 55 at Calle 48, is across the street from the railroad station and is an oddity in this age of highway and air travel — a newish hotel constructed to serve the needs of rail travellers. It is admittedly quite some distance from the plaza, but this could be an advantage under crowded conditions that can fill all the hotels in town mighty sudden. Regard the Central as an ace-in-the-hotel. Moderate.

The *Hotel D'Farahon*, on Calle 65 between Calle 56 and Calle 54, is a climb-one-flight-to-the-lobby sort of place with the redeeming virtues of low rents and convenience. The other buildings in the block are being rebuilt one at a time and I have a feeling that the D' Farahon will shortly be renewed out of business, or at least into a couple of price ranges higher, but until that happens it is one of the better low-budget hostels. Inexpensive.

The *Hotel America*, on Calle 67 between Calles 58 and 60, is a few blocks off the plaza, but not far enough to take the glow off the price. Inexpensive.

The *Hotel la Paz*, on Calle 62 between Calles 65 and 67, is a big old barn of a converted town house. It's about the same vintage as the ridiculously expensive hotel Colón a few blocks up the street and there the similarities end. The Paz is essentially a family hotel for the unrich people from Progresso who arrive by bus, and is a rarity this close to downtown because it is inexpensive.

The *Hotel Oviedo*, on Calle 62 between Calles 65 and 67 in the same block as the Paz, is a little fancier but also a little more expensive as well. Popular with European travellers, but I have never encountered an American on the premises, and I don't know why. Moderate.

The main bus station in Mérida has been there long enough to accumulate a number of small hotels.

Turn right on Calle 68 as you leave the station and the *Hotel Alamo* is at the end of the block. During the summer vacation rush the Alamo is very likely to be full, but it is always worth a try because it is inexpensive and economy hotels aren't really all that thick on the ground in Mérida these days.

Across from the entrance to the bus station on Calle 69 is the *Hotel San Jorge*, all new and blue tiled. Looks expensive, to say the least, but surprisingly it isn't. Recommended, but if you're bothered by noise, take a back room. (Calle 69 carries most of Mérida's heavy bus traffic, although there are no night buses and the station actually closes up tight during the wee small hours.) Moderate.

Also across the street from the entrance to the Central de Autobuses is the tiny lobby of the *Hotel San Fernando*, easy to overlook in spite of the coating of blue and white paint on the facade. Usually full, but like the Alamo, worth a try. Inexpensive.

On the corner to the left of the bus station from the entrance is the *Hotel San Pablo*. It prefers family rentals, but outside the busy season occasionally rents both singles and doubles. The white with brown trim paint job doesn't do much for this Mexican Monstrosity, but then, what could? Inexpensive for groups.

Places to Eat

The best shot for an economical breakfast for the early-risers are the two bakeries near the plaza. The one on the plaza itself at the corner of Calle 63 and Calle 62 is better known and has a larger assortment of goodies, but the other one, on Calle 61 between Calles 58 and 60, has a refresco machine so that their customers can buy a bottle of Coca or whatever to wash down their pan dulces. Very inexpensive.

As always the market is the place to go for really low-cost eating. There are really two markets in Mérida. The one fronting on Calle 60 is called a 'bazar' and sells clothing, shoes, hardware, etc, and very little in the way of food.

The other market is behind the bazar and handles the food items. Walk over on Calle 67 and continue straight up a ramp and into the market building. At the head of the incline turn left and you will find a row of food stalls selling both Mexican and Yucateco dishes. Good place for arroz con pollo, liver and onions, eggs ranch style and so on. Inexpensive. (If you turn right at the top of the ramp you will encounter another well-stocked artesanias complex, this one mostly specializing in silver, watches and other costly gift items.)

Les Balcons Pizzeria y Restaurante and Health Foods Place is on Calle 60 between Calles 57 and 59. I like this one — it is so seldom that one encounters a sign in three different languages! This is an upstairs joint, rather more interestingly furnished than the usual Mexican hash house. It is also more expensive than most vegetarian restaurants, and they sell wine and beer, plus some meat dishes for the omnivorous among us. Menu in English (sort of) and Spanish.

The *Plaza Hidalgo* (Plaza de Jesús, etc), on Calle 60 between Calles 59 and 61, has been upgraded by paving the street level with the curbs and barring motor vehicles except for taxis supposedly delivering passengers to one of the hotels on the plaza. The paved-over space has been converted into a sort of sidewalk cafe sans sidewalk. Depending on where you choose to sit, your food and drink will be brought to the castiron tables from either the Hotel España or the Hotel Caribe. As with all setups along these lines it is more a place for chatting, smoking, talking and drinking than it is for serious eating, but a very enjoyable place to idle away a few evening hours.

Los Almedros, located out toward the railroad station on Calle 59 between Calles 50 and 52, is easily the best-known restaurant in Mérida. The famous local specialty, poc-chuc, originated here, and if you like poc-chuc this is the place for you, but it is just one of the things the Almedros does right well. It has atmosphere in abundance and isn't all that expensive, much cheaper in fact than dozens of other places around town that give you less and charge more. Expensive, and worth every peso of it.

Mexican cities with extensive bus traffic and centralized bus stations ordinarily sprout small eating houses like porcupines sprout quills, but Mérida has very few restaurants in the station area, and not because the bus station restaurant is so good, either.'

The best place near the station, and a pretty good workingman's restaurant in any league, is the *Restaurant y Cocteleria la Terminal*, to the right and across the street as you leave the station it is about 75 metres away but can't be seen from the station exit. The 'Cocteleria' part of the name refers to seafood cocktails (not the martini variety), and the Terminal is one of the few restaurants that clings to the fine old Latin-American custom of giving the customer a snack with his bottle of beer. Inexpensive and recommended.

The food at la Terminal is well worth crossing the street for, especially when compared to the horrible concoctions at the bus station greasy spoon. Most of la Terminal's customers are people who live in Mérida, and not necessarily bus passengers. For economical eating during the evening, a good bet is *Las Mil Tortas* on Calle 62 between Calles 65 and 67, across the street from the Progresso bus station. There are only 15 tortas, not 1000 as indicated by the name, but they are real whoppers, piping-hot filling on a heated bolillo. Very inexpensive.

The little restaurant on the ground floor of the *Hotel America*, on Calle 67 between Calles 60 and 58, is another place to have a reasonably economical evening meal. It will cost a bit more than Las Mil Tortas, but the menu is somewhat more extensive. Another place that does liver well, and I have had excellent huevos motuleños several times. Inexpensive.

Getting There & Getting Around

To get downtown from the main bus station, turn left as you leave the building, then right at the corner on Calle 69. In four blocks turn left on Calle 62 and follow it three blocks to the plaza. Walking time is 15 minutes.

If you happen to arrive somehow for the first time from Progreso on a bus, simply turn right as you leave the station and the plaza is a couple of blocks straight ahead. Walking time: five minutes.

Arriving in Mérida by air is increasingly popular, especially from Miami and other southern US cities. The regular fares are relatively economical because of the short distances involved, and discount fares bring the price down even more. From Yucatán the flight to Oaxaca avoids a long and often uncomfortable bus ride, and Mexico City is only a couple of hours away by jet, whereas the trip by bus or train can eat up the best part of a couple of days. Consult your travel agent for latest schedules and fares.

Railfans will enjoy the train trip between Mérida and Mexico City; most people won't. The pullman fare (at present) is M\$1201, but the first-class fare is only M\$412. If you must cut expenses to the bone, and have survived the trains of Turkey, India or Indonesia, you can pay only M\$246 for second-class but this is a hard way to travel.

Regardless of where you ride on the train, be sure to pack a good-sized lunch that will hold you for a couple of days. There is no dining car on the train, of course, and the hawkers who swarm aboard now and then never seem to be around when the hunger pangs strike. The schedule calls for a 37-hour trip, but I have never heard of the train actually arriving in Mexico City on time, and five to eight hours off the advertised is about par for the course.

To get to the plaza from the railroad station, go out the front of the building and through the gate on your right and keep right on going on calle 55 to Calle 60. Turn left on 60 and three more blocks will bring you to the plaza. Walking time: 20 minutes.

PROGRESO, Yucatán

Very few visitors to Mérida make the short 33-km trip down to Progreso. In fact, not too many of the travellers have even heard of the place, which is a pity because it makes an enjoyable side trip for people who have seen too many ruins and are tired of loafing around the Plaza Hidalgo.

Progreso was, up until the late 1940s, a wealthy and thriving community, its economy based on henequén, one of the most profitable and least labour-intensive of all agricultural crops. Because the slope of the pretty, sandy beach is so gradual, one of the last things Progreso did before the bubble burst was to construct a long concrete finger pier that can handle several of the largest ocean-going freighters at a time. The pier juts about two km into the Gulf of Mexico and is a fine place to fish.

The henequén industry was killed by the development of synthetic fibres, but not before it had made millionaires by the dozen. Many of these wealthy families built palatial homes on Progreso's Malecón, along the shore to the right of the main street as you approach the ocean. Although a few casual travellers wind up in Progreso, rarely do they discover these beautiful old mansions. Most take one look up and down the unimpressive main street and head back for Mérida.

For the beach enthusiast Progreso has many km of fabulous south-sea-island-type beach, with palm trees that sway in the trade winds, smooth sand, and a sloping bottom that allows you to wade out 300 metres in places before the water gets up to your shoulders. The best of the beaches are found out toward Chicxulub, five or six km along the beach to the east of Progreso. A good road parallels the beach.

I learned about Progreso from two young travellers who come to Progreso every winter and spend three or four months camping on the beach, coming into town every three or four days for supplies, which didn't cost them very much because they were both enthusiastic fishermen.

Places to Eat
Most people don't spend enough time in Progreso to discover the really good restaurant on the zócolo. The *Córdobes* is famous among the better-heeled locals. Most seaside restaurants specialise in sea food and pretty well neglect anything else, but the Córdobes has a rather extensive menu and its prices are surprisingly reasonable. Moderate.

On the main drag as you come in from Mérida, on the right hand side, is a new-looking seafood restaurant with lots of plastic in the decor. This is *Soberanis*, part of the chain of sea food restaurants that started in Mérida and now even include a resort hotel or two. The Soberanis is higher in price and a little lower in quality than the Córdobes down on the square, but appeals to people more satisified with Denny's and Howard Johnson than funky Mexican restaurants. Expensive.

Getting There
Most people get to Progresso on the shuttle buses that leave Mérida from their own station on Calle 62 between Calles 65 and 67. Several buses an hour make the 30-40 minute run down to Progreso.

The railfans occasionally catch a local train from the railroad station on Calle 55 at Calle 48. This is a slow, slow train, usually taking a couple of hours or more.

CHICHÉN-ITZÁ, Yucatán
This is one of the best-known, most popular, and attractive ruins in Mexico and its very popularity contributes greatly to its attraction because the site is such a money-maker for the Republic that a good deal of money is expended in maintaining the grounds, thus making it ever more attractive to more and more visitors.

Chichén-Itzá is one of the premier Maya — and Toltec — ruins, and if you are only going to see one ruin in Southeast Mexico, then by all means make it Chichen.

There are guidebooks in Spanish, English, French and German available both in Merida and at the site itself. They go into a great deal of detail and are heartily recommended, but in case you don't get a guidebook, here are a few 'must see' highlights:
El Castillo The largest building in the complex, built atop still another pyramid with rooms within. The Castillo was, among other things, important in astronomical calculations.
Chichan-Chob Hieroglyphic on inside of the upper chamber, thought to be pure Mayan.
El Caracol So called from its snail-shaped interior stairs. Astronomical observatory with holes in the walls here and there that were used in making calculations.
Temple of the Warriors Really a complex in itself, with courtyards, colonnades, pyramids and so on.
Ball Court Two walls 83 metres long, and the usual stone rings approximately 7.3 metres above the ground and 46 cm inside diameter. The object of the game was to drive a ball through the ring using only the elbows, feet and knees. The captain of the losing team lost his head.
Cenote Of great interest to the modern tourist, for in order to propitiate the gods all sorts of valuable items were thrown into its depths, including gold, silver and jade jewellery, and young virgins (female I assume). One Edward Thompson, who bought the whole shebang for US$75 in 1885, dredged the Sacred Well and brought up buckets of skeletons, medals, gold bells and a large quantity of jade. He shipped the bulk of his finds to the Peabody Museum in Boston; not too long ago the Peabody sent some of the treasure back to Mexico.

Places to Stay

There are a number of hotels in the area because Chichén is a fantastic people magnet, but they are too expensive for my taste, some of them running to over M$1000 a day.

I prefer to get a bus to Piste, check into the *Posada Novelo* and use it as my base of operation, rather than to commute from Mérida every day. The Novelo is certainly no Rodeway Inn, but it is moderately priced and only about 3½ km from the site, less than an hour's walk.

Another way to go that several wayfarers have recommended is to book a room in Valladolid and then commute the 30 km to the ruins by bus. I have been told that there is no problem in finding a moderately priced room in Valladolid, but I have never had occasion to try this scheme for myself.

Getting There

Chichén-Itzá is about 122 km east of Mérida on the heavily-travelled road to Valladolid and Cancún, a route with considerable through bus traffic, so ordinarily getting out to the site from Mérida is not a problem. When things are crowded, as can happen during the summer and winter 'seasons', taking a more expensive tour out from town may be preferable to standing and sweltering for several hours in the non-air conditioned bus station with not even a fan to stir the hot, sticky, smelly and humid air.

UXMAL, Yucatán

Uxmal, about 60 km south of Mérida, is much smaller than Chichén-Itzá, and a great deal more has been done to make it attractive to the visitor. For instance, there are two light-and-sound shows every evening, the first at 7 pm in Spanish, the second at 9 pm in English.

Because it covers such a small area, about 1000 by 700 metres, it is easy to take in Uxmal in a single day, and if you have only a day to spend I'd choose Uxmal and see all of it, rather than going out to Chichén-Itzá and only seeing a part, and a small part of it at that.

Uxmal is somewhat harder to reach than Chichén, as it is not on a main-travelled road. There are buses but not all that many. From Mérida, catch a bus bound for Hopelchen, Campeche, or a Campeche bus that goes down highway 180. Buy a ticket to Uxmal if they will sell it to you, or Santa Elena, 14 km beyond, and unload at the ruins.

Most of the buses that ply this part of the world don't adhere to any particular schedule, so you may have quite a wait on the return leg of the journey. Alternatively, you can continue on to Campeche after you've finished ruin-seeing.

There is no nearby town to Uxmal (such as Piste near Chichén), and though hotels have sprung up over the years to milk the tourist traffic they have all been dreadfully dear at M$500 a day or more. The restaurant situation isn't much better, and this is another place where a well-planned picnic lunch is definitely in order.

Because of the transport problems, Uxmal is one of the few instances I would recommend taking a tour at any time of the year, mostly for the transport end of the deal. I try to avoid getting a tour with lunch included, preferring to take my own. There are lots of tour companies in Mérida, so shop around. I have had the best luck with the Yucatán Travel Service, with a main office up on the Paseo de Montejo at 475-C, Suite 12. (They have a toll-free US telephone number: (800) 241-7257.) The Uxmal tour from Mérida will cost about US$20, without lunch.

IZAMAL, Yucatán

Izamal is only about 70 km by road from Mérida, but it might just as well be on the other side of Mars as far as the average tourist is concerned. It appears in few guidebooks which is a great shame, because Izamal has a good deal to offer.

The principal item of interest is the great Convent of Izamal, built on a huge Maya pyramid on the theory that the existence of a Christian church could discourage the Indians from their 'devil-worship'.

The Convent has a huge open patio surrounded with portales, and has a sort of restful calm reflecting its great age — it was built in the middle 1500s and is one of the oldest convents in the Americas. It is located along one side of the plaza, and some distance across the plaza from the convent is a mostly-unrestored pyramid called Kinch-Kama.

There are lots of pyramids in the area (there are thousands on the Yucatán Peninsula) and if you can persuade the sexton to permit you to climb up in the tower of the church you will be able to see mound after mound, each covered with lush jungle growth, and every one representing a Mayan pyramid or other structure.

There is a park beside the convent, and the new market-place is on the street that runs between the convent and the park.

Getting There

The best way to get to Izamal is by the mixed train that leaves from Mérida station at Calles 55 and 48. You don't have to be a railfan to enjoy this little narrow-gauge lechero as it winds through flat henequén fields, likely stopping at such places at Tixkob, Cacalchén and Tekanto to load and unload freight and country people bearing immense bundles of henequén fibre, hats, or huipils, with now

and then a live turkey or a few hens or fighting cocks thrown in.

Unless you'd like to repeat the trip I suggest you make the return leg by bus. You can catch a bus direct to Mérida, or if the wait happens to be too long, catch a bus by the plaza for Hoctún.

Hoctún is on the Mérida-Valladolid road and catches a lot of traffic. The buses to Hoctún from Izamal go two different routes, either 23 km via Kimbila, or 38 km via Kantunil.

CANCÚN, Quintana Roo

Cancún is really two separate places. The resort area is a sandspit called the Zona Hoteleria, located on a former island sticking out into the clear waters of the Caribbean Sea. The other Cancún is the Zona Comercial (or Comercio) which is the business and residential area for the employees of the big hotels, plus a huge number of stores selling duty-free merchandise.

Some years back the Mexican Government commissioned a computer study to determine the ideal location for all-new resorts, and Cancun came up heads! Since then, construction has gone on apace, and today there is practically a solid line of huge, expensive hotels along the Zona Hoteleria. The fancy hotels start at about M$750 a day and up — way up! — and are kept full by an astute publicity campaign that never ends, witness the 'Third World Conferences' in late 1981. (For these conferences, by the way, the regular paying guests were all evicted.)

If it weren't for the original resort at Isla Mujeres (described later) the whole eastern end of the Yucatán Peninsula would be a total loss for the casual wayfarer.

If you go out of the bus station and around the left end of the building, across the heavily-travelled street and then turn left again, you will be on a shopping street where everything from an otoscope to a Crescent wrench is available at about 50-100% over State-side prices. This is a free zone and the merchandise is intended for consumption by Mexicans who often come great distances to do their shopping along here. Many US tourists on package tours really lap all this up, apparently under the misconception that they are getting a bargain. They aren't!

Places to Stay & Eat

The hotels out in the Zona Hoteleria are, of course, breathtakingly expensive, but the mainland hotels are expensive, too. The cheapest room I could find was M$300 and booked solid for the remainder of that year and part of the next.

The answer to this sad state of affairs is to go out to Isla Mujeres and commute. You will get the same water and identical sandy beaches, but different hotel rates.

The eating situation is somewhat rosier because although the local people never stay in a hotel, they do eat in low-price restaurants.

To start with the *bus station restaurant:* usually crowded with refesco drinkers. As a place for anything else it is definitely not recommended!

If you go left out of the bus station, around the side, and look across the busy street (technically it is Uxmal, but Cancún hasn't gotten around to installing street signs) you will see a store called El Triunfo. The restaurant *Leonardo* is on the other side of the Triunfo, a ray of hope for the bus travellers who need a fairly quick meal. Leonardo specialises in such Yucateno delecacies as cocinata de la plancha and the inevitable poc-chuc. And best of all, the Casablanca fans under the palapa lean-to not only stir up a much-needed breeze but also manage to hold the flies at bay. A restaurant with class aspirations, Leonardo even has custom-made ash trays emblazoned with its

name. Moderate.

If you go right from the bus station instead of left, and then turn left on the boulevard, you will be on Avenida Tulum. Go along Tulum about two blocks and you will come to a big bakery that has everything you can imagine in the way of baked goods, from bread to exquisite pan dulces, for an economical picnic. Inexpensive.

A few doors beyond the bakery is the *Restaurant Veracruz* which rarely ever sees a tourist. Strictly a local for locals, and more Mexican than Yucateco, its the kind of place where the lady who cooks will waddle out of the kitchen if she suspects you didn't enjoy your order. Best go in Cancún Comercial. Clean unisex toilet (bring your own paper, of course). Moderate.

If you continue walking for about 10 minutes out Tulum toward Puerto Juárez you arrive at the cross-road where the Juárez road branches right. Here you will find the *Centro Comercial del Crucero*, a small public market, and at the far end of the complex there are a number of typical market-place food stalls. I like the *Restaurant Iciatel*, even if it doesn't sell beer and has a gigantic juke box prominently displayed (although I have never seen anyone play it). Very inexpensive.

Getting There & Getting Around

Cancún has a busy international airport, with flights to various places in the US and Europe, as well as Mexico City and other spots in the Republic. Local carriers also fly to Cozumel, which can be a great time-saver over a bus down to Playa del Carmen, some 70 km, and then waiting for the ferry to Cozumel before finally embarking on the 50-minute voyage out to the Island.

Cancún is the terminus for buses from Mérida on the east and Chetumal on the south, and there are regular buses for Mexico City. Persons intending to stop off at Palenque or Oaxaca are best advised to buy a ticket to Villahermosa and catch another bus to their destination.

At the end of the curve that brings Uxmal into Tulum street, near the Mexicana office, there is a shop renting small, fat-tyred Honda 90 motorcycles. This is the economical and time-saving way of exploring Cancún, Cozumel and the surrounding country, including the several Mayan ruins. But bear in mind that motorcycles are designed to carry one person and not to be ridden two-up. If there are two of you, rent two scooters — the additional safety factor is well worth the slight extra cost.

PUERTO JUÁREZ, Quintana Roo

Because of the tourist development, Cancún has greatly outgrown Puerto Juárez, and it will probably come as a surprise to many visitors to the area to discover that Puerto Juárez is far the older of the two. It is about three km from Cancún and is the place to get the ferry to Isla Mujeres.

Places to Stay

The *Motel Isabel* is the type of business that springs up to take advantage of people in a bind. Their customers are travellers who miss the last boat to Isla Mujeres and have to stay on the mainland, so the Isabel charges Cancún Comercial hotel rates and give as little as legally possible in return: no towels, no hot water, no pillow slips, inefficient maid service, and rates that are ridiculously expensive.

Slightly better, but not much, is the *Los Faroles* which at least has hot water most of the time. Both the Isabel and the Faroles are hard by the ferry landing.

The moral of the story: don't miss the last ferry, which leaves for Isla Mujeres slightly before dusk — the boats don't run at night.

Getting There

There is city bus service from Cancún direct to the ferry landing. To get out from Cancún catch a Ruta 3 bus on Avenida Tulum or Avenida Cobá, the road that runs out along the sandspit among the fancy and expensive hotels. To get into Cancún from Juárez, catch a Ruta 3 Hoteleria bus where it turns around in the parking lot by the ferry landing. Tell the driver when you board whether you are going out to the Zona Hoteleria or just into the town of Cancún — the trip out to the hotels calls for an extra fare.

Puerta Juárez is the end of the line for many long-haul buses coming from Valladolid, Chetumal and Mérida, rather than Cancún proper, so getting there is no problem at all for many tourists.

When arriving at the Cancún bus station it will be necessary to go out one of the front doors and turn right across the divided boulevard and catch a bus going from right to left. It will be necessary to walk with the flow of traffic a little distance to the bus stop — parada.

ISLA MUJERES, Quintana Roo

There are a couple of stories about how this island got its name, both aphocryphal. The first tale has it that when the Spaniards arrived on the scene they found a number of terra-cotta figurines, most emphatically feminine. The second relates how the old-time pirates used to leave their women there while they went to sea. Personally, I lean to the first version, but vouch for neither.

Isla Mujeres is the nicest place on the Yucatán Peninsula from the point of view of the average traveller. Progreso is superior in many ways, but in Progreso you have to speak Spanish, be a loner, or import a companion, whereas in Isla Mujeres you can always find someone to talk to in your native language.

One of Mujeres' attractions is that

although it has allowed itself to succumb to a considerable extent to the lure of the Yankee dollar — and the French franc, British pound, Swiss franc and what have you — it still derives its primarly income from the sea. Aquatic-minded visitors find the fantastically clear surrounding waters the ideal place for skin diving, either off the beach or off a rented boat. This being Mexico, nobody seems to have given serious consideration to scuba diving facilities. There are lots of beaches within easy walking distance of the low-priced hotels near the ferry landing.

Aside from sun, sea and sand, there isn't a hell of a lot to do on Isla Mujeres.

The popular excursion is to go out to the 'fort', supposedly built by a slaver named Mundaca. This is the romantic story. (The real story is perhaps more romantic.) Mundaca was a slaver, all right, but when the US abolished slavery and the black ivory business fell on its face, Mundaca retired to Isla Mujeres and built himself an elaborate hacienda. Following the custom of the times and the Latin temperament, his house was his castle and was built as one. He was supposed to have fallen in love with a lady who married another, and shortly thereafter he died, though of a fever rather than unrequited love. He expired in Mérida, and eventually the purpose of his abandoned hacienda was forgotten and people started calling it a fort. Today the place sits in isolated splendour on the opposite end of the island from the town, and Fermin Mundaca de Marechaja, according to his wishes, lies in the little graveyard on the island.

A bit beyond the fort, at the southern tip of the island, there is a lighthouse and a small site of Mayan ruins. The ruins are said to have outlasted no less than four lighthouses. Just before reaching the lighthouse is a fairly secluded beach, Garrafon.

Isla Mujeres is really a rather small island, being only about eight km long and rather less than half that wide and shaped a bit like a lacrosse racquet. For practical purposes it is surrounded by beaches.

The town and the island carry the same names, but somehow this never seems to cause any confusion. The town has a plaza, but unlike most Mexican communities this is not the focus of the town; the ferry dock is, and it is possible to spend a week's vacation on Isla Mujeres and never visit the plaza.

Because of the almost total lack of activity, reading is a popular pastime on Mujeres, and there is even a book store there, of sorts. To the left and across the Malacón as you leave the passenger ferry is the Flea Market, a sort of weird general store carrying all kinds of gimcrackery and a fair assortment of English-language paperbacks. Also, some of the more thoughtful inkeepers make a practice of collecting books left behind by departing guests and reserving them for future arrivals.

Places to Stay

Because the airport on Mujeres is too small to accommodate the larger planes, the island is not afflicted with too many wealthy travellers or package tour operators, with the result is that Mujeres has a goodly supply of reasonably-priced housing, in marked contrast to Cozumel and Cancún.

Straight ahead as you leave the passenger ferry is the *Hotel el Paso*. It has no electric sign, so it might be a little difficult to locate in the dark if you happen to catch a late last ferry, but during the day the white front with red trim will help you locate it.

The bulk of the viajero hotels are pretty close together on Madero, reached by going left on the Malacon as you leave the passenger ferry dock, then right up the next street.

The *Hotel Ma Jose*, called 'Maria' by the islanders, is about 15 metres up Madero. Don't be discouraged by all the weary bicycles in the lobby and out front. They are for rent and do not belong to the guests. Almost all the rooms have their individual balconies. The hotel is a concrete block construction, beige with tile trim. Moderate.

A few metres beyond the Maria is the *Hotel Martinez*, with pale green front and brown and yellow tiled patio perimeter. It makes a point of saving books left behind for future roomers. I saw books in English, Spanish, German, French and Italian. Moderate.

On the corner above the Martinez is the *Hotel Osario*, the best hotel in the immediate area. The Osario is well maintained, and looks somewhat newer than it actually is. Expensive, but good value for money.

In the upper end of Madero is the *Hotel San Luis*, which looks like a motel but isn't. It is a member of the Mexican Hotel Association that actually charges reasonable rates. Unfortunately it is set up for the family and group trade and accepts no singles when things are busy. It's another place with the foresight to establish a small paperback lending library. For groups who split the tab among themselves, the San Luis is inexpensive.

If you turn left when you come to the Hotel San Luis, and then right at Ciro's Lobster House you will find the *Poc-na* on the right side of the street at the end of the block. This is a hostel-type operation, extremely popular with European travellers who are more inclined to carry sleeping equipment than Americans. There is a pleasant palapa-shaded patio for eating, drinking and making new friends. Meals, beer and wine are available. For those with their own sleeping bag, the Poc-na is inexpensive; without sleeping equipment it can be downright expensive.

Places to Eat

If you continue straight on past Ciro's Lobster House, away from Madero, you will find yourself at the city market in a couple of blocks or so. Not a very big market, but then, Mujeres isn't a very big town. Fish is naturally a big item with the lunch stands, and very inexpensive.

Across the street is the sit-down restaurant *Loncharia Chely*. In common with the rest of Mujeres' restaurants this is primarily a sea-food establishment, but they also do a prime job with their breakfast eggs. Unusual for this leisurely end of Mexico, the Chely opens bright and early. Inexpensive.

As you stroll off the ferry dock you will see the restaurant *Villa del Mar* on the corner of the Malacón in front of you. This is a good spot for a cooling draught taken in air-conditioned comfort, but other than this, I'd skip the Villa del Mar as the service is slow and the food over-priced. Expensive.

If you turn right as you leave the ferry, at the end of the block on the Malacón you come to the *Restaurant Tropicana*, a true-blue seafood house that doesn't even bother to list that Mexican standard, encheladas, on their menu. Most of the patrons are local workmen, fishermen and boatmen. Moderate.

Straight up the hill from the dock, past the Hotel el Paso, is an *ice cream parlour* that has been turned into a restaurant by a Japanese-Mexican family, probably because they ran out of ice cream. The upper walls are lined with intriguing posters advertising such specialties of the house as '3 marias', 'Dixies' and 'La Copa de Olvida'. (This was apparently non-alcoholic, but the very name, 'The Cup of Forgetfulness', bothers the hell out of me. I've tried for years to get any one of the above, but the answer is always 'No hay' which in Mexico deserves to be set to music.) Widely varied food menu. Moderate.

If you feel in the mood to put on a bit of dog, *Ciro's Lobster House* is a good choice. Food and service are the best in town short of going out to one of the fancy hotels. Convenient to all the hotels mentioned above. Expensive.

Up on Madero, in the next block above the Hotel Osario, is the wee *Panadería la Reina*, a small bakery popular with wanderers and residents for the reasonably-priced bakery items and for its table and chairs where customers can have coffee and consume their purchases on the premises — the nearest thing Isla Mujeres has to a coffee house. Very inexpensive.

Getting There
It is possible to fly to Isla Mujeres from Cancún by air taxi, though I must admit I have never met anyone who has done so. It is somewhat more practical to fly from Cozumel to Mujeres because both are islands and getting from one to the other will take a minimum of around three hours by surface transport, but again I have yet to meet a person who has done so. The carrier is Aerocaribe.

Several passenger ferries and one car ferry haul thousands of passengers a day each way from Puerto Juárez to Isla Mujeres. The trip through the clear blue water takes 45-55 minutes.

Passenger ferries run about every hour. The fare in 1981 was M\$20. They habitually run grossly overloaded and there is no evidence at all of life preservers.

The US-made automobile ferry doesn't actually leave from Puerto Juárez — it docks at Punta Sam, a few km farther along the beach. The car ferry hauls passengers at a lower rate than the passenger ferries, but the dock is rather hard to reach and the ferries sail only about three times a day, so it strikes me that this is rather a hard way to save M\$10.

Although Isla Mujeres isn't very big, lots of visitors rent bicycles to get around and to visit the fort, Garrafon or the lighthouse. The bicycles don't cost too much on a per-day basis, but if one will be needed for any great length of time it is advisable to buy one and resell it when parting time arrives. A couple of locals rent little Honda nifty-fifty step-through motorcycles.

COZUMEL, Quintana Roo
The third of Mexico's Caribbean resorts is located on the Isla Cozumel, a fairly large island about the same distance from the mainland as Isla Mujeres. It is Mexico's largest island and was occupied by a few fishermen and a small military and airforce detachment until 'discovered' by Holiday magazine.

It was originally discovered by the Spaniard Juan de Grijalva in 1518 and was at that time occupied by a few Mayas. There are many ruins on the island, indicating that there was at one time a fairly large population. During WW II the US built an airfield on the Island — Mexico was one of the Allied Nations — and the same field, somewhat enlarged, is in use today.

Until the relatively recent popularity the town of Cozumel was known as San Miguel, or San Miguel de Cozumel, and you will still hear the old name once in a while, but mostly it is known as Cozumel by native and foreigner alike. The plaza is straight up the street from the dock and isn't really up to the prosperity of the town, but then most of the people who come to Cozumel by direct flight from such places as Houston, Miami and Los Angeles, probably don't have any particular feeling for plazas.

As with the rest of Quintana Roo, the island is still a free zone insofar as customs duties go, even though Quintana Roo has been a state for several years now. There are a number of 'Importaciones' shops that do a thriving business with the package tour customers, but Mexicans rarely make the trip out to the island as everything there is available three times over in Cancún with a lot less hassle.

In common with the rest of the Caribbean, the waters around Cozumel teem with marine life, and the water is warm and crystal-clear. Diving is excellent and scuba and other equipment can be rented. The Mexican government has conservation laws prohibiting the taking of certain marine animals, and these laws are enforced. Find out what is permitted before you put a spear through a fish or break off a coral branch. Remember, Mexicans don't believe in rehabilitating an offender, but they do believe in punishment as a deterrant. A foreigner who runs afoul of the conservation laws is unlikely to repeat his error when he hits the street again some time later.

Cozumel has miles and miles of white-sand beach, and by federal law the beaches are public property and anyone can use them. Some of the most attractive beaches are quite isolated, and many foreigners are tempted to try nude bathing. My advice: don't. The same thing that happened to the party of foreigners in Puerto Peñasco can happen in Cozumel, although I will agree that the Islanders are somewhat more blase about the antics of gringos than most Mexicans.

Places to Stay & Eat
You might expect Cozumel to have lots of facilities for the unrich, but such is far from the case, and the few small hotels with anything at all like peoples' prices are not only usually full but also have length waiting lists. In all probability there will be no economical rooms available. On two recent visits I've tried to locate an inexpensive place to stay with no luck at all. For what it is worth, there is the *Posada Letty* on Calle 1 Sur, not far from the

zócolo, it is very expensive, which is economical in Cozumel.

The *Hotel Posada Cozumel* is two streets to the left on the Malacón as you leave the ferry dock. It is built around a patio in the old style, although it is not all that old. I have always found it full, so I've never stayed there. This hotel much prefers not to rent to singles — they prefer to rent the same room to two people for 50% extra. Very expensive — when available.

I've been eating off and on at *Pepe's* since the days when fishing was the main industry in this part of Quintana Roo. It is expensive, like almost everything on Cozumel, but gives good value. Now one has a choice of eating out under the umbrellas à la St Tropez, or inside where the food is the same but the help is dressed a little fancier. It is near the ferry dock and expensive.

By the time you get to Cozumel you are likely to be hungry or thirsty or both, and right across the Avenida Melgar from the ferry dock is the *Restaurante las Palmeras*. The Palmeras serves standard Mexican fare plus a few regional dishes, and is relatively cheap, probably because it is naturally air-conditioned. Moderate, and therefore a rarity that probably won't last on Cozumel!

Some travellers are tempted to camp on the beaches to beat the high price of accommodations, but I don't believe this is too practical because the impoverished local sees even the poorest of the tourists as enormously rich, and now and then someone camping on the sandy shore gets robbed of everything he or she has, or raped.

In these respects Cozumel is like Acapulco, and for precisely the same reasons.

Getting There
The usual way of getting to Cozumel is by passenger ferry from Playa del Carmen. There are only three ferry

trips a day each way, and the voyage takes 50-60 minutes. The first morning boat leaves around 6 am; if you miss it you will have a four-hour wait for the next trip, at least. Only 25 years ago the ferry to Cozumel only made about one trip a week, sailing from Puerto Morelos, which is still the port for the automobile ferry. In those days the trip out to the island took a good three hours.

There is a shuttle plane at the little Carmen airport that will enable you to 'do' Cozumel in a single day, and do it thoroughly. It leaves every half hour or so.

As Cozumel doesn't really have all that much to offer — less than Isla Mujeres, in my opinion — recommend spending only part of a day there, even if it means indulging in an airplane flight, which isn't all that expensive, really, because of the short distance involved.

Some of the buses down from Cancún are scheduled to connect with the passenger ferries, and often do.

TULUM, COBÁ & XEL-HA,
Quintana Roo

Tulum differs from the usual Maya ruin by being built as a fort on the coast, rather than a ceremonial city. It is about 115 km south of Cancún on the road to Chetumal, and readily accessible from either city.

The road to Tulum is well signed, and the ruins are about one km off the main highway.

Pack a lunch before starting out. Food and drink are available around the entrance to the site and along the road to the main highway, but choices are limited.

A detailed description of Tulum would take too much space for a book of this nature, so I suggest you get one of the guidebooks that are sold at the ruins.

Cobá is probably the least-visited ruin in Mexico that is actually on a

paved road. The turn-off is about one km south of the Tulum junction, but whereas the ruins of Tulum are only about one km from the main road, Cobá is something on the order of 50 km. Most people reaching this site have done it through their own efforts because there are almost no buses and not enough traffic to make autostopping practical. There are some tours run from Cancun and Playa del Carmen.

All in all, I would advise visiting Tulum which is in the open and close to the ocean, and has fairly frequent bus service, and skipping Cobá. The latter is surrounded by breeze-stopping jungle and is hot and muggy and buggy. It is also not very big and I regret both the trips I made there. If you do go to Cobá, pack a lunch. The one or two little stores on the road are not reliable.

Xel-ha is a swimming hole located about 15 km north of Tulum, and is the regular cooling-off place on the way back for people who have visited either Tulum or Cobá.

Getting There

If you go down to Tulum by bus from Cancún, pocket your pride and take a second-class bus — they are much more frequent and holding out for a first-class bus could cost considerable time.

Returning to Cancún presents more of a problem. During the afternoon, which is when you'll probably return, the buses often run with capacity loads and may not stop to pick you up. Expect the bus that does stop to be crowded.

There are almost no buses to Cobá.

The turn-off to Xel-ha from the Cancún-Chetumal highway is signed, and it theoretically should be easy to reach Xel-ha by bus from Tulum, but in fact it is almost impossible at worst and impractical at best. And hitch-hiking in this part of the world is difficult because of the paucity of private vehicular traffic. It is cheap and easy to visit either Xel-ha or Tulum by bus, but not both.

I get down from Cancún on a rented 90cc Honda motorbike, but it is common for groups of intrepid ruin examiners to pool their resources and drive down in a rented automobile.

The little Hondas plug at an easy 50 km per hour or so and I ride down to Tulum in about 2½ hours, which compares favourably with the bus when allowance is made for the waiting time. And the bike beats the bus all hollow on the return. If you go by motorcycle, remember it must have its tank filled for the return at the station at the Tulum intersection.

With your own wheels, stopping at Xel-ha is no problem.

CHETUMAL, Quintana Roo

Chetumal is one of those out-of-the-way places most people visit on their way to somewhere else, in this case Belize. Which is not to say anything against the town itself. It is a nice, clean-looking little place, due to a series of hurricanes, the most recent in 1945, that fair destroyed it.

Back in the days when Quintana Roo was a territory it was a free port to encourage commerce, and now it has become a state the government hasn't thought to change the rules. There are dozens of shops carrying everything under the sun that can be manufactured in far-away places: canned hams from Denmark and Poland, Scotch shortbread, socket wrenches from West Germany. All this and a great deal more in one shop — stores in this part of the world don't specialise.

This merchandise is considerably more expensive than in the US and really isn't intended for tourist consumption. Mexicans and Belizians buy most of it and in turn smuggle it back into their own countries.

Chetumal is a prosperous town, as are most border cities in Mexico, and such things as portable radio/cassette players for M$14,750 and scuba outfits for M$21,000 are not at all unusual.

Chetumal is not the place for sightseeing. For practical purposes it is a one-street city, with most of the businesses, including hotels, restaurants and the bus stop, clustered along the Avenida de los Heroes which for the traveller starts at the big CFE generating plant and ends at a typical monument on the shore of the Mar del Caribe, about one km.

Places to Stay

Considering how much money is at large in Chetumal, it is surprising to find as many low-priced hotels as there are, the only problem is that they're usually full. Since many people going to Belize City have to stay overnight, it is wise to nail down a room as soon as possible. I've wound up sleeping on the concrete bench across Heroes from the bus station a couple of times when I arrived too late to secure a room. (Not especially uncomfortable; the weather was warm and things get quiet when the bus station closes sometime before midnight.)

Most of the hotels are to the right of the bus station as you leave, but there is one to the left. To reach it, turn left as you leave the station, then right at the first cross street. It is then about a block to the hotel with the fascinating name, the *Ucum*. Actually it is more of a motel than a conventional hotel, with lots and lots of secured and guarded parking space. Expensive, but it often has rooms later than others because many casual travellers never find out about it.

Directly across from the Terminal de Autobuses on Avenida Heroes is the strictly deluxe *Hotel Continental*, a shining example of modern design. The plain brown front gives no clue to the size of the house. You just about need a map or a guide to find the bar,

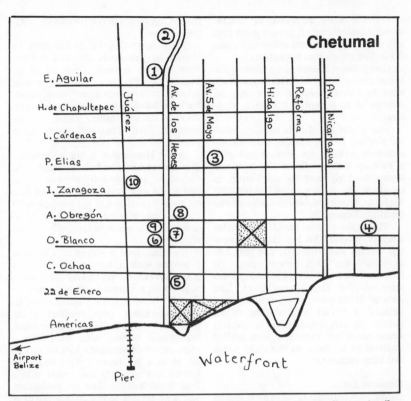

Chetumal

let alone the Restauarant la Cascada. It has everything from an outdoor short-order stand to a disco-joint complete with auto-triggering strobe lights, and goes like Gang-busters hours after the Presidente up the street closes up. One bar with an intriguing name, the Switch Bar. Ridiculously expensive, of course.

The *Hotel Tulum* is actually above the Terminal de Autobuses, but the noise should not be too serious a consideration here because the bus business begins to slow down about 9 pm and by midnight the station is locked. Moderate, and among the first in town to fill.

To the right as you leave the bus station and across the street is the *Hotel Brazilia*. It is actually on Aguilar, but easily visible from the front of the bus station across the little plaza. Moderate.

Next comes the *Presidente Chetumal*, the quasi-government hotel. It has the earliest bar and restaurant closing hours in town, and Chetumal is a place that burns the candle at both ends. Small for a Presidente, and gets most of its custom from tour groups. Ridiculously expensive.

On down Heroes and to left on Quintana Roo is the little *Hotel Quintana Roo*, small and inconspicuous and easy to overlook, as the sign merely says 'Hotel' and not very loudly at that. Moderate.

On the same street is the three-storey *Hotel Barod*. It gives a good first impression with its tiled lobby and clean floor. Fairly new and expensive.

Going down Heroes some more is the *Hotel Doris*. I stayed there some years back and there seem to have been no changes at all except in the price. Moderate.

The *Hotel Big Ben* is another hotel on Heroes. It is a newish, three-storey structure without an elevator and with a walk-up lobby. I figure the reason it looms so high over its neighbours is to allow the owner to sell advertising space on the highly-visible sides of the building. Expensive.

The *Azteca* is a hard-to-find hotel roughly behind the bus station. Leave the station and turn left, and turn left again by the CFE power house. (If it is dark you will hear it rumble.) Turn right at the first cross street. The Azteca is another new building and painted a bright and shining cream colour. Its only disadvantage is that it is above the Chez Farook, a joint greatly inclined to loudness as the night wears on. Very expensive.

Places to Eat

Eating in Chetumal is somewhat less of a problem than sleeping. Again starting in front of the bus station, the first restaurant is *La Japonesa*, right by the door. The Japonesa earns most of its money through the sale of soda pop, but it is capable of whipping up a filling late-night snack for a reasonable price. It is open 24 hours. Moderate.

A little to left on Heroes is the *public market*, quite a bit different from the usual Mexican market. (Can you picture a public market selling hand-painted silk-and-ivory fans from Spain, Korean ginseng, Dutch gouda cheeses and canned iced tea from Hayward, California?) A good place to get a meal both tasty and cheap, but you won't enjoy it unless you eat at a stall with a big paddle fan to chase the flies away. Very inexpensive.

Restaurante Grijalva, to the right on Heroes as you leave the bus station, then left on Avenida Cardenes, is recognizable by the peculiar colour scheme with orange store front, cream walls, red-bottomed chairs and international orange table 'cloths'. More Mexican than Yucateco dishes. Inexpensive.

Along Heroes past Avenida Cardenes, the *Restaurant Baalbek* has such odd dishes — for Mexico, anyway -- as taboli and pita bread. It has Bogart fans to discourage flies and is a good place to find a late evening domino or backgammon game. Unexpectedly good. Moderate.

The last time I stayed in Chetumal I awoke with a burning desire for a good breakfast, preferably of huevos motelenos, a Yucatan specialty made — usually — with refried beans, tortillas tostadas, green peas, various chilis, plus what ever else falls ready to hand, the whole topped with fried eggs. I tried various restaurants with no luck at all, so as a last resort I went down the hill to *El Presidente* and ended with a fine breakfast, cooked to perfection, and with service to match, but the price was very expensive. However, it is possible to eat quite reasonably in El Presidentes if you stick to the basic breakfast of coffee and fried eggs.

Getting There

Chetumal is an eight-hour ride on the bus from Mérida, and it takes just about as long to get to Puerto Juárez at the other end of the state. As I said it is the last place in the world one would pick for a destination. You can also fly from Mérida but this is seldom done by tourists since the only reason to visit Chetumal is to stop over on the way to Belize, and it is usually easier to fly to Belize direct.

To get from Chetumal to Belize City

catch the direct bus, which usually runs several times a week, or take a cab the six km to the border crossing, enter Belize, and depend on local transport in that country. There are usually rattle-trap buses and trucks fitted with plank seats, from the border to Corozal Town, and from Corozal to Belize City. The fare from the Mexican border crossing to Belize City should run around $3 or $4 (Belize currency). The adventure-some can go by public transportation on to Guatemala if the border isn't closed and time is no object.

Sometimes you can catch a ride on a produce truck. If you're fortunate enough to be offered a ride, expect to pay. In Belize there is no free lunch, and no free rides as a general rule.

Cuernavaca, Morelia & the Mexican Riviera

CUERNAVACA, Morelos

Cuernavaca has always been a haven for the wealthy who have preferred Cuernavaca to Mexico City. First it was the Aztec rulers, then the Spanish beginning with Cortés himself, and after Independence, it was rich Mexicans and their families. Of recent years Cuernavaca has become the home-away-from-home for a good number of Americans, and it is generally conceded that Cuernavaca has the second-largest American colony in the Republic — after Guadalajara/Chapala.

A contributing factor to Cuernavaca's present popularity as a retreat is the closeness of Mexico City; it doesn't take very long to drive 75 km on a divided highway. And due to the ridge surrounding Mexico City, very little of the obnoxious smog for which the capital is infamous manages to waft itself down to Cuernavaca.

The Borda Gardens are Cuernavaca's best-known feature. These were built by the French prospector and miner José de la Borda with his Taxco-derived riches.

The park is a shining example of a very rich, self-made man's open-handed generosity toward his adopted land. And it is huge. One pool, for example, is about 120 metres long, and there are winding pathways, fountains and more fountains — one of the very few formal old-world gardens open to the public in the Republic.

The gardens are reputed to have cost a million or so pesos, and originally were absolutely magnificent, but as with most Mexican operations, were allowed to deteriorate and at one time were all but abandoned, with the premises occupied by the usual motley collection of squatter's shacks occupied by families with lots of children, no visible income and an appreciation of a good downtown location.

Of recent years the gardens are being rehabilitated, a process marred by the incredibly poor workmanship that is far, far below the original standard. The electrical work is especially bad.

Considering how short Cuernavaca is of green recreational areas the gardens are remarkably little used. Probably this is accounted for by the M$10 admission fee, a high price for a stroll in a public park, but it does make the gardens the ideal place for a lazy, fairly private, afternoon picnic.

The Jardines de Borda are on Morelos at the end of Hidalgo, and the entrance is by way of a standard flat-fronted building that could be the home of a tyre repair shop, and then through two patios. The Tourist Office is in one of the rooms in the double-patioed entrance building.

Contributing to the incidence of Americans in Cuernavaca are the language schools teaching Spanish by the immersion method wherein the student boards with a local family and hears nothing but Spanish, a system that seems to work extremely well. Information is available from the Tourist Office. (For a ripping good read, I recommend *Please, Write for Details* by John D MacDonald, a story describing the founding of a summer art school in Cuernavaca.)

Cortés' Palace is now the Museo de Cuauhnahuac, and well worth the M$10 admission. Much more diversified than most local museums, and not too heavy with pictures of by-gone politicians, although there is an excellent Diego Rivera, the bill for which was footed by Charles A Lindberg's father-in-law when he was ambassador to Mexico. It is heavy on the nuts and bolts of daily colonial life, such as sugar-cane squeezers, ox bows, stills, weapons,

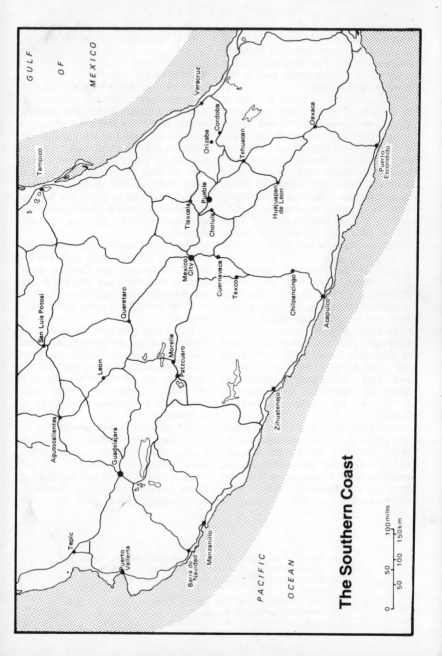

The Southern Coast

armour, diligencias and tools. Anyone with a modicum of curiosity will spend at least three hours here, and probably the whole day. The Museo is on the plaza which in Cuernavaca goes by the name of Jardín Juárez.

The FONART complex on Salazar by the side of the Palacio/Museo has an all-too-rare preoccupation with useful everyday ceramic household items, but it also has some non-utilitarian ceramic art, plus cloth, woodenware and even bamboo birdcages. All in all it is a worthy selection and should be visited by anyone who is thinking of picking up some local native handicrafts. Even if nothing is bought from FONART it will give a good idea of what the better-quality merchandise looks like.

Also in the FONART complex is the Ceramica Gres with an entirely different line of merchandise. The Gres specializes in modern, high-tech dinner-ware and some of their dinner sets are remarkably attractive examples of con-temporary Mexican design. But then at M$21,000 for a 12-place setting one can reasonably expect good design and high manufacturing standards! These are intended for local customers, by the way, for the Gres sees very few tourists.

The plaza is really a two-part affair. The small square to the north of the Jardín Juárez is the Parque Alameda, and it is here that the mariachi groups gather of an afternoon across the street from the Multibanco Comermex. They often pass the time before starting the

evening's work by practicing new tunes — in effect a free concert for passers-by.

Places to Stay

Prices in Cuernavaca have skyrocketed of recent years, partially because of Mexico's vicious inflation, and partially because of the new motorway which has made it practical for many people to commute daily to Mexico City, and has also led to a booming week-end trade with refugees from the capital. This means that not only do prices tend to be high, but also at times it is next to impossible to find a room during the weekends. Don't say you weren't warned!

The *Hotel Posada de Cortez*, directly in back of Cortés palace, on Leyva between Salazar and Las Casas, is proof positive that there are still low-priced hotels in expensive Cuernavaca. Frankly, all it has going for it is the price! Inexpensive.

In the very next block is the *Casa de Huespedes Dora*, on Leyva between Las Casas and Abosolo. About the same social level as the Cortez, but with the Dora you can be reasonably sure of a hot bath — there is a bath house operated in conjunction with the Dora. Inexpensive.

You might logically assume that all the hotels in the vicinity would be in roughly the same price bracket, but you would be very, very wrong!

On the next corner past the Dora, at Leyva and Abosolo, is *La Posada de Xochiquetzal*, which from the street

A Many hotels started life as the mansion of a wealthy family. This is the patio of the Hotel San Francisco in El Fuerte, Sinaloa.

B Most of Mexico's older Moorish style homes are built around a patio.

C The interior of the 'Los Balcons Pizzeria y Restaurante and Health Food Place' in Merida.

A
B C

looks to be a hole-in-the-wall but is something else again once you are past the front door. It has an elegant lawn in the sunken patio with a restaurant/bar under the portales, leather-topped bar tables and table lamps made of — among other things — antique Kahlúa bottles. There are surgically-clean sanitary facilities off the bar, just in case of emergency. And of course the Xochiquetzal is ridiculously expensive.

Just north of the Borda Gardens, on Morrow near Tejeda, is the *Hotel Colón* with its peeling beige facade and painted imitation stone lobby. Overall an air of benign neglect, and it really looks as if it should be a low-price house, but this is another case of appearances being deceptive for the Hotel Colón y España, to give it the full name, is expensive, but you can usually get a room here.

The *Hotel del Parque*, on the Parque Alameda over the old theatre, looks fairly new, but it has been in operation for some 25 years. With absolutely no consideration for charm or ambience, it is primarily a mid-city hotel intended for travelling salesmen and the like. It is one of the last hotels to fill because it is expensive.

The *Hotel los Canarios* at Morelos and Fabregas, about three blocks above the Flecha Roja bus station, could as well be called a motel with its parking area around a core of buildings within the huge patio. This is another instance of appearances being deceiving, but in the right way. You might expect it to be expensive, but this one is a real sleeper and the best value for pesos in

town. Moderate.

The *Casa de Huespedes Marilu*, the *Hotel America*, and the *Posada San' José* are within 50 metres of each other on Aragon y Leon between Morelos and Matamoros. They differ in detail, but not much. The Hotel America, for instance, has two storeys and may clutter up its patio with a few guests' cars. The Marilu has a cheerful two-storey patio with full size trees growing in crimson oil drums. Both the America and the Marilu are moderate. The San Jose is a European-type pension, with meals and a favourite with hucksters and buskers; and inexpensive.

On the same block, but a notch or two lower on the social scale, is the *Casa de Huespedes Buen Veccino*, very easy to overlook. This is another favourite of the street peddlers. Inexpensive.

All four are among the first hotels in Cuernavaca to put up the 'lleno' signs. This is not due to the tourist business, because with the possible exception of the America and the Marilu, none of them gets much action from foreigners.

Laundry There is a laundromat on Morrow just down the hill from Morelos, but it is not a coin-op as it would be in the US. Here it is a laundry that uses household type washing machines. Quick service and gentle on clothes.

Places to Eat
Eating is a somewhat better proposition in Cuernavaca than sleeping because the hotels get filled quite often, seem-

A Market scene in Oaxaca.
B In another market.

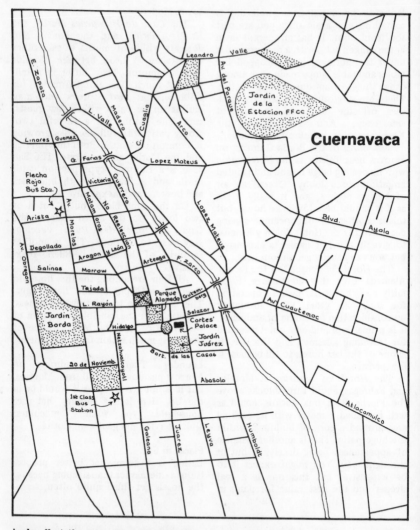

ingly all at the same time, while there is always a place to get an economical meal, starting with the *Tacos Cabellero* in the Flecha Roja second-class bus station, a bit above most Mexican bus station operations and a good place for a snack on the run. Very inexpensive.

On Rayón near Galeana are a couple of worthwhile restaurants. The one closest to the Jardín Juárez, the one with the small-tiled front is the *Restaurant Bar Acuario*, and a little further along and on the other side of the street is *El Tepa*, which on first glance could easily be mistaken for a torta joint because of the tacos-al-carbon set-up in the front, but it is really a full-fledged restaurant. Both rely to a considerable degree on the patronage of the government employees from the brown piles fronting the Jardín and are quite similar in most respects. Perhaps the Acuario does have a shade more class, but then the Tepa has a little better service, as a rule, and the Tepa is very slightly cheaper most days. Both are moderate.

Vegetarian restaurants in Mexico are usually a pretty good go, reasonable in price, with better than average cooking. But the *Vegetariano* on Salizar near Cortés' palace is a notable exception to this sweeping generalisation. It is a very pleasant place, a shady patio beneath the FONART handicrafts emporium, but the prices are flat out of reason.

Another bummer in the same neighbourhood is *El Arbol,* in the lower patio of FONART by the Vegetariano. Actually a bread, cheese and cold-cut place, and grossly overpriced.

The *Restaurant Vienes,* on Tejeda at Comonfort, is multilingual — French, English, Spanish and German — with an emphasis on Austrian entrees. If the place appears full from the sidewalk, you will probably find a table in the upstairs dining room, except around 3 pm. Expensive, but worth the price.

The *Cafe la Cueva,* on Obregón below Rayón, is my favourite for breakfast. It is much larger than it appears from the street, with a back dining room. As well as breakfast, the Cueva has a complete midday menu, often including such Norteno items as cabrito al horno and barbacoa, both rare this far south. Moderate.

Practically next door to the Cueva is a large bakery with a small supermarket as part of the overall operation. Meat, bread, cheese, wine — all the classic ingredients for a picnic, under one roof, and the Borda Gardens are only four blocks away. Very inexpensive.

For a really grand assortment of things edible and otherwise, try the *Aurrera,* below the Flecha Roja bus station. Just turn right as you leave the station and it is in the next block. The Aurrera is a giant supermarket and the most general of stores. There you can have a Yale key made, buy a pair of jeans, get the wine, bread and cheese for a picnic, or have a hamburger with a malt chaser right in the store.

If you get a craving for something a little more sophisticated than standard Mexican cooking, the Sunday buffet at the *Posada de Xochiquetzal,* over on Leyva at Abosolo, is ridiculously expensive at M$200 but is about the best value for an expensive meal in town, and the surroundings are downright de lujo. Very popular with members of the American Colony, which just might give you an opportunity to practise your English.

Getting There & Getting Around

Bus service to Cuernavaca from Mexico City is fantastic, with all the buses leaving from the Terminal del Sur, but they arrive at three different bus stations in Cuernavaca.

I prefer to catch a Flecha Roja bus from Mexico City because it lands in the middle of the low-rent district. Autobuses Pullman de Morelos' station is at the corner of Abosolo and Netzahualcoyotl, which is about the same distance from the Jardín as the Flecha Roja station. The Estrella de Oro stops way down south on Morelos about one km from the centre of things. This is a first-class operation and the way to go for those heading down to Acapulco or Zihuatenejo. Taxco is such a short distance — only about 100 km — that it doesn't make much difference whether you go first or second-class, and generally the extra convenience of the Flecha Roja station tips the balance in its favour.

To get to the plazas from the Flecha Roja second-class station, go out the front door and turn right on Morelos and follow it four blocks to Lerdo de Tejada. Turn left on Tejada and the Parque Alameda is two more blocks.

TAXCO, Guerrero

Taxco is another of Mexico's colonial monument cities where all new construction must be in the colonial style, and permits for any building at all are very difficult to obtain.

The beauty of the old buildings, coupled with their picturesque setting, make Taxco a photographer's paradise, in my opinion superior in this respect to Guanajuato or San Miguel, both of which to a certain extent have the same history and setting.

Taxco actually isn't very old, nowhere near as old as it appears. Although silver mining in the modern sense began in the days of Cortés, the town really dates from 1716 with the arrival of José de la Borda, a French prospector and miner. He had previously had more financial ups and downs than a roller coaster, but at Taxco he had a magic touch, and located one rich silver vein after another and he wound up one of the richest men in a country where the rich were — and are — very rich indeed!

Taxco owes a large part of its attraction to the hills on which it is built, and it does seem at times as if there are only two directions, uphill and downhill.

The wealthy miners built as grandly as the limited amount of land would permit, and their homes have been tastefully restored in recent years to their original aspect, giving the town a 'colonial' look unmatched anywhere in the Republic. The old-world appearance is enhanced by the cobblestone streets, far and away the best cobble-laying I have ever seen, and the only place I know where the streets routinely have two-tone designs — crosses, arrows, etc.

The mines began to play out during the early years of the 20th century and the finishing touches to Taxco's prosperity came when the country lapsed into anarchy about the time of the revolution. Today there is one active mine, across the Carretera from the town — you can see it from the Estrella de Oro station. Using all new and modern equipment and techniques, it doesn't look much like the usual Mexican mine which tends to date back several hundred years and shows it.

With the failure of the mining industry, Taxco began to lose population as families were starved out, and the abandoned buildings became more and more decrepit until it began to take on the aspect of a ghost town like Real de Catorce and Pozos.

This was the situation when a young Yale graduate, William Spratling, came to town to write a book. He fell in love with the place and eventually settled there. Recognizing that something must be done to provide an economic base if Taxco was not to wind up a pile of rubble, he hit on the happy idea of making silverware and jewellery. He also began to train the young men of the area in silverworking, and at one time his operation, the Taller de Delicias, employed several hundred barefoot apprentices, many of whom went on to become today's wealthy businessmen.

From that modest start in the mind of a single gifted individual, in about 50 years the silver business has come to dominate the city and silver shops stand shoulder to shoulder, with sometimes as many as five or six in one block. The silver does not come from Taxco's mines. Perhaps at one time it might have been possible, but today Taxco is no longer a major silver producer and the metal is bought on the open market.

Spratling had the ill luck to be a better teacher, designer, inspirer and dreamer than he was a business man, and he eventually lost control of the business he had founded. He died in an automobile accident in the late 1960s.

Borda had a pet saying, 'God gives to Borda; Borda gives to God'. He put his money where he put his mouth by underwriting the Church of Santa Prisca on the tiny Plaza Principal to the tune of around M$7 million — a huge amount at the time. Borda insisted on overseeing the actual construction of the church, which gives it a unity of design rare in Mexican churches of this size which often take a hundred years or more to finish. Santa Prisca took a mere seven years.

Today the view of the church is blocked somewhat by the ubiquitious Indian laurels on the plaza, but it is still an impressive structure. The proper name is the 'Inglesia de San Sebastián y Santa Prisca', and it is often miscalled a cathedral on the basis of its size.

The Museo de Guillermo Spratling is directly behind the church and easily identified by the plaque on the wall. I understand it has some excellent examples of pre-Columbian art, along with considerable Taxco memorabilia and artifacts pertaining to its recent history, but this is another well-known museum that I've never found open.

It is almost a necessity to prowl around Taxco on foot. For one thing finding a parking spot is next to impossible. For another, the narrow streets were laid out for pack trains and horses, and for some years wheeled vehicles were not even permitted in town, which would be a good idea today. The streets are mostly one-way, confusing and seem to spiral off in all directions. Between stone walls about 4½ metres apart they carry two-way traffic plus foot traffic on both sides, with no curbs or sidewalks on most of the streets, either.

Taxco has a peculiar method of installing water pipes on hilly pedestrian walkways. Instead of running them to one side, or burying them well out of the way, they're placed in the centre, often on the surface. This means that a person coming downhill can easily put a heel on an exposed pipe instead of the expected rough cobble and take a header, and on Taxco's steep hills a fall is deadly serious.

Cobblestones and women's high heels don't mix very well. The most practical footgear seems to be flats, with made-for-work huaraches a close second. The soles should be stiff because cobblestones are noted for inflicting painful stone bruises to tender feet. The local girls wear spike heels, even while pregnant and/or carrying a baby, but they fall, too, now and again.

Visiting the silver shops is the big thing to do in Taxco — after all, it is famous throughout the western world for hand-made silver. Most of the shoppers who scurry from one store to another are convinced they will somehow get a bargain if they buy from the 'factory', but that isn't the way it works. The only advantage shopping in Taxco has over buying Mexican silver in Mexico City or Tijuana is the fantastic assortment, and the prices are actually inclined to be a bit higher in Taxco than the same goods in far-away places.

Nevertheless, I make it a point to visit the *Plateria Gloria*, on the Plazuela San Juan, across from the Hotel Santa Prisca. The Gloria has about the finest collection of silver, brass and tin-plate artifacts in town. Belt buckles by the dozen, brass vases, gargantuan tin-plate masks — you name it, if it is made from flat or round stock the Gloria has it. Even if you are totally disinterested in shopping, the Gloria is definitely worthwhile, and it isn't necessary to stop looking with the Gloria, because there must be half a dozen silver shops in that one short block!

Almost every shop has a sign saying

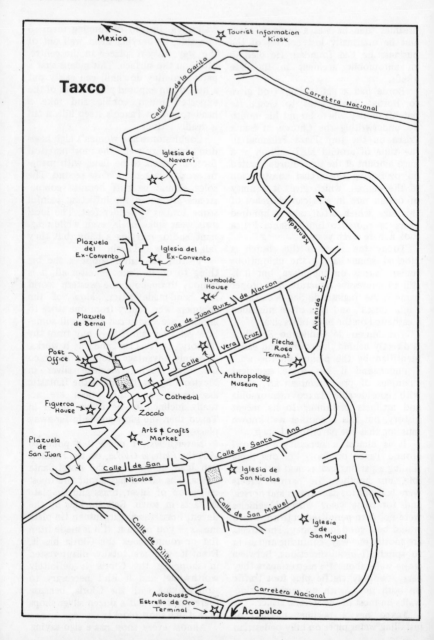

Taxco

Mexico

Tourist Information Kiosk

Calle de la Garita

Carretera Nacional

Iglesia de Navarri

N

Avenida F. J. Kennedy

Plazuela del Ex-Convento

Iglesia del Ex-Convento

Humboldt House

Calle de Juan Ruiz de Alarcon

Plazuela de Bernal

Vera Cruz

Flecha Rosa Terminal

Post Office

Calle

Anthropology Museum

Figueroa House

Cathedral

Zocalo

Plazuela de San Juan

Arts & Crafts Market

Calle de Santa Ana

Calle de San Nicolas

Iglesia de San Nicolas

Calle de San Miguel

Iglesia de San Miguel

Calle de Pilita

Carretera Nacional

Autobuses Estrella de Oro Terminal

Acapulco

'Fabrica de Plata', or 'silver factory', or both. This is mostly hyperbole and the majority of shops are simply retailers who tend to charge exactly the same prices as their next-door neighbours, by agreement. (In Mexico this isn't illegal as it would be in the US.)

Places to Stay

The *Casa Grande* is an old, old and confusing hotel on Plazuela San Juan. The problem is not with the hotel itself, which is perfectly straightforward, but with the entrance which it shares with the movie house beneath it and which bears only the Cine sign. Once the puzzle is solved you find still another hotel in a once-magnificent old private home. It is moderate, convenient and recommended.

The *Casa Melendez*, between Plazuela San Juan and the zócolo, is an old reliable house for experienced foreigners and well-to-do Mexican families. As the third generation of the Melendez tribe is currently the resident manager, close attention is paid to the service. Expensive.

The *Hotel Jardín*, in the street to the left of the church as you face it, is a nice little place that may not get as much business as it would like simply because it is rather difficult to find. There is only a small unnoticeable sign to indicate its presence. Moderate.

The *Hotel del Monte* on Calle Juárez across from the post office, is a small family operation with the grandchildren crawling around the lobby. Rooms are large and airy as befits a hotel in a mostly unconverted colonial home. A real rarity in expensive Taxco, it is inexpensive.

Even harder to find than the Jardín is the *Casa de Huespedes* (no other name). The easiest way to reach it the first time is probably to branch off the zócolo to the right of the church as you face it. Watch on the right side of the street for the Centro de Artesianas and go down and continue past it to the steps. Continue down to the Templo Bautista and turn left and go down some more steps. The Casa de Huespedes is a rambling multi-storeyed building that looks like an illustration from a 19th-century edition of Don Quixote. It is the most economical place to stay in Taxco — if they have room — that I've been able to locate. Inexpensive.

Places to Eat

Because Taxco has so many tourists, it has a large number of restaurants, one or more to fit each purse.

In the Plazuela San Juan the modestly-priced *Casa Grande* hotel has a striking restaurant on the premises. It is located on the second floor front, with two small balconies which provide a pleasant place to sit at sunset and watch the lights go on around the Plazuela. Expensive.

Continuing on toward the zócolo, we come to the *Hotel Melendez* with its dining room looking down on half the tiled roofs of Taxco. This is one of the better places to eat, especially for the guests, and particularly good for breakfast. The Melendez comes awfully close to serving an English breakfast, except the toast is hot. Breakfast is moderate in price, other meals are expensive.

Further around the plaza is the *Pizza Dama*, near the Hotel Agua Escondido. La Dama not only serves a wide assortment of pizzas (cooked in a real pizza oven), plus spaghetti and hamburgers, but it also has that internationally-known Texican delicacy, chili con carne. This is the only place I have ever encountered it in Mexico. There are two varieties: if you look like a New York or California gringo you automatically get the milder, flatter variety; if you look like a Texan or a Mexican you get the real stuff, the kind that will grow and/or curl the hair on your chest. Eat on the balcony during the evening and enjoy the night view of the town.

The *Restaurant los Candiles* is sort of a nuisance to find, which may very well be why there are usually local people there. Go down the street to the right of Santa Prisca and watch for the Centro de Artesanieas, below you on your right. The Candiles is entered through the crafts shop. There are tables on the balcony looking down on the red-tiled roofs of old Taxco. It is unusual in that in addition to the standard fixed menu of Mexican dishes it offers daily specials, also 'pozole nearly every day!' Expensive.

The market ladies, as always, are the best shot for cheap eats. To reach the market, face the Hotel Melendez and go down the hill on the street on its right. One whole floor of the market is practically devoted to prepared foods, from pan dulces to restaurant stands. Very inexpensive.

Getting Around
The first-class bus station in Taxco is a pseudo-colonial gem of a building with leather-bottomed chairs and a table. Other good things for the bus passengers, such as a branch of turismo, make it easily the nicest little bus station in Mexico. To get from the station to the plaza, simply go straight across the street and start up the cobble-stoned hill that slopes up and up in front of you like a cow's face. Keep climbing until you hit a square right-hander and there is the Plazuela San Juan. If you go straight across the little plaza in front of the Casa Grande and out the other side, in approximately 100 metres you find yourself on the Plaza Principal. Walking time is about 10 minutes.

To get uptown from the Flecha Roja bus station, go right on the heavily-travelled road in front, the Carretera Naciónal a Mexico. At the IMSS hospital turn right and begin climbing. Follow this street without deviation

and you will come to the Plazuela San Juan. Leave the little plaza by the street to the right and you will soon be on the Plaza Principal. Walking time is 15 minutes.

CHILPANCINGO, Guerrero
Chilpancingo may very well be the most un-touristed city in Mexico. Located 133 km and about a three-hour bus ride from Acapulco on the way to Mexico City it is rich in history but only moderately attractive otherwise. But it does have one great advantage over Acapulco — its altitude (1100+ metres) gives it a far superior climate. Some people who take their vacations in the summer at the beaches at Acapulco spend their last night in Chilpancigo where it's ever so much cooler, and continue on to their destination the following morning feeling no end refreshed.

In Chilpancingo, across the street from the Estrella de Oro bus station there is an older pseudo-colonial house, the *Hotel Posada Melendez*, with its huge, tiled, spic-and-span lobby and big, olde-time rooms upstairs. It looks as if it would be ridiculously expensive, and would be if it were in Acapulco or Oaxaca, but here it is merely expensive.

MORELIA, Michoacán
Morelia is another town that has become a national monument, which means that it remains pretty much as it was before Morelos became a national hero and the Spaniards still called the city Valladolid, after the city in Spain where Fernando of Castile wed Isabela la Catolica.

After the revolution, when it became popular to tack the names of the new crop of heroes onto the existing names of cities, Valladolid went the whole hog and changed its name completely. More than patriotism played a part in the renaming, for Mexico has several Valladolids large and small, notably the one in Yucatán, causing no end of confusion.

Morelia has a large quantity of colonial buildings, most of them quite charming, but for the tourist it is mainly a place to stop overnight on the way to somewhere else.

Enterprising entrepreneurs peddle maps of Morelia from the sidewalk under the portales alongside the zócolo.

The cathedral facing the Plaza de Los Martires is one of the most beautiful in Mexico and one of the few that started out with one unifying style and stuck to it, even though its construction took more than a century. It is made of the usual trachyte, in this case more brownish than pink, in pure Plateresque style, and in excellent proportions.

The interior was originally as impressive as the exterior, and the huge open centre of the building is still striking, but the solid silver communial rail was removed and confiscated by the government when the church refused to pay a war assessment about the time of the Reformation. The interior decorations are in excellent taste, but only go back to about 1900. It is well worth while spending an hour or so admiring this beautiful work of art.

The Hotel Soledad is a ridiculously expensive place to stay, but this should not discourage the wayfarer from stepping inside and savouring the exquisitely-done restoration. Around Christmas time the children of the employees and guests have their own celebration in the Soledad's patio, complete with blindfolds, clubs and piñatas filled with candy and trinkets — a heartwarming thing to witness and a barrel of fun for the kids.

The Palacio del Artesano, really a part of the old San Francisco Church, is on Frey J de San Miguel one block south of the main drag, Madero. San Miguel changes its name when it crosses Madero and becomes Dominguez. The Church of San Francisco is one of the oldest in Mexico, which doesn't of itself make it very interesting, but the Palacio del Artesano more than justifies the six-block walk from the plaza. A fantastic assortment of hand-made Michoacán goods is on display, including lacquerware, copperware, birdcages (sans birds), pottery, clothing and everything used by the country people. Everything is for sale and every piece is price-marked. This is a much better place to buy than the public market, and as a general rule better merchandise is available here than in the villages where it is actually made. The Palacio occupies three large rooms and is quite extensive. Not a place to spend a quick five minutes!

Morelia's market is called the Mercado Independencia and it is not really all that worthwhile, but for those market aficionados it can be reached by going out Madero to Vaso de Quiroga and turning right, then left on Cárdenes — the market is then two blocks away.

Places to Stay

Morelia has lots of economy hotels, although most guidebooks see fit only to mention the Soledad, and others of that ilk.

The *Hotel Allende*, on Allende between Cuatla and Bravo, has an unprepossing, dingy exterior that conceals a two storey open patio planted with flowers and tropical shrubs. This is a real find in a largely overpriced town. Moderate.

Hotel Fenix is on Madero between Guzman and Farias. Its only real disadvantage is an unfortunate habit of using the patio for a public parking lot, but it is an extremely rare bird — an inexpensive hotel fairly close to downtown.

The *Hotel Orzco*, almost next door to the Fenix, does not use its patio for a parking lot, which may explain why their charges are slightly higher than the Fenix. Moderate.

And then there is the *Hotel Señorial*, on Tapta between Farias and Guzman, about 1½ blocks from the bus station. This is another old family home gone into trade. They have been redoing the exhausted patio for some time now and when the job is completed they will probably up the tab, but for now it is inexpensive.

Stand outside the bus station and look around and you will see several medium-budget hotels. My favourite is the *Hotel Plaza*. Like the others in this neighbourhood it is fairly new and with a pretty good restaurant on the premises. Expensive.

Places to Eat

The restaurant situation in Morelia is nothing to write home about, but there are quite a large number of low-cost restaurants.

Natural-food addicts will do well to try *Señor Sol* across the street from the big crafts shop on Faria between Madero and Tapta. The usual assortment of fruit and vegetable salads, Yogurt, queso fundido and lots of other healthy things. Close to bus station. Moderate.

The *Restaurante Boca del Rio*, on Farias at Tapta, is a first-rate seafood joint hundreds and hundreds of km from the nearest salt water. Mexicans do wonderful things with fish, especially considering that they are not seafaring people. The kitchen crew is dressed up like British ward nurses with white headdresses to keep things sanitary, something that is not generally a consideration in Mexico. Expensive, but good value for money. However, do not order any wine by the glass. The Boca del Rio buys its house wines in big jugs and as Mexicans generally aren't big wine drinkers the jug can sit opened on top of the bar an awful long time before the last drink is sold.

The Morelia *bus station* restaurant is

one of the poorest in Mexico. If you step out the front door of the station and look up and down the street you will see about half a dozen beaneries that will feed you better and cheaper than the cafeteria behind you.

Getting There & Getting Around

Morelia is the transport hub of the region, and at the inconvenient little bus station you can catch a direct bus for Patzcuaro, Manzanillo, Guadalajara, Mexico City, San Luis Potosí — in fact just about anywhere in the northern or western part of the republic.

It is about 385 km from Morelia to Mexico City, and takes about six hours by bus, with a stop at Toluca, so unless you want to get into the capital pretty late it is best to catch an early bus. I try to leave around 7 am or even earlier.

The rest rooms in the Morelia bus station are to the left or right as one enters the building from the bus stalls — awfully easy to overlook, especially if one is in a tearing hurry.

To get downtown from the bus station in less than 15 minutes, go out the front of the station and turn left, then right at the corner. Turn left when you come to the street with the arch-topped stone wall and go to the third street and turn right. Another couple of blocks will put you past the Hotel Soledad to the plaza.

PÁTZCUARO, Michoacán

Pátzcuaro is the ideal small Mexican town that has everything; climate, lakeside location, fairly flat site, history and great beauty, yet the tourist business hasn't had much influence on the day-to-day life of the inhabitants.

Pátzcuaro is unique in that the founders laid the foundation for great growth and provided it with two plazas, rather than the usual small town's one. The larger one, called either the Plaza Principal or the Plaza Grande, is almost the size of the zócolo in Mexico City, while even the minor plaza, the Plaza Chica (officially called the Plaza Bocanegra), is still larger than the teensy square at Acapulco, a city ten times the size of Pátzcuaro.

The life of the city centres on the Plaza Chica. It is here that most of the buses load and unload. The market starts at the Plaza Chica and runs back for a couple of blocks or so. Here are most of the economy hotels and restaurants. And when the locals feel like taking a bit of rest they usually do it on one of the benches in the shade of the trees on the Plaza Chica.

On the other hand the Plaza Principal, at least four times the size of the Plaza Chica, ie essentially a public park. Because it doesn't attract many people, and the few it does attract are simply lost in its immensity, the Plaza Principal is always an uncrowded place for reading, napping, courting or just plain loafing.

One of my favourite Mexican museums is the Museum of Popular and Regional Arts, at the corner of Arciga and Quiroga. More like a large country home than the usual museum, it is located in what was the College of San Nicolás, later moved to Morelia. It has an unusual entrance, being at the corner, rather than a street-facing wall. The patio has an operating well, the old-fashioned kind with a bucket and a rope to draw water. Among the other exhibits is a replica of a 16th-century kitchen that looks as if it only needs charcoal and a match to begin boiling a cazuela of beans.

Another don't-miss is the Casa de Once Patios, on Larin between Ensenanza and Cos. Once it was a Catherine convent, today it is filled with the clackety-clack of the traditional wooden, foot-powered looms weaving cloth to be sold at one of the nearby shops. The Casa de Once Patios is not a museum, but rather a small shopping

centre, and is occupied by stores selling cloth, lacquerware and beaten-copper cookware. There is even a restaurant which I have yet to find open for business. One of the Turismo offices is here, and I haven't found it open either. But even if you're not in a buying mood, this place is definitely worth a visit simply to enjoy the ambience of a well-constructed building some 400 years old.

Beautiful lacquerware is made in and around Pátzcuaro, but of recent years much of it is of inferior quality, on the well-verified theory that the average tourist for whom the work is intended won't know the difference anyway.

High-quality lacquerware is made by applying numerous coats of different colours, topped with a jet-black layer. The design is then made by cutting away the various layers until the desired colour is arrived at. This is a tedious and time-consuming operation, and an expensive one. Much of the lacquerware sold now is made by simply laying on a coat of black lacquer and allowing it to dry thoroughly, and then adding the design as if the artisan were painting a teacup, or making an ordinary painting. Obviously this is a much cheaper process and, if it can be sold for the same price as the genuine article, quite profitable.

Another thing to remember about lacquerware is that it is extremely fragile, at least as fragile as the equivalent in porcelain, and it must be packed very carefully to withstand handling by the baggage-smashers.

Everywhere you go in Pátzcuaro you will see references to Don Vasco de Quiroga. He was sent from Spain in 1540 to replace another Spaniard named Nuño de Guzmán. Guzmán was renowned for his cruelty, and this in a hard-bitten land. At one time he was the kingpin of the region centering on Lake Pátzcuaro, and among other things he roasted the chief of the local

Tarascan Indians to death over a slow fire in an attempt to force him to divulge the source of his tribe's gold. The official Spanish policy was never one of mistreatment of the Indians, and when word got back to Spain of Guzmán's activities he was dismissed and Vasco de Quiroga, one of the great men of the Conquest, was delegated to replace him.

Don Vasco started out in life as a lawyer, and a successful one at that. He took religious vows late in life, and although he rose rapidly through the church hierarchy, he was 68 when he became bishop. His wisdom and compassion endeared him to the Indians as much as Guzmán was detested. He provided Patzcuaro with a potable water system that served the community well for about 300 years. He also founded the College of San Nicolás.

His crowning achievement was the construction of the Cathedral. The building was begun in 1540, and much is made of the fact that Don Vasco never lived to see it completed. But then, neither did anybody else. It was damaged by an earthquake while under construction and the tremendous dome was never built. The present façade is an afterthought. And it never became a cathedral, although it was finally raised to colegiata in 1907. Today most people refer to it as 'La Basilica', which is as good a name as any.

The Basilica is the focal point for pilgrims, and they come for hundreds of km by tour bus to venerate the Virgin made of corn-stalk pith and orchid juice. The story is that she was discovered floating in the lake. The Indians are supposed to say 'She is dark just like us' and come in from the aldeas to venerate her on the eighth of every month.

Bishop Quiroga's ashes are kept in a safe in a small chapel behind the altar in the Templo de la Compañia de Jesús, about two blocks to the south of the

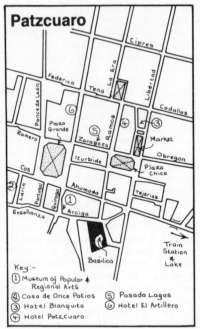

Key:-
① Museum of Popular & Regional Arts
② Casa de Once Patios
③ Hotel Blanquita
④ Hotel Patzcuaro
⑤ Posada Lagos
⑥ Hotel El Artillero

Basilica on the opposite side of the street.

Most visitors to Pátzcuaro go out to one of the inhabited islands in the lake, the most interesting of which is Janitzio, more like an island town in the Mediterranean than a Mexican Indian village. On the top of the Isla de Janitzio is a huge statue of Morelos by Guillermo Ruíz. This concrete and stone abortion is surely one of Mexico's monumental mistakes. To put it another way, the town of Janitzio is interesting but the statue isn't worth walking across the street to see, let alone up a steep hill.

Boats for the islands leave from the Embarcadero, one km or so from the plazas off the road to Morelia by car or direct from the Plaza Chica on foot.

Places to Stay

Pátzcuaro is well blessed with low-cost hotels and attracts large numbers of foreign tourists as a result.

The *Hotel Blanquita* must be the best-kept secret in town. Although it is small, clean, quiet, comfortable and convenient I have yet to see a tourist there. It is beside the upper, concrete building at the end of the market. Inexpensive.

The *Hotel Pátzcuaro*, less than a block from the Plaza Chica on Ramos between Tena and Zaragoza, has a peculiar 'rustic-trimmed' lobby complete with non-operational fireplace, but except for the slabs tacked around the lobby it is a standard small viajero hotel. Inexpensive.

Posada Lagos is on Zaragoza between the two plazas. The long narrow lobby is really a hall leading to the two-storey patio out back around which the hotel is constructed. Sign at rear of lobby over patio door says 'Hotel y Restaurante' but there's no restaurant. Otherwise it is another standard small hotel, but if you share W C Fields' dislike of children stay away from the Lagos. Inexpensive.

Hotel El Artillero, on Quiroga between Zaragoza and Tena, is another hotel in a rebuilt mansion, complete with French doors opening onto iron-railed balconies. Moderate.

The *Hotel Meson del Gallo* is on Cos off the Plaza Principal. By both location and appearance you would expect the rooster to be another reasonably-priced house, but this establishment caters to the package-tour groups travelling the high-on-the-hog route, and is ridiculously expensive.

The *Hotel Posada de la Rosa*, the *Hotel San Augustine*, and the *Hotel Concordia*, on the Plaza Chica opposite the Flecha Amarilla bus station are upstairs hotels over stores, and all three are about the same type and quality. This is the heavy-traffic Plaza in case you're bothered by noise, but you can't have a more central location. Inexpensive to moderate.

Places to Eat

I swear that every last restaurant in the region, from Morelia to Urapan, features the pez blanco that the Indians catch in the lake using the photogenic butterfly nets. They are on the order of medium-size herring but far less tasty.

The restaurant in the *Hotel Blanquita*, hard by the concrete market building, is in the hotel building but otherwise has no connection. Being by the market, and serving well-prepared food at reasonable prices, it does a lot of business with locals, but it is probably too far off the plazas for the floating foreign population to locate it, and I have yet to see another tourist there. Inexpensive.

The market itself is, of course, a logical place for economy dining, and the little market at Pátzcuaro has a number of food stalls that are more a part of the Plaza Chica than the market itself. Very inexpensive.

The *Gran Hotel* on the Plaza Chica has a restaurant reached by going through the lobby toward the back of the building. Both the hotel and restaurant are expensive, but both also offer quite good value for money. The chef does especially well with soups.

The restaurant in the Posada San Rafael, on the Plaza Principal, is another excellent choice, especially if you get the urge for an 'American Breakfast' which they do very well. Moderate.

If you really want to put on the dog some evening, try the restaurant at the *Hotel Meson El Gallo*, on Cos near the Plaza Principal. First make sure, though, that there's no tour bus in! Very expensive and with lots of hokey atmosphere.

Getting There

Pátzcuaro has direct bus service from such far-flung points as Guadalajara,

Querétaro and Mexico City, but don't worry about a direct bus, unless one is due to leave right away. Get a ticket to Morelia and catch a bus from there to Pátzcuaro. There are dozens of buses every day, and at least half a dozen bus lines. The Flecha Amarilla has the most buses.

Pátzcuaro is the originating terminal for buses going to dozens of small, isolated places, such as Tacámbaro, Pedernales and Inguarán.

There are daily train services to and from Mexico City, the fastest of which is advertised to take ten hours and the slowest a full day. Only a committed rail fan would even consider taking the train. In Pátzcuaro the railroad station is a considerable distance from town, requiring most passengers to take a cab.

One final remark: Pátzcuaro regards the Fiesta of the Immaculate Conception with great seriousness, and at that time thousands of pilgrims converge on the little city. Unless you want to sleep in one of the plazas — as a great many families do — I suggest that around December 8 you make a day trip to Pátzcuaro from Morelia or Urapan. Both are about 50 km, and there are lots of buses.

PUERTO VALLERTA, Jalisco
Some 20 years ago, Puerto Vallerta was described by one writer as 'a remote, charming fishing village' and 'Mexico's nearest equivalent to a quiet Mediterranean village, even to the tourists who are beginning to discover it'. That is still true except that the tourists have now discovered Puerto Vallerta in a big way.

Modern Puerto Vallerta is an excellent illustration of what publicity can do to a community. When Taylor and Burton were filming 'Night of the Iguana', they kept the gossip writers busy for months, and every story went out datelined Puerto Vallerta. The town at that time was not to be found on

most highway maps!

From that day on Puerto Vallerta has had a mystique that has brought tourists in ever-increasing numbers, and the town's population has multiplied about 25 times in 20 years, making it Mexico's fastest-growing city. But Vallerta is not running only on the momentum generated by 'Night of the Iguana' — it has one of the most aggressive tourism departments in the Republic.

Basically it is a small town, and people still go out in the wee small hours to catch the fish that form one of the staples of the diet of the poorer families. Renting a sport-fishing boat is no problem at all, just go down on the Malacón (Diaz Ordaz) at 31 de Octobre, by the Hotel Rosales, and make the best deal you can. These are large cabin cruisers, but the economy-minded can usually find a small open outboard boat, such as the local fishermen use, for about a quarter the price.

Because Puerto Vallerta's basic industry is servicing the tourists, it really isn't too good a town for shopping when it comes to handicrafts. This is a fine place, though, to buy tourist-oriented merchandise, and there are 'cowboy' shops that don't sell reatas, 'onix' stores, boutiques, and antique shops — Mexico has lots and lots of antiques! To top them all is the little shop called Aquí es José, mistranslated on the sign as 'Here is Joe'!

Even in tourist towns it is sometimes difficult to find books in English, but not in Vallerta. As you stroll north on Insurgentes across the Rio Cuate bridge toward the mini-zócolo you will notice on your right a little shop called Las Tejas, and if you read Spanish you would never in the world guess Las Tejas sells English-language paperbacks and magazines, also Beech-nut Chewing Tobacco, pipe cleaners, and enough made-in-Mexico brands of pipe tobacco to embalm the taste buds of every pipe smoker in North America and the British West Indies.

The Laundrymat Nelly, on Hidalgo near Guerrero, gives good service, although it is not exactly what one would be led to expect from the sign. Recommended.

The most popular beach is the Playa del Sol, less than one km from the centre of town. To reach it, go south on Insurgentes and National Highway 200 to Pulpito and turn right. The beach is about two blocks straight ahead. Technically the Playa del Sol starts at the big dock, Muelle los Muertos, but I couldn't see much difference in the water or the sand on the north side of the dock.

Something that has always intrigued me, and for which the locals have no sensible explanation, is the openwork crown on the tower of the church by the zócolo, certainly a unique way of finishing an otherwise pedestrian structure.

It really doesn't take very long for the quiet delights of Puerto Vallerta to pall on the average, or non-reading visitor, so nearly everyone takes a day trip out to Yelapa. This is a small village accessible only by boat. Yelapa has a beautiful white sand beach and all in all is pretty much like one of the South Seas paradises of story and fame. There is also a rather primitive Indian suburb of the same name a short walk away. To get to Yelapa go out the Malecón to 31 de Octobre to the dock where the larger sport-fishing boats land. There are regularly scheduled ferry boats aimed at the tourist trade. All are expensive, but some are more expensive than others, the price essentially determined by whether or not there is a bar. Ask around and you can usually get a ride to Yelapa for a third the cost of the ferry price from one of the other boats making the run down with freight, mail, etc. But be sure your return trip is included, and that the boat is returning the same day.

Shortly after leaving the wharf the boat to Yelapa will pass Los Arcos, a peculiar water-sculpted rock formation within Banderas Bay. Watch for it.

Places to Stay

Madero, the street crossing Insurgentes to your left as you leave the Tres Estrellas and Pacifico bus stations, is the street of economical hotels in Puerto Vallerta.

On Madero, between Insurgentes and Constitución, is the *Casa de Huespedes Garcia Altos*, above a Mexican-style fast-food joint. The overall effect isn't helped a bit by the restaurant's ventilation duct being led up the front wall. But as you go up the stairs to the lobby you realise the off-white tile is spotlessly clean. Moderate.

Next door to the Garcia Altos is the white-fronted *Casa de Huespedes Hortencia*. This one, too, is spic and span. Initially the Hortencia was a ground-floor-only operation, but business was good and recently the Hortencia added a couple more floors a project that looks to be completed by the time this is published. I don't doubt the Hortencia will then become a hotel and jack up its rates, but currently it is moderate.

Across the street from the Garcia and the Hortencia is the *Águila*, over the TNS bus station. The location is no particular disadvantage in this case because there aren't all that many TNS buses arriving and departing. The Aguila doesn't call itself anything, but rents rooms and apartments. Good for a long stay. New, with largish rooms. Moderate.

The previous three are all very conveniently located within 50 metres of Insurgentes.

The *Hotel Lina*, on Madero between Insurgentes and Aguacate, is on the way up to the Analiz. It doesn't seem quite as clean or as well run as some of the others on Madero, and the price isn't

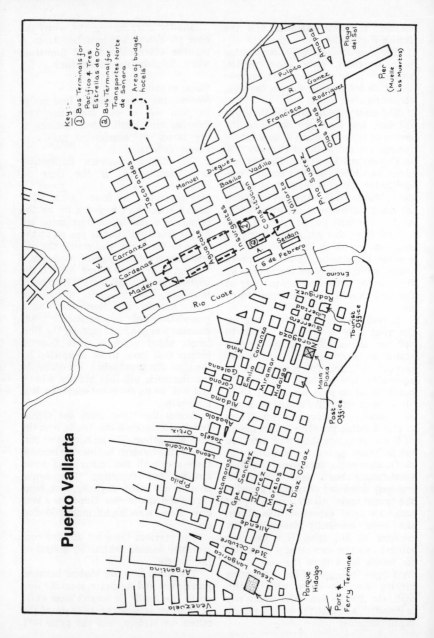

Puerto Vallarta

Key:-
① Bus Terminals for Pacifico & Tres Estrellas de Oro
② Bus Terminal for Transportes Norte de Sonora

Area of budget hotels

right, either, but it is pleasant and built around a large and airy patio and the rooms are ample. Expensive.

Farther up Madero is the *Hotel Analiz*, between Aguacate and Jacarandas. There is nothing at all pretentious about the Analiz, just a typical clean, small establishment surrounding a tiny, white-painted patio containing a few plants in 20-litre cans. Competently managed by simpatico people. Moderate.

Casa de Huespedes Bernal is next door to the Analiz, and more of a hotel than a run-of-mill casa de huespedes. The two-storey white front overlooks the little-travelled street. Moderate.

Across the street from the Analiz and the Bernal is the much larger *Villa del Mar*, identified by the jumping marlin in tile beside the front entrance. Over the years I've stayed at both the Analiz and the del Mar, and I'm well satisfied with both. Three storeys with tall palms growing in the patio. Moderate.

There is a beach about 15 km south, where the road turns inland, that is popular with tenters. Get there by second-class bus which leaves from a station on Madero on the water side of Insurgentes. Don't try camping on the beach without an insect-proof tent unless you are one of the lucky people that mosquitoes dislike.

Places to Eat

There is a tipico restaurant serving authentic Mexican food that's leagues ahead of the 'Mexican' in the US. It is on Serdán near Insurgentes — Serdán is the next street north of Madero, which in turn is the next street to the left of the Tres Estrellas bus station. Watch for the sign touting the Herreria El Arte Colonial — the restaurant is in the front half of the blacksmith's shop. Try the birria de chivo, a specialty of the house and about as Mexican as you can get short of menudo! Inexpensive.

As you cross the bridge on Insurgentes over the Rio Cuate going toward the plaza, you can't miss *Henry's Restaurant Bar and Cafeteria*. Henry's has everything from machaca to bean sprouts, yoghurt to wholewheat bread — this last rare in the Republic. Natural juices. Sandwiches — you name it. I've snacked here several times and have no complaints at all. Moderate.

The *city market* is at Insurgentes and the Rio Cuate, and as usual the best place for economical eating. Here the food counters are on the top floor, rear. At least once each time I'm in Puerto Vallerta I eat at the *Cenaduria Elodia*. I suppose a cenaduria technically is a place that does suppers only, but the Elodia is open all day. Very inexpensive.

If you cross the Rio Cuate on Insurgentes and turn left alongside the market you will shortly come to the *Restaurant Mi Tierra* at Matamoros. A no-frills eating house catering to the hardworking men of the vicinity and their families. Lots of lazy paddle fans discourage flies and mosquitoes. Moderate.

Benitos, on Zaragoza between Juárez and Morelos, opposite the plaza, is a pizza and spaghetti joint that also serves a number of Mexican dishes and sea food. It is efficiently operated and very popular with local families — Mexican kids, like kids everywhere, go for pizza in a big way — but liable to be crowded Sunday afternoons with large family groups. Moderate.

One block south of the Tres Estrellas bus station, on the corner of Insurgentes and Cárdenes, there is a fair-size supermarket, the best of its kind in town. The cheapest way to eat well and heartily is to buy the necessities here and meander down to the beach.

Getting There

There is no central bus terminal in Puerto Vallerta, although one is sorely needed, but the various stations are fairly close together. Most foreign bus travellers arrive by Pacifico, Tres Estrellas de Oro or Transportes Norte de Sonora.

The Pacifico and Tres Estrellas stations are on Insurgentes between Madero and Cardenes. To get downtown from either, go out the front door and turn left. Cross the Rio Cuate, turn left and go along the right side of the market to Juárez, the third street. Turn right and you will be at the plaza in three blocks (but watch carefully, for the plaza in Vallerta really doesn't amount to much). Walking time is 15 minutes.

The TNS station is on Madero close to Insurgentes. To get to the plaza, turn left on leaving, then left on the first street, Insurgentes, and proceed as above.

There is frequent bus service to Guadalajara, Mexico City, Tepic and Manzanillo. Coming from Mazatlán and points north, service is less frequent, so I suggest you get the first available bus to Tepic and change there to the Vallerta bus. From Tepic to Vallerta is only 169 km, but it is 463 km to Mazatlán, an eight or nine-hour bus ride, and the break at Tepic provides a welcome opportunity for leg-stretching.

Puerto Vallerta has no railroad, but it does have a twice-weekly ferry to Cabo San Lucas and Cabo San Jose on the tip of Baja California. There isn't much of anything in that part of the world, more than 200 km from La Paz, and it is far more convenient to cross to or from Baja California by either the Santa Rosalia-Guaymas or the La Paz-Matzatlán ferry, and catch a bus for the rest of the journey. Frankly, I recommend the ferry be regarded as the last resort.

Although Vallerta is pretty small as cities go, it has excellent air service and an international airport with flights to Tucson, Phoenix, Los Angeles, San Francisco, Guadalajara, Mazatlán and Mexico City, among other places.

BARRA DE NAVIDAD, Jalisco

Barra de Navidad is easy to each, either from along the coast or from Guadalajara, and I am at a loss to know why it is visited by so few foreigners — it is certainly popular with Mexican families who flock down from Guadalajara in droves, especially on weekends.

The town is built on a small peninsula and has the blue Pacific almost all around it, with a long, almost deserted, white-sand beach.

Barra has no organised tourist activities, except for fishing. Instead it is the epitome of tropical towns, with palm trees, palapa shacks, an old movie set, open-air restaurants, and a hotel that looks as if it were left over from the movie 'Rain'. (It wasn't.)

The movie set is the Bar Grif which was built for a movie that was to have been called 'Cabo Blanco', starring Chas Bronson and others of like stature. For some reason it was never released in the US, but the well-made set still stands. It was intended to represent a South Seas saloon and the barroom, and is two storeys high with a balcony running around the inside perimeter. Today it stands just as it was when the last scene was shot on the main street just past the Hotel Tropical from the bus station. It is supposed to be locked up, but getting inside for an inspection is no trick at all.

Places to Stay

I have never seen Barra run out of hotel rooms, but I suppose it could happen, especially if some movie outfit were working in the neighbourhood, which happens all the time because of the beautiful tropical scenery. But there are quite a few hotels.

Step out of the front of the bus station and across the street on your right is the big, white, three-storey *Hotel Barra de Navidad*, a beach-front hotel that is nowhere near as rapacious as the Tropical. Palm trees grow tall in the patio, and the surf just outside doesn't make the usual hissing noise — it booms on the steep beach, at times jarring the whole building. The bar and restaurant are inclined to close a little early for my taste, but quite good value by local standards. Very expensive.

Turn to your left as you leave the bus station and across the intersection is the little *Hotel Guadalajara*, at present the cheapest house in town. It is usually full but worth a try. Inexpensive.

Keep going a couple of blocks past the Guadalajara and you'll arrive at the *Hotel Tropical*, a rather pretentious beach hotel. This one catches the movie trade and, as a rule, the better rooms are taken first, but they charge as much for their cold-water rooms as they do for their very best. The Tropical originally offered excellent value for money, especially compared to the waterfront hotels in Manzanillo up the road. Not only have the rates sky-rocketed over the years, but the Tropical is not above charging singles at the posted doubles rate now and again. Ridiculously expensive and not a lot for the money.

If you turn left on Sonora, the street that branches off the main street just before you reach the Tropical, and follow it to the bottom and turn left again, you will shortly arrive at the *Hotel Delfin*, a typical tropical hotel of more or less contemporary design. Four storeys, arched balconies outside the rooms. Very expensive, but a far, far better deal than the Tropical.

A short distance farther along and across the street is the *Sands* hotel, almost exactly the same price and very popular with the up-at-4 am sportsfishermen. Ridiculously expensive; try the Delfin first.

Somewhere along the way Calle Sonora becomes Calle Morelos, and if you continue past the Delfin and Sands

far enough you wind up behind the reception desk of the *Hotel Jalisco*, for years the bargain of Barra de Navidad. It had oodles of hot water and the other little amenities so appreciated by the wayfarer, such as toilets that flushed reliably. Unfortunately the Jalisco closed shortly before this was written, but several local residents have told me it will reopen at about the same old prices. Moderate.

Places to Eat

The bus station, being a private operation, has a pretty fair restaurant that gets most of its business from the locals, not the passengers. Inexpensive.

If you go left as you leave the station, on the next corner is the restaurant in the *Hotel Guadalajara*, open to the breezes on two sides. It does a bang-up job with seafood and is a popular place for breakfast, but if more than ten people arrive within five minutes the rush simply overwhelms the leisurely operation and the service, always haphazard, goes all to pot. Inexpensive.

The best place in town is *Pancho's*, beyond the Tropical, so well appreciated that a good share of its trade comes from families who make the 285-km drive down from Guadalajara just to put their feet beneath Pancho's table. Pancho's sign states 'the best of the sea for you' and they ain't kidding. The restaurant doesn't get up a head of steam until 8 pm. Moderate.

The restaurant in the Hotel Tropical is called *La Bugambilia* and regardless of my remarks about the hotel, the restaurant is not too bad and is the only place in town where you can get an American-style breakfast any hour they're open. It is only a little more expensive than Pancho's, and the food is almost as good, with white table-cloths and everything. Expensive.

(Don't order a drink at La Bugambilia. A copita of Viejo Virgil brandy will cost a whopping M$75, a ridiculous price, even if you do get two for the price of one during the evening happy hour.)

Getting There

Barra de Navidad has direct bus service from Guadalajara, Manzanillo and Puerta Vallerta, making it easy to get to. The 280-km trip down from Guadalajara takes six to eight hours over a twisty road that drops about 1500 metres in the process. It is only 73 km from Manzanillo along the coast, but to Puerto Vallerta it is almost 200 km, over an up-and-down road that in at least one place rises to about 700 metres.

MANZANILLO, Colima

Manzanillo has one of the best harbours on Mexico's pacific coast and there has always been a settlement there. It is believed that the local Indians had contact with Chinese traders around the 12th century. When Cortés visited the place he realized immediately it was the ideal place for a shipyard, and to this day there are boatyards there.

It does less business than Acapulco, which is odd because Manzanillo has a railroad connection with the interior, whereas Acapulco doesn't. Manzanillo today is the seaport for Guadalajara, and to a lesser degree, Morelia. Shipping is the principal business, with tourism and boat-building trailing by a considerable margin.

The town itself gives the impression of age, and there are a number of buildings dating from colonial days, but there has been a great deal of new construction, and the ancient part of town is pretty much concentrated aound the Jardín de Obregón, the official name of the plaza. Manzanillo is a seaport pure and simple, and looks it.

Most of the tourist business isn't in Manzanillo at all, it is at Playa Azul, about 10 km south of town. Here are most of the super-expensive hotels and restaurants.

The well-publicised Las Haidas, is located near Playa Azul. Developed by the Bolivian tin magnate Antenor Patiño, Las Haidas was intended to be a haven for the wealthy jet-setters, but it didn't take off as there aren't too many ordinary people willing to pay thousands of pesos for a hotel room. Eventually the Mexican Government took over the operation, which didn't make business one whit better, and now it mostly a monument to one individual's optimism.

Although the beach at Manzanillo is popular with the locals, foreigners staying in town mostly go out to the Playa La Audencia or Playa San Perdido, about one km from the plaza on the north. Of the two, I prefer Perdido because it has a gently-sloping beach and is the closest to the plaza.

There is a sheltered lagoon on the inland side of Manzanillo, and the residents use it regularly, but I wouldn't recommend it because the town has no sewage treatment plant.

Places to Stay

Manzanillo is booming, and the rooms are usually full of longshoremen, fishermen, sailors, railroad men, campesinos and all the rest of the people it takes to operate a busy port. Low-priced rooms are at a premium and especially so near the plaza.

My perennial favourite is the *Hotel Miramar*, upstairs on Juárez at 21 de Marzo, across the street from the Turismo office. The sign on the side of the building is plainly visible from the plaza. The Miramar has been popular for years with seafaring folk who don't mind climbing the flight of steps to the lobby, and is very well managed by people who are even helpful when the hotel is full which, frankly, is most of the time. Moderate.

The *Hotel Savoy*, on Davalos at Puerto, is overpriced by a factor of

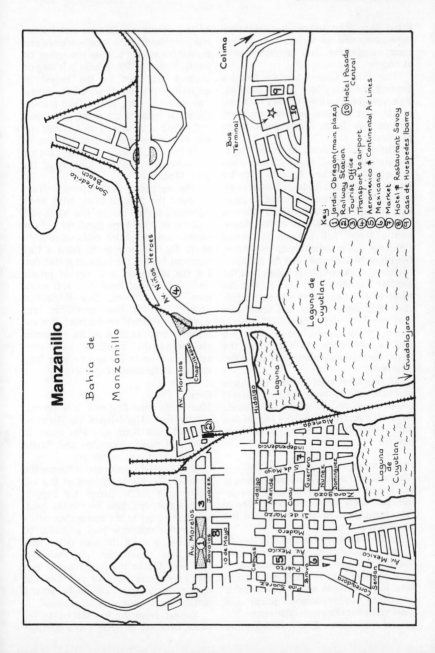

Manzanillo

Bahia de Manzanillo

San Pedrito Beach

Laguna de Cuyutlan

Laguna de Cuyutlan

Laguna

Key:
1 Jardin Obregon (main plaza)
2 Railway Station
3 Tourist Office
4 Transport to airport
5 Aeromexico + Continental Air Lines
6 Mexicana
7 Market
8 Hotel # Restaurant Savoy
9 Casa de Huespedes Ibarra
10 Hotel Posada Central

three. Should be inexpensive but is very expensive, and is included as a last-resort suggestion, not a recommendation.

The *Hotel Emperador*, on Davalos beyond the Savoy is a pretty good go. Fair size rooms, three storeys with balconies, and a cream and maroon paint job on the front. Quite good value. Moderate.

The *Hotel Colonial*, on 10 de Mayo, is only a block off the plaza and without question the best hotel in town by far. It has the attributes we have come to expect in a Mexican hotel of its class: high ceilings, large rooms, small windows in proportion to the size of the rooms, and a lobby full of psuedo-colonial furniture. It is ridiculously expensive, but much better value than the Savoy.

There are a couple of hotels near the Central Camionera. If you go out the front of the Camionera and turn right, then right again at the first street you will come to the *Casa de Huespedes Ibarra*, three storeys, cream paint job and in my opinion a cut above the Savoy downtown at about half the price. Moderate.

If you keep right on past the Ibarra and turn right at the next street you will soon come to the *Hotel de Posada Central*, directly behind the bus station and visible from the bus stalls. Inexpensive.

Places to Eat

Manzanillo, like most seaport towns is not noted for the excellence if its cuisine, but there are a number of pretty fair, low-priced restaurants around the plaza.

At the corner of Davalos and Mexico is an easy-to-miss small restaurant without a name. It looks more like a soda fountain but it really is a restaurant. It owes most of its considerable popularity to reasonable prices and good value for the pesos. Moderate.

The *Restaurante Savoy*, at the corner of the zócolo on Davalos and Puerto, has been feeding the local workmen and myself for as long as I can remember. Of course, being in Manzanillo it is long on seafood but not to the extent of neglecting the remainder of the menu. The Savoy is not a health food place in the usual sense of the word, but it puts out a fruit salad served on a platter and has everything available in the way of local fruit. And the big ceiling fans are a Godsend a good 11 months of the year. Moderate.

The restaurant in the *Hotel Colonial* is easily the best in town, with white tablecloths that match the white-clad waiters, colonial-type furniture and the chairs even have thick cushions. Chilled mugs for the beer come from a tiny barroom behind the restaurant that during the afternoon is a sort of private club for the affluent and influential men of the town. The Restaurant Colonial is for that inevitable time when you yourself need a treat. It is not a tourist trap, as most of the customers are well-to-do localities and their families. It could use some ceiling fans, though. Ridiculously expensive.

Getting There

Manzanillo has first-rate bus service, mostly from Guadalajara via Barra de Navidad, but there are also buses to Colima, Urapan, Acapulco and Puerto Vallerta, among other places.

The Central Camionera in Manzanillo is easily the most grasping of the lot. There is a M$20 charge for baggage checking service, M$1 to use the head, and just to get in the bus station sets a prospective customer back a tostón (50 centavos). But on the plus side I have never seen the station very crowded, nor have I seen the interminable lines one encounters all over the Republic during the summer, so maybe all this pettiness serves some useful purpose.

To get from the bus station to the plaza, turn left on leaving and continue on the same street to the second set of railroad tracks. Turn right and follow the tracks to the first cross street, Juarez. Turn left and the plaza is in the second block. Walking time: 15 minutes.

Occasionally a railfan or a masochist arrives by the train that originates in Guadalajara and stops at Colima for a while. This is supposed to be an 8¼ hour trip, but it usually takes longer, sometimes a lot longer!

Manzanillo has an international airport, with regular flights to Guadalajara, Mexico City and Los Angeles.

ZIHUATANEJO, Guerrero

A mere 25 years ago Zihuatanejo was a sleepy little fishing and banana-shopping port of about 1400 souls. Electric power came from a little Cat light plant that (usually) ran from sundown until 11 pm or thereabouts.

Little by little the idyllic tropical town has been 'discovered' by sun-worshippers and now it has zoomed to about 15,000 while still maintaining much of its original charm.

Zihuatanejo has no intriguing colonial buildings because it was only established around a century ago, but much of it is of the frame construction utilised by the French in their tropical operations, and the town has a most un-Mexican aspect as a result.

There are a number of beaches at Zihuatanejo, separated by rocky out-croppings. The beach right in front of town is sheltered, but Madera, La Ropa and Las Gatas beaches are more popular and open to the Pacific combers. They are reached by going down to the water-front and walking around to the left as you face the water. Madera is below the Hotel Madera, and La Ropa is the one by the Hotel Catalina. Many visitors simply take a boat from the waterfront out to Las Gatas and make a day of it. Food and drink are available from stands.

It is possible to charter or rent boats for fishing and other acquatic activities, but so far there are no parachute rides or water skiing, though I expect both these activities to arrive any day and turn Zihuatanejo into a full-fledged Mexican resort, right up in the same league as Puerto Vallerta and Acapulco.

Places to Stay

Although there aren't any organised entertainment activities, there are enough foreigners who like the South Seas ambience, warm and sunny weather, and sandy beaches, to fill every available room during the winter, and recently the same thing has been happening during the summer vacation months. This is one place where it pays to make paid reservations.

But even with all the tourist activity, there still remain a few reasonably-priced hotels from the old days, and they are right in town where they do the most good. Zihuatanejo is so small that the whole downtown is less than 500 metres from salt water.

The *Hotel El Dorado* is a small house on one of the shopping streets well away from the beach, and the more distant the beach the less money, as a rule. This is reflected in the price of the rooms! moderate.

The *Hotel Guadalupe* looks dingy from the outside, although it is really about average clean, which is quite clean indeed in Mexico. It is one of the last places in town to fill, probably because of the lack of visual appeal to foreigners. Moderate.

The *Casa Aurora* is practically next door to the Guadalupe, but otherwise they have nothing in common. The Aurora is neat and intelligently managed and often full. Moderate.

Go out the front door of the Estrella de Oro (not Tres Estrellas) bus station and a few metres to the left is *Casa de Huespedes Lupita*. Not much of a place, but for such low prices you can't expect the Dorchester. Inexpensive.

The *Posada Laura*, a block from the market on the way downtown, is a two-storey building with a veranda running the length of the front with a functional balcony above, a unique combination in Zihuatanejo. White, unpeeled paint job. The very best shot in town for those fortunate enough to land a room. Moderate.

Places to Eat

There are lots of restaurants in Zihuatanejo. As usual, the cheapest, and far from the worst eating, is in the market, but there are a couple of others that I patronise each time I'm in Zihuatanejo.

The first is *El Tapatio*, across the street from the Hotel El Dorado. Well-equipped with overhead fans, it isn't cheap, but it does a nice unhurried breakfast while the paddle fans keep the flies at bay. The help is helpful and the food is typical Mexican, heavy on fish. Moderate.

My other selection is one that I usually patronise just once each stay. *La Mesa del Capitan*, at Bravo and Guerrero, is a deluxe place that caters to the package tour customers who are fed up with hotel fare, and is the best place to eat in town if price is not a consideration. The wines are domestic and trustworthy, or at least I have never had to send a bottle back.

Getting There

Getting to and from Acapulco is a cinch, as is going up to Mexico City, but Manzanillo is more difficult as very few buses run beyond Lázaro Cárdenes, and it may well be easier to go up to Urapan and then double back to Manzanillo. This is a main route and there are lots and lots of buses every day.

There are two bus stations. The second-class Flecha Roja station is on

the other side of the market from town. Taxis are available, but it is only a 10-minute walk. Go out the front door and straight ahead to the main street. Go right, then left a few metres farther along. Pass the market, then turn right on the street by the Posada Laura. A couple of blocks more will bring you downtown.

The Estrella de Oro, or first-class bus station, is almost downtown. Go out the front door and turn left, then left at the next street.

The more affluent tourists fly to Zihuanatejo from Mexico City and there is talk of instituting direct flights from the US West Coast.

PAPANOA, Guerrero

Papanoa is a town about a fifth as large as Zihuatanejo and about 60 km along the coast on the way to Acapulco. Very popular with surfers who prefer to camp on one of the beaches rather than staying at the costly Club de Papanoa. But even for non-surfers some of the prettiest and most unpatronised beaches are near here. All supplies are available in Papanoa, which simplifies camping out.

ACAPULCO, Guerrero

Almost as soon as the Spanish took Tenochitlán they discovered the superb harbour at Acapulco. Immediately recognizing its worth, they established a shipbuilding business on the shore. The first two ships were christened in 1532, the *San Marcos* and the *San Miguel*, and were intended for use in an expedition of exploration by Hurado de Mendoza. In 1533 ships sailed from Acapulco to Peru, and in 1565 Fray Andrés de Urdaneta opened commerce between the Philippines and Mexico via Acapulco.

Until the early 1800s Acapulco was a lusty, brawling seaport through which most of the trade with the Orient was conducted, but apparently the profits went elsewhere, because Acapulco has very few of the fine old great houses of most older Mexican cities.

Came the revolution and Mexican independence, and the trade dried up. Acapulco slipped into the lethargy that lasted for over a hundred years. The pack routes running north to Mexico City were disused and overgrown, and by the early 1920s Acapulco was just another forgotten seaport, about as important as San Blas or Altata and certainly of far less account than Salina Cruz.

Acapulco would still be dead except for the road built in 1928 that allowed the first motorized vehicles to serve the town. Once the road to the interior was improved and reopened, it was again possible to haul freight, and the ships started arriving, first one or two a month, and in a few years they came in fleets. Today Acapulco is Mexico's second port, and Mexico City's seaport on the Pacific, and its tonnage is only exceeded by Veracruz, its counterpart on the Atlantic side.

And for some unfathomable reason, there is still no railroad!

Most people think of Acapulco as strictly a resort city that has always been a tourist-oriented, but it wasn't until just before WW II that the first of the fancy resort hotels was constructed, and there really wasn't much business until well after the end of the war.

After the tourist business started with a trickle clever advertising and promotion kept it growing, and I don't know of a time since 1950 that there has not been at least one luxury hotel under construction. But even with all the tourist activity Acapulco is first an and last a seaport, and it is not unusual to see a couple of huge freighters tied up along the Costera Alemán, a few hundred metres from the zócolo, with half a dozen more waiting for berthing room.

Of recent years Mexico has been assiduously promoting Acapulco and the other Pacific Coast towns, such as Manzanillo and Puerta Vallerta, as the 'Mexican Riviera'. Another shot in the arm for the tourist business has been the successful television sitcom, 'Love Boat', probably the best free advertising any country ever received. (It is perfectly suited to the tastes of the people Mexico needs — moderately well-off, older people who buy an all-inclusive package-tour package tour that insulates the tourists from all contact with the sometimes-unwashed local people, and generates the maximum profits for the operators.)

The harbour at Acapulco is one of the finest and most interesting on earth, and the way to get an overall view of Acapulco is not to go up on a hill and look down on it, in my opinion, but to eyeball it from the water. Several boats offer cruises around the bay, leaving from a pier immediately southwest of the zócolo. The best time is late afternoon when the city is illuminated by the setting sun coming from behind you. There are also evening cruises, intended for dancers and lovers young and old who appreciate each other, and by night Acapulco is even more beautiful than the real Riviera. The blue-white and orange of the street lighting, the brightly-illuminated hotels, and the rank on rank of workers' homes blanketing the hills all combine to make an unforgettable sight, one that by itself comes close to making the trip worthwhile.

The little Fort San Diego, on a hill just above the Costera Alemán, is a working military post and usually closed to the casual visitor. If you go up and wander around you might be fortunate enough, as I once was, to be invited inside, but don't count on it. The fort has a long and violent history. It is actually the second fort in Acapulco. The first was El Castillo de San Diego which was flattened by an earthquake back in 1776 — the only instance to my knowledge of a Spanish fort that was damaged, let alone destroyed, by an earthquake.

This didn't discourage the Spaniards however, and they promptly built the present one, El Fuerte de San Diego, with an unusual — for the Spanish — star configuration. During the revolutionary war the little fuerte was attacked by Morelos and a force he thought would be overwhelming. Overwhelming or not, the seige lasted four months before the Spanish were finally forced to run up the white flag, so the unusual shape can be counted a successful design.

The beaches at Acapulco start right at the zócolo and are much frequented by local families, although generally overlooked by tourists. For the price of a local bus ride you can go down on the Costera and catch a bus out to the Caleta and Caletilla beaches, only a couple of hundred metres apart, or you can go the other direction to still more beaches along the south side of he bay.

Caution! Sunburn in Mexico does more harm than all the turista cases ever joked about!

Everybody goes out to see Acapulco's famous boy high divers. This show takes place every evening. Catch a Quebrada bus out Quebrada and get off at El Mirador, or walk — it's only about 1½ km. To reach Calle Quebrada, go through the zócolo and past the cathedral on the street along the right side of the zócolo, Independencia, and Quebrada is the second street. Turn left. Walking time from the plaza: 20 minutes or so.

It is easy to forget that a great deal of fish are caught commercially at Acapulco, and if you happen to be an early riser you can saunter down on the Costera Alemán and watch the men launch their boats and later bring in their catch. The boats are stored well

above high water, and come launching time are put on wood rollers and wheeled down the beach. Landing is much the same thing, except more people are required.

Those odd boxes-on-wheels along the sidewalk are used to unload the catch and cart it up to the fish buyers who congregate well before sunrise along the water side of the Costera. The bargaining involved in selling and buying the catch would do a Syrian arms peddler proud. This all takes place just below the Fuerte San Diego, a few hundred metres from the deep-water berths where the big ships unload.

Every movie shot around Acapulco has at least one scene of either the Quebrada divers or the parachute riders as a locating shot. It isn't too practical to try the high diving, but the parachute rides go on all the time. They aren't dangerous, although every time I try it I get the living beJazus scared out of me. If this is your bag, or you just want to spectate, catch a 'Cine Rio-la Base' bus at the stop above Sanborn's. Just past the Estrella de Oro bus station it turns down to the right and winds up running along the Costera Alemán past a lot of exceedingly expensive hotels. Get off at either the Playa Condesa or the Centro de Convenciónes. Stand on the sand a few minutes and odds are that you will be hustled by a prachute-ride salesman. Try it — you might like it.

Sanborn's is, as always, the place to get English-language books and periodicals, but I'll bet dollars to pesos they are out of Guerrero and Acapulco maps.

Places to Stay

Acapulco has probably the largest collection of low-price hotels in the Republic short of Mexico City. They aren't out on the points among hotels that go for M$1500 or more a day, but they are mostly a lot better positioned

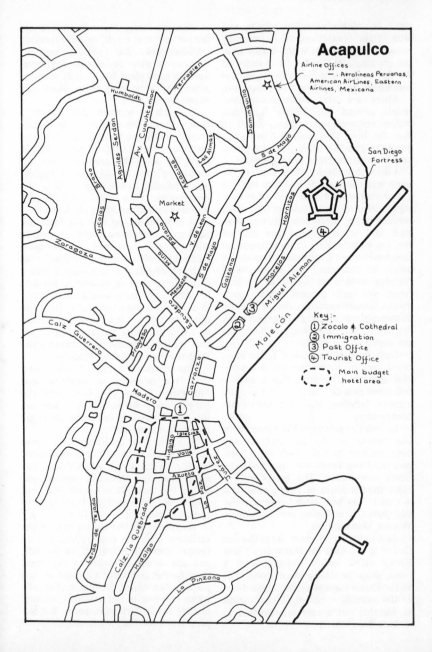

Acapulco

Airline Offices
— . Aerolineas Peruanas,
American Airlines, Eastern
Airlines, Mexicana

San Diego
Fortress

Humboldt

Terraplen

Domingvillo

5 de Mayo

Las Almas

Av. Cuauhtemoc

Aguiles Serdan

Acacias

Hornitos

Bravo

Market

V. de Leon

Nicolas

Zaragoza

Mina

Dolores

S de Mayo

Galeana

Morelos

Mendez

Miguel Aleman

Escudero

Progreso

Calz Guerrero

Malecón

Carranza

Madero

Key:-
① Zocalo & Cathedral
② Immigration
③ Post Office
④ Tourist Office
- - Main budget
hotel area

①

Hidalgo

Iglesias

Valle

Azueta

Juarez

Paz

Lerdo de Tejada

Calz. la Quebrada

Hidalgo

La Pinzona

right downtown near the zócolo, and with these hotels go the matching comedores familiares where mama does the cooking and the daughters and sons do the serving and the washing-up and sometimes sleep in the dining room, too.

There are also some economical hotels around the Flecha Roja bus station and the market. These aren't all that far from the centre of town but generally give less value than the places near the zócolo. There are exceptions.

Leave the Flecha Roja station the same way the buses do and turn left. Go a few metres and you will come to a street divided by a concreted creek running right down the middle. Turn right and in two blocks you will see the *Amueblados Familiares Economicas Comfortables — Logement a Loyer*. No name except the hard-to-see word 'Tomles' welded to the top of the iron fence. Not really a hotel, but an apartment house suitable for a family contemplating a fairly long stay, say for the winter. Inexpensive when costs are shared.

Next door is *La Casa del Rio* identified by an inconspicuous black-on-blue sign over the gate. This is an old-fashioned casa de huespedes that readily accepts families, but is usually full. Inexpensive.

Or you can go out of the Flecha Roja bus station by the bus entrance and keep walking past the pedestrian overpass until you reach the corner and the *Hotel San Carlos*. The San Carlos is older than it looks at first glance, and it usually has hot water because it also sells baths, a common combination in Mexico. Moderate.

Across the street/creek from the San Carlos is the *Casa de Huespedes Marie Elonia* in an office building with a paint shop on the ground floor. The Maria Elonia occupies one whole floor of the building — not at all uncommon in Europe, but a rare arrangement in Mexico. Inexpensive.

The big *Hotel Playa Hornos*, a bit farther up the creek, is an expensive establishment that prefers not to rent to singles or casual wayfarers, but is a good place for a family contemplating a fairly long stay. Quiet and expensive.

But it's downtown and a sling's throw from the zócolo that hotels giving good value for the money are to be found in quantity. By a coincidence they are also the most conveniently located places to stay in Acapulco, much handier to the focal point of the community than the large luxury hotels scattered out along the beaches.

A few blocks up the hill from the Sanborn's downtown outlet at Costera Alemán and Escudeos is the blue-fronted *Hotel Sanchez Romero* at Roberto Posada No 9, a short distance from the grotesque cathedral. No sign is visible from the sidewalk immediately in front; you can only read it from the opposite side of the street! Meals are served in the large patio and there is a fine loafing balcony overlooking Calle Roberto Posado. A find. Moderate.

The *Hotel del Patio*, a block or two from the cathedral at Guerrero and Progresso, is up the hill from the Sanchez and lower in quality. Rooms on the inside opening onto the patio are nicest. Inexpensive.

The blue *Casa de Huespedes Concha* at 25 Quebrada looks like a small-town house on a side street, which it was. The doors open on a verandah running clear across the front. It is usually full, but people do come and go from time to time. Inexpensive.

As you go up the zócolo toward the cathedral from the Costura you will see several streets running off to the left, and the second is called La Paz. Turn onto La Paz and about a block from the plaza is the *Hotel California*. The off-white exterior is not matched, unfortunately, by a dark pink patio, but the price is not too bad. Moderate.

A little farther along La Paz, at Valle, is the *Hotel Isabel* with its mostly stuccoed pink and white facade. It is designed to take advantage of the chimney effect to draw cooling evening air into the lobby, and is the only hotel in Mexico that deliberately uses this practical system. The Isabel is only two streets off the zócolo. Not air-conditioned, but the big, lazily-turning ceiling fans do a good job of agitating the air and the rooms are comfortable enough so that I usually stay at the Isabel if they have a room available. Moderate.

Going up the hill and away from the plaza is almost like entering a separate small town, a town where money goes a long way. Stand on the corner of Hidalgo and Quebrada, for instance, and there are no less than six hotels in plain view, mostly moderate.

The nearby *Hotel Mariscal* only rents to two or more people, but the *Hotel Pachis* just beyond is happy to room a single. The Pachis has a tiny dining room occupying half the small lobby and does a pretty fair inexpensive meal. The hotel itself is moderate.

The *Casa de Huespedes Alicia*, Azueta No 9, near La Paz, is really for families, but if you happen to be part of a group and split the bill the Alicia would probably be the cheapest place to stay in Acapulco. Large rooms, some with three twin beds. Try early — the Alicia is a bargain, but no secret!

Places to Eat

Acapulco is famous for its high-priced restaurants, such as the elegant *Normandie* and the high-camp *Carlos 'n Charlies*, but there are probably more good inexpensive restaurants in town than there are deluxe establishments worth their elevated prices.

The restaurant in the *Estrella de Oro* (not Tres Estrellas de Oro) bus station is better than most bus station restaurants and a safe bet for an early breakfast. Moderate.

For really down-to-earth eating the *market* in Acapulco is, as usual, a pretty good choice. To get to the market, go out of the back of the Flecha Roja bus station where the buses enter and turn left. Cross over the pedestrian footbridge by the OB clinic and the market and its pleasures are all around you. Very inexpensive. This market is both wholesale and retail and gets a very early start. It is a good place for a cheap eye-opener before the rest of Acapulco awakes.

Competing with the market in price is a ramshackle restaurant opposite the Canada shoe and to the right of the bus exit from the Flecha Roha bus station. It runs 24 hours and does an enormous business, much of it to-go, but also has tables and chairs as well. The specialty of the house is a sort of open-face taco called a 'sope', as filling as a gordita, which it greatly resembles. Two or three of these and a coke will hold most people the rest of the day.

But take heed: this restaurant makes its own red sauce with chilis árboles which are among the hottest on earth, about on a par with the chilis habanos of Yucatán. If you really aren't up to the genuine article in Mexican labourer's provender I suggest you order yours 'sin salsa colorado'. Very inexpensive.

On toward town, *Sanborn's*, a couple blocks short of the plaza, has the usual Americanized Mexican menu — or Mexicanized American menu — for the benefit of those who value apparent cleanliness and decor similar to the better type of Stateside small-town restaurant. Clean restrooms. Expensive.

The downtown *Denny's* — there are others in town — is located on the left of the zócolo at the corner of Juárez and is the exception to my laudatory remarks about the fine state of their sanitary facilities. These are admittedly cleaner and better kept than the bus station johns, but not by all that much. Expensive.

The *Restaurant San Carlos*, on Juárez across the street from the back of Denny's and about 35 metres from the zócolo, is a tightly-run establishment that puts the lie to the fable about Acapulco being strictly a deadfall for tourists. I've eaten here a number of times over the past few years, and I doubt if I've seen more than a dozen travellers in the place, although it is fairly well patronized by foreigners who spend any length of time in town. The decorations consist mostly of red pillars and a large parilla at the front. Nothing obnoxiously fancy. The San Carlos serves both meat and seafood, and does both right well. Most things are cooked al carbón, and a mechanical breeze blows through the place, cooling the customers and wafting the good cooking smells out onto the street.

For a top-hole seafood dinner without paying uptown prices, try the *Mariscos Milla* Go through the zócolo and turn left at the cathedral. Continue to Azueta (née Arteaga) and turn left again; the white-fronted Milla is on the next corner. This is the place for the main meal of the day, say from noon to around 4 pm, and the Milla often closes very early for a Mexican restaurant, say 7 pm. Expensive, but good value.

There are a number of low-price restaurants on Azueta near the Milla, with little to choose among them. Most feature seafood simply prepared and all are in the inexpensive to moderate range. They usually chalk the day's offerings on blackboards outside.

There is a small bakery/grocery store on the corner of Hidalgo and Azueta, and are also several grocery stores nearby that can be combined for shopping purposes to knock the stuffing out of the high cost of living.

Also in the vicinity are a *casa de Huespedes* or two which insist on renting on the American Plan (ie meals included) when they can get away with it during the busy seasons, but they can be very inexpensive indeed when the price of meals is factored in.

Getting There & Getting Around

Most of the people who come to Acapulco by bus come by way of Mexico City, Cuernavaca and Taxco, and there is practically a shuttle service between the Central del Sur in Mexico City and Acapulco. Both first and second-class service are offered, with all sorts of variations on the first class, such as 'de lujo' and 'Pullman'. Personally I take the first available seat on a first-class bus and let it go at that.

I don't recommend the second-class bus service on that route. There is very little difference in cost between first and second-class, and the second-class buses stop and pick up people along the road constantly, detouring around the plaza of every collection of huts within 10 km of the highway.

To get downtown from the second-class Flecha Roja bus station, take a bus marked 'Zócolo' or 'Centro' near the bus exit from the station. If you want to walk, leave the way the buses do and turn left. Go a few metres to the street divided by a creek and turn right. Follow this three blocks to the Costera Alemán, the main-travelled boulevard paralleling the beach, then follow this for about 30 minutes to the zócolo.

To get downtown from the Estrella de Oro first-class bus station, catch the bus that runs past the front door from right to left as you leave. The station is about four km from the zócolo, about a 40-minute walk. If you decide to hoof it, go out the front door of the station and turn left. Stay on this street until it crosses a road divided by a creek and turn left, then right on the Costura.

To get back to the first-class bus station, catch a 'Cine-Rio' bus at the next bus stop above Sanborn's. The buses make a left off the Costera by Sanborn's and often won't bother to pull over for a mere one or two passengers. The locals are well aware of this and catch the bus at the next stop.

The Estrella de Oro bus station in Acapulco is pretty well closed up during the night for ticket sales, and if you want to take the 7 am bus for Mexico City you won't be able to buy a ticket immediately before the bus leaves, so buy one a day or more in advance. If you don't have a ticket you can still pay the driver in cash for the journey to the first open ticket office, probably Chilpancingo, where you will be expected to buy a ticket for the balance of your trip.

Acapulco has a busy international airport, and is served by several airlines, both foreign and domestic. It seems that a new carrier adds Acapulco to its list every few months and promotional fares and excursions offering cut-rate tickets are constantly being offered. Check with your travel agent, preferably one with some knowledge of the area, to get the lowest prices and latest schedules.

PUERTO ESCONDIDO, Oaxaca

The Spanish laid out their towns systematically, following approved-in-Spain plans, and using surveying instruments to make sure the streets intersected at correct 90° angles. But Puerto Escondido just grew, and the lack of planning and a central plaza shows! The main street is called Perez Gasga, I'm told, although there are no street signs at all. It roughly parallels the beach at some distance inland so there is plenty of room for buildings along the west side. It is a good place for high-speed sightseeing — about five minutes will pretty well suffice for viewing the whole town.

Escondido today is about what Puerto Vallerta was two years before 'Night of the Iguana'. Not much to do except loaf, enjoy the trades, sleep during the afternoons as any civilised person should do, read, fish and surf. Probably the surfing is Escondido's great single attraction, and any dedicated surfer you meet has surfed at Puerto Escondido at one time or another.

Because Puerto Escondido attracts so many young and literate travellers from the US, and they have a lot of reading time available during their television-less stay, there is an excellent book store on Gasga. It is called The Paperback Shack and it is right over the pharmacy, with a branch at the local airport (!). The Paperback Shacks are operated by an American, Dr George Bennett, who can be a fountain-head of information about Escondido and environs, and Mexico generally.

Places to Stay

It is difficult to believe today that only 25 years ago Escondido didn't have a single hotel to its name, and anyone staying overnight had to make arrangements with a local family for lodgings or content himself with sleeping on the beach with the mosquitoes for company.

On the main drag is the *Hotel Masón* with its sign in front of the thatched-roof barroom. The Masón itself is a newer building up the hill behind the saloon. Inexpensive.

A few metres down the hill is the *Habitaciones Amuebladas Precios Economicos.* This one traces its lineage back to the days when families stretched their meagre income by taking in travellers, and is pretty ancient for Escondido. Entered through a builder's workshop. An inspection is recommended prior to booking a room. Inexpensive.

You can see the tile-roofed water tank and sign of the *Hotel Paraiso* from the hill by the bus station, although it is entered from the main street not too far from the Habitaciones Amuebladas. The Paraiso is an antique — for Puerto Escondido — with a tile roof.

It looks as if it would be a nice, moderately-priced establishment, but it very definitely ain't. The asking price is ridiculously expensive, although you could probably bargain a bit.

Further down the hill, the *Hotel Roca Mar* is three storeys of green paint with no sign at all. The first floor is now made up of aluminium and glass store fronts which I suppose will eventually be rented. The office is in a concrete pillbox — very obviously an afterthought — on the left side of the building. Get a top floor front room to take advantage of such breezes as may occur and the ocean view. Moderate.

Places to Eat

There are several restaurants in town, of course, but one of my personal favourites is the *Colonial* on the water side of the main stem. This is primarily a seafood restaurant, which comes naturally in Escondido. The tar-paper roof makes it unbearable in the afternoons, although things are better in the early morning and after the sun sinks.

Absolutely the best place to eat in Escondido is the *La Palapa*, on the hill side of the street above the Roca Mar. The palapa top which gives it its name would make for afternoon coolness, but for some reason it is only open during the evening. As with every other eating house in the area, the Palapa is long on fish, shrimp and langosta, this last being called 'lobster' on the US west coast. Meat is only for testing the sharpness of tooth and strength of jaw. Expensive but worth it.

Getting There & Getting Around

The best way to get to Puerto Escon-dido is to fly down from Oaxaca on a Oaxaquenas DC-3. If you are lucky, it will come via Salina Cruz and then fly up to Escondido along the beach, which makes a grand sightseeing trip. Several flights a day, usually three. Fare is M$600.

A distant second is by bus, and the simplest route is via Oaxaca because the service along Highway 200 on the coast is infrequent. Bus routes in Mexico are generally set up to haul people back and forth to the interior and/or Mexico City. There is a fairly frequent service from Acapulco.

From Puerto Angel and Salina Cruz there is supposed to be one bus a day, but lots of days it doesn't make it.

The principal bus line in this part of the world is Flecha Roja, and the Flecha Roja operation in Puerto Escondido must be seen to be believed. Flecha Roja is one of the worst bus lines in the Republic, and its low point is reached at Escondido. The published schedule is an imaginative work of fiction, the ticket agent usually doesn't sell tickets, the fans in the waiting room don't work, and to top it off there are no rest rooms and the paying customers are expected to avail themselves of the facilities of the bit Pemex gas station across the lot. To put it bluntly, the Flecha Roja is a second-class operation all the way.

To get downtown from the Flecha Roja bus station, pass around the back of the little Pemex gas station and go downhill and across the paved road (Mexico 200) and continue on the dirt road that curves around the hillside to your right. In another curve or two this becomes the main drag, although it never does get paved or sidewalked.

Glossary

Albóndiga Meatball, usually cooked in soup or stock.

Arroz Rice, a staple of the Mexican diet.

Arroz con pollo Rice with chicken, one of the more popular dishes.

Barbacoa Barbecued meat, usually well spiced.

Bifstek Beefsteak, but don't expect it cut US style!

Billete Banknote (not ticket, as in Spain).

Bimbo White balloon-type bread, sliced. Found all over Mexico. Avoid of course.

Birria de Cabro Goat stew. One of my favourite dishes.

Bollio An oblong raised bun made of white flour. If you feel it necessary to eat white bread in Mexico this is the way to do it. Universally excellent.

Burrito Not all that 'Mexican'. A popular dish near the border and widespread in 'Mexican' restaurants in the US. Consists of a flour tortilla wrapped around a filling.

Caballeros Literally 'horsemen' but as meaningless as 'gentlemen' in the USA. Usually found on men's room doors.

Cabrón Literally 'little goat', but that ain't what it means. The best definition I know is: A cabrón is a man whose best friend is screwing his wife — and he does nothing about the situation. Either avoid the word altogether or say it with a friendly smile!

Cabrito al horno Baked kid, a delicacy popular in the north.

Café Coffee.

Café con leche Coffee with milk. Made with strong coffee and hot milk, served in individual clay pitchers; it is a wonderful way to start the day.

Calle Street.

Callejón Usually an alley, but can also be a small, narrow or very short street.

(al) Carbón Literally, charcoal. Usually refers to food cooked over charcoal.

Carne Asada Roasted or grilled meat, usually beef.

Cazuela Clay cooking-pot, usually sold in nested sets. One of the world's best cooking pots.

Cena Supper.

Cenaduria A restaurant that serves suppers, but in Mexico can be found applied to any restaurant.

Central Camonera Central Bus Station.

Central de Autobuses Central Bus Station.

Central de Camiones Central Bus Station.

Cerveza Beer or other malt beverage.

Chicharrone Crackling, the pork skin or other part that has had the lard rendered out. Often sold on street corners and occasionally served as a soup.

Chiliquilie A sort of thick soup essentially made from corn tortillas and a stock base.

Chili Rellonos Literally, stuffed chilis. Made from the large mild ancho chilis with the seeds removed, stuffed, dipped in batter and deep fried. Not at all 'hot'.

Chimichanga Sort of like a deep-fried burrito. Delicious when made from the huge thin Sonora tortilla. Mostly a regional dish in the states of Sonora and eastern Baja California.

Churros Made from dough squeezed out of a pastry bag and deep-fat fried. The cooked churro is then coated with coarse sugar and served. Also applied to a 'donut' in some areas.

Cigarros Cigarettes.

Coca Coca-cola.

Cocida de rez Beef stew, which no two cooks make the same way!

Comal A clay griddle.

Comida Lunch or dinner.

Comida corrida A multi-course meal usually much cheaper than the cost of its components when ordered separately. Usually available for lunch, but sometimes carries on into the dinner hours.

Conquistador The early Spanish explorer-conqueror.

Damas Ladies. Usually found on loo doors.

Desayuno Breakfast. In Mexico, the lightest meal of the day.

Diligencia Stagecoach or vehicle of like ilk. These were popular and widely used in Mexico before the Pilgrims wore out their welcome in the Old Country!

Descompuesto Broken, a far from uncommon state of affairs in Mexico.

Embarazada Literally, embarrassed. Usually means pregnant.

Estación Ferrocarril Railroad station.

Excusado Toilet. In most of Mexico 'bathroom'.

Ferrocarril Railroad.

Flan Desert custard, one of the few Spanish dishes in Mexico.

Frijoles Beans, usually pintos. A staple, especially in the north.

Frontera Border between political entities.

Guayabara (also Guayabarra) A thin man's shirt, more or less a 'dress' item, with pockets and with two appliqued designs running up the front, over the shoulders, and down the back.

Guarache (also huarache) A sandal made of woven leather, with a sole of retired automobile tire.

Hamburguesa A hamburger by another name. Not to be confused with a Big Mac. At best, more like a wimpy.

Hay A verb meaning 'there is'. Mostly encountered as 'No hay', which means 'there is none'.

Higado Liver.

Hombres Men.

Hot Kakes Pancakes.

Huarache See guarache.

Huevo Egg.

Jabon Soap. Easy to confuse with the next word.

Jamon Ham. Genuine ham is scarce in Mexico. What you usually receive instead is 'pressed' ham.

Larga Distancia Long distance telephone.

Leche Milk.

Lechero Milk train.

Lista de Correos General delivery or poste restante. Literally means 'mail list' because names of people with letters on hand are often posted on a list, supposedly updated daily.

Lonche A pochismo meaning 'lunch'.

Loncheria or luncheria Lunch room.

(de) Lujo Deluxe. As in the US more often used than is warranted!

Lleno Full.

Mariscos Seafood, usually shellfish.

Machaca Shreaded meat, either dried or pre-roasted.

Menudo A tripe soup or stew, something on the order of tripe à la mode de Caen with oregano and cumin. Popularly supposed to be a specific for crapulence.

Mexicana Literally 'Mexican'. Applied to food implies a method of seasoning heavy on tomatoes and spices, but not necessarily 'hot'.

Molé Usually a sauce made of chocolate and spices, mostly served over fowl.

Mordita Literally, the little bite. This is the trifle you pay a traffic cop in lieu of receiving a ticket.

Mosaico Pressed luncheon meat. Also mosaic.

Mujeres Women. Another sign often seen on loo doors.

Palapa Thatched, usually thatched roof.

Pan Bread.

Pan Dulce Sweet bread, usually served in the form of assorted buns in a basket on the breakfast table. Eat as many as you will and be charged for those actually consumed.

Papel Higiénico Toilet paper. In Mexico it is in short supply.

Parada A bus stop, usually for city buses.

Picadillo, picadilla Spiced minced meat. Also occasionally applied to hash.

Plazuela A small plaza.

Pochismo A word 'poached' from another language, usually English. 'Autobus' and 'trucka' come readily to mind.

Portales Arches supporting a roof extending over a sidewalk. Arcade.

Postre Dessert.

Pozole A soup or stew containing hominy and usually based on calves or pigs' feet, and/or other outside parts, such as tails or snouts.

Presidio Usually a fort or the garrison thereof.

PRI Stands for Party of the Revolutionary Institution, the dominant political party of the country. You will see a PRI sign on at least one wall in every village in Mexico, and in the larger cities PRI slogans can be seen strung side by side for many km.

Propino, propina A tip or gratuity. Not quite the same as 'mordita', and not to be confused with 'propio' which means proper, or one's own.

Puro Cigar.

Quesedilla A folded-over, deep-fried taco. Usually.

Queso fundido A Mexicanized fondue, nothing at all like the stuff served around Zurich!

Rejas The handsome wrought-iron window guards that are the first thing the salvage artists take when stripping a ghost town.

Rico Generally means delicious, but although most places advertise Rico Menudo or Rico Pozole their claims are as much to be believed as political promises.

Salsa Sauce. Molé is a salsa. So is the stuff that appears in little dishes on tables. Approach warily.

Sanitario Toilet. Also sanitorium.

Simpatico No equivalent English word. Translated variously as sympathetic, amiable, friendly, likeable and so on. Means all of the above, and more.

Sopa Soup.

Supermercado Supermarket. Can be a small mom-and-pop backstreet shop, or a veritable department store.

Taco A small corn tortilla folded or wrapped around a filling. Anything folded over.

Tacos al pastor Tacos made from strips of meat piled on a vertical spit and cooked in front of an up-and-down grate. As the spit revolves the outermost meat is browned, then it is trimmed off to make the filling for the tacos. Of the thousand and one tacos of Mexico, the taco al pastor is my hands-down favourite. Not generally street-corner food.

Taller Shop or workshop. A 'taller mechanico' is a mechanic's shop, usually for automobiles, and a 'taller de llantos' is a tyre repair shop. And so on.

Templo Church. Can be applied to a wayside chapel, or a very grand structure.

Tipico Typical, characteristic of a region. Often applied to shirts, belts and pistol grips.

Tocino Bacon.

Tostón A fifty-centavo coin. In Yucatán, Campeche and Chiapas it can refer to thin-sliced plantain, batter dipped and deep fried.

Torta A sandwich, usually made on a bollilo that has been sliced lengthwise and some of the bread removed to make way for the filling.

Torta a la plancha A sandwich as above that is 'ironed' in a sort of smooth waffle iron. A sort of grilled sandwich.

Tortilla A flat, round unleavened bread made from either wheat flour or more likely, yellow field corn (maize). The basic item in the Mexican diet. In Mexico it is never an omelette!

Viajero A traveller, although some writers tend to use it pejoratively. It merely means traveller, and that is the way I have applied it in this book. It can also mean 'passenger', but this is relatively rare in Mexico.

Zaguan Usually vestibule or foyer, but occasionally porch.

Index

LONELY PLANET NEWSLETTER
We collect an enormous amount of information here at Lonely Planet. Apart from our research we also get a steady stream of letters from people out on the road — some of them are just one line on a postcard, others go on for pages. Plus we always have an ear to the ground for the latest on cheap airfares, new visa regulations, borders opening and closing. A lot of this information goes into our new editions or 'update supplements' in reprints. But we want to make better use of this information so, we also produce a quarterly newsletter packed full of the latest news from out on the road. It appears in January, April, July and October of each year. If you'd like an airmailed copy of the most recent newsletter just send us A$1.50 (A$1 within Australia) or A$5 (A$4 in Australia) for a year's subscription.

OTHER LONELY PLANET PRODUCTS
We have Lonely Planet T-shirts (A$5, state size and colour preference) and self-adhesive LP stickers (A$1 for two).

Africa on the Cheap
Australia — a travel survival kit
Burma — a travel survival kit
Bushwalking in Papua New Guinea
Canada — a travel survival kit
Hong Kong, Macau & Canton
India — a travel survival kit
Israel & the Occupied Territories
Japan — a travel survival kit
Kashmir, Ladakh & Zanskar
Kathmandu & the Kingdom of Nepal
Korea & Taiwan — a travel survival kit
Malaysia, Singapore & Brunei — a travel
    survival kit
North-East Asia on a Shoestring
Pakistan — a travel survival kit
Papua New Guinea — a travel survival kit
The Philippines — a travel survival kit
South America on a Shoestring
South-East Asia on a Shoestring
Sri Lanka — a travel survival kit
Tramping in New Zealand
Trekking in the Himalayas
Thailand — a travel survival kit
USA West
West Asia on a Shoestring*

* Formerly Across Asia on the Cheap

Lonely Planet travel guides are available around the world. If you can't find them, ask your bookshop to order them from one of the distributors listed below. For countries not listed or if you would like a free copy of our latest booklist write to Lonely Planet in Australia.

Australia Lonely Planet Publications, PO Box 88, South Yarra, Victoria 3141.
Canada Milestone Publications, Box 2248, Sidney, British Columbia, V8L 3S8.
Denmark Scanvik Books, Sankt Annae Plads 30, 1250 Kobenhavn K.
Hong Kong The Book Society, GPO Box 7804, Hong Kong.
India UBS Distributors, 5 Ansari Rd, New Delhi.
Japan Intercontinental Marketing Corp, IPO Box 5056, Tokyo 100-31.
Malaysia MPH Distributors, 13, Jalan 13/6, Petaling Jaya, Selangor.
Nepal see India
Netherlands Nilsson & Lamm bv, Postbus 195, Pampuslaan 212, 1380 AD Weesp.
New Zealand Roulston Greene Publishing Associates Ltd, Box 33850, Takapuna, Auckland 9.
Papua New Guinea Gordon & Gotch (PNG), PO Box 3395, Port Moresby.
Singapore MPH Distributors, 116-D JTC Factory Building, Lorong 3, Geylang Square, Singapore 1438.
Sweden Esselte Kartcentrum AB, Vasagatan 16, S-111 20 Stockholm.
Thailand Chalermnit, 1-2 Erawan Arcade, Bangkok.
UK Roger Lascelles, 16 Holland Park Gardens, London W14 8DY.
USA (West) Bookpeople, 2940 Seventh St, Berkeley, CA 94710.
USA (East) Hippocrene Books, 171 Madison Ave, New York, NY 10016.
West Germany Buchvertrieb Gerda Schettler, Postfach 64, D3415 Hattorf a H.